# Education Issues in Creole and Creole-Influenced Vernacular Contexts

# Education Issues in Creole and **Creole-Influenced Vernacular Contexts**

EDITED BY

## IAN ROBERTSON

AND

## HAZEL SIMMONS-McDONALD

THE UNIVERSITY OF THE WEST INDIES PRESS
Jamaica • Barbados • Trinidad and Tobago

The University of the West Indies Press
7A Gibraltar Hall Road, Mona
Kingston 7, Jamaica
www.uwipress.com

A catalogue record of this book is available from the National Library of Jamaica.

978-976-640-463-5 (print)
978-976-640-471-0 (Kindle)
978-976-640-479-6 (ePub)

*Cover illustration*: Detail of a mural on the wall of the Registry, University of Guyana, Turkeyen. The mural was done by art students at the University of Guyana in 1995, with different students doing different sections. The section shown is signed by D.Munroe.

Cover design by Marsha Pearce and Robert Harris
Typesetting by The Beget, India
Printed in the United States of America

# Contents

# Foreword

Zellynne Jennings-Craig
University of the West Indies, Mona

> *For life itself is a word, true*
> *without speaking, an ecstasy without singing*
> Dennis Craig, *Tribute*

Dennis Craig's research and publications on educational issues in creole contexts and their contribution to the thinking of applied linguists, sociolinguists and educators are well acclaimed. Indeed, Jeff Siegel acknowledges the "groundbreaking" nature of his early publications in *Language Learning* in the newly emerging field of second-language acquisition. The significance of Dennis's contribution to language learning in creole contexts is evident not only in his academic publications but in the extent of his work in curriculum development, in which he applied principles from his research to the development of reading materials, particularly at the primary level. Most notable among these is Primary Language Arts, a series of teachers' guides and pupils' materials for the primary school which he co-authored with Don Wilson and Peggy Campbell. This became the reading primer used in Jamaican primary schools for over twenty years. With Hilary Sherlock, he wrote four introductory books of the *New Caribbean Reader* series. In the mid-1990s he was retained by the Belize Ministry of Education as consultant and general editor of a self-contained course on the teaching of the language arts at the primary level, to be delivered by distance methods to Belizean teacher trainees. He was the writer of the most extensive module of this course. In 1998–99, he was consultant to the CARICOM Secretariat in a programme for the determination and measurement of desirable learning outcomes in the language arts in the school systems of CARICOM member states. In 1980, with Grace Walker Gordon, he wrote books 1 and 2 of *New World English*, and in 1983 and 1985 he wrote books 3 and 4 respectively of the same text. This was a language course for secondary-school children in non-standard language contexts.

Dennis's major focus, as Jeff Siegel rightly states in chapter 1, was on the specific problems of teaching standard English to speakers of English-lexified creoles. Apart from his search for a methodology of teaching English in a Caribbean context, especially Jamaica, Beverley Bryan (chapter 2) credits Dennis with key contributions to language education in the Caribbean. These include the notion of an "interaction area" or "mutual interference" as the learner combines structures from two different linguistic systems, and that of the "creole-influenced vernacular". Bryan also underscores the contribution that Dennis was able to make to policy which influenced the teaching of literacy in schools. He had a burning desire throughout his life to improve proficiency in standard English at all levels of the education system. This explains the amount of time he spent developing materials for the teaching of standard English. He often expressed disappointment that all his efforts seemed to come to naught. There were a number of reasons that he felt accounted for this, but two in particular seemed to frustrate him most. First of these was the fact that the books were not used as intended. For example, the teachers' guides for the Primary Language Arts series proved too costly to reproduce and so most teachers did not benefit from the wealth of instructions and ideas on the use of the pupils' materials. Second, he bemoaned the fact that those with the power to influence the teaching of language and literacy in the schools were trained in situations where English was a first language, and so they advocated the use of teaching methodologies (for example, communicative language teaching) which he did not consider appropriate for creole-speaking contexts.

Dennis's love for research and writing was evident in other ways. He started writing fortnightly viewpoints for the Guyana Broadcasting Company in 1989. When he became vice chancellor of the University of Guyana in 1991, he gave up doing these, so as to concentrate on the demands of his new job. Seven months later, he resumed the viewpoints because he found it impossible to divorce issues in higher education from the local issues that intrude in the business of the university and that, in his own words, "beg for the public expression of rational opinion". Several of his viewpoints were on the topic of education. For example, on 15 November 1993, he addressed the complaints about university graduates and their deficiency in general education character-istics, as evidenced by the roughness of their speech and their inability "to put two sentences together". But these were the very complaints, Dennis wrote, that were levelled against school leavers, including those from the very best second-ary schools. Teachers at that level blamed the deficiency on weaknesses at the primary level. Dennis traced the deficiencies in the education system to broad societal changes that had taken place over the past sixty years. These included the rapid democratization of education that had taken place in the postcolonial era, which had given access to secondary education to children in the lower socio-economic classes. These children had brought with them cultural habits "including language that were once frowned upon and suppressed in traditional middle and upper class society". However, non-standard speech (such as Guya-nese Creolese) had become accepted as a legitimate form of language not to be treated as "bad language". At the same time, Dennis added, a grammar-oriented approach to English teaching had gone out of fashion and had not been replaced by the adapted second language which was most appropriate. He concluded: "Do not express shock therefore that secondary schools and the University are affected. If our graduates had been taught to write Creolese, they would write you much better reports in Creolese than they can now write in English."

Dennis's passion for his discipline remained with him to the very end. I recall one day, about three months before his passing, when on our visit to his doctor we happened to meet in the surgery a politician with responsibility in education. Though in obvious pain, Dennis could not resist the opportunity to engage the politician in discussion on the importance of monolingualism in the home language, as opposed to the full bilingualism advocated by the Bilingual Education Project that was being tested in some primary schools in Jamaica at the time. Whether or not the politician was convinced, as Siegel notes in chapter 1, "where teaching standard English to speakers of a related vernacular . . . is occurring, models of monolingualism in standard English or monoliterate bilingualism are still being followed. Therefore, the methodologies, curricula and classroom activities developed by Craig for such situations still remain relevant, and will remain so for many years to come."

Dennis was also a poet. He won the 1998 Guyana Prize for Literature for the best first book of poetry. Originally, he wanted his book of poems to be entitled *Seeds by the Wayside*. This may be an appropriate title for the volume of his life's work. Perhaps intuitively he perceived the legacy of his work. His ideas, like seeds, were scattered. Some took root and were acknowledged by scholars, but others fell by the wayside, unnoticed, even forgotten. Siegel notes that "unfortunately, Craig's work has not received the recognition it deserves in writing on standard dialect teaching." Bryan, on the other hand, gives examples of Dennis's lasting impact. She asserts that inadvertently, he may have influenced the Bilingual Education Project: "Craig's inclination to privilege the vernacular is being taken to its logical conclusion." She concludes that "Craig's work is inspiring departures" and that "his research was of the greatest significance to educators, as his insights from research always focused on what was most socially useful for teachers and what was essential for learners."

A linguist, a language educator, a mind with a fount of knowledge about educational issues, a poet, a man of simple pleasures, a remarkable intellect to the very end. Such was Dennis. I was blessed to have shared the latter years of the life of this quietly brilliant man – a gentleman in the true sense of the word – who would have felt humbled by the honour that his colleagues and friends have bestowed on him in this book. A writer of so many words, he would have been lost for them.

On his behalf, I say to you all, a thousand thanks.

# Preface

Professor Dennis Roy Craig was, without a doubt, an outstanding Caribbean educator. Born and raised in a working-class environment in his native Guyana (British Guiana), he managed, by the end of his life to become an outstanding language educator, education planner and advisor, manager of tertiary-level institutions, and a highly respected Caribbean academic.

Dennis Craig was passionate about the teaching of language and, in particular, English language to what he termed towards the end of his career speakers of creole-influenced vernaculars (CIV). He worked tirelessly at researching the various Caribbean language learning and teaching situations and at developing and sharing materials appropriate for these contexts. In this, he made excellent use of his experience teaching at secondary, teacher training college and university levels in the region. He trained, mentored and guided a large number of Caribbean academics, who are all in his debt.

Professor Craig served as dean of the Faculty of Education at the Mona campus of the University of the West Indies and also as the first university dean of the three Faculties of Education which existed at that time on the three campuses of the University of the West Indies. He returned to Guyana where he served as the first director of the National Centre for Education Research and Development. His last major academic appointment was as vice chancellor of the University of Guyana.

Professor Craig was central to the establishment of the Society for Caribbean Linguistics, which he served as the first secretary/treasurer and later as the vice president and then president. Dennis Craig also wrote poetry and won the Guyana prize for his first collection of poetry, *Near the Seashore*.

Contributors to this volume are among the large numbers of academics and students who came to respect him for the manner in which he wore his considerable talents and achievements with a simplicity and humility that could only be equalled but never bettered.

# PART 1

## DENNIS CRAIG IN CARIBBEAN LANGUAGE EDUCATION

# 1

# Dennis Craig's Contributions to Applied Creolistics

JEFF SIEGEL

*University of New England (Australia)*

The most important area of applied creolistics is concerned with the role of creole languages in formal education. Dennis Craig was a leader in this field. Throughout his distinguished career, he worked both at the local level to improve the education of speakers of creole languages in the Caribbean and at the international level to promote research on educational issues as an integral part of creolistics. Craig critically assessed the various teaching methodologies used to teach creole speakers and suggested practical, but theoretically grounded, alternatives. In contrast to most other creolists, Craig also went beyond pronouncements and academic papers to produce useful teaching materials and run workshops for teachers. His work had wider implications for speakers of creoles outside the Caribbean region and for speakers of marginalized vernaculars, such as African American English. This chapter reviews Craig's contributions to applied creolistics in these four areas: promotion, analysis of methodologies, practical solutions and wider implications. It is written from my own point of view, as someone from outside the Caribbean who has been a long-time admirer of Craig's work and of his steadfast commitment.

## Promotion

In addition to dozens of publications in Caribbean journals, Craig's many book chapters and articles in international journals have brought educational issues in creole contexts to the attention of not only creolists in general but also applied linguists and sociolinguists. His chapters in the influential early volumes on pidgins and creoles (Craig 1971, 1977, 1980) established a place for applied creolistics as part of the discipline. Chapters also appeared in volumes on varieties of English around the world (1986, 1997), bilingualism and bilingual education (1978a, 1978b, 1988a), and language and inequality (1985). Craig's articles in *Language Learning* (1966, 1967) were groundbreaking in the newly emerging field of second language acquisition, and later articles in the *International Journal of the Sociology of Language* (1976, 1984, 1988b) demonstrated the importance of creole language situations in sociolinguistics. His final publication was a chapter on pidgins and creoles in education in *The Handbook of Pidgin and Creole Studies*, which appeared in 2008.

From 1968, Craig also presented dozens of invited papers on educational issues in creole contexts, not only throughout the Caribbean but also in the United States (Texas, Arizona, Hawai'i, Illinois, Michigan, Washington, DC), Canada (Ontario, Quebec), Britain, Austria, Germany, India, Kenya and the Seychelles.

Worth mentioning also were his many contributions to the *Pidgins and Creoles in Education (PACE) Newsletter*, which was distributed to educators around the world from 1990 to 2003. In the late 1990s he also established the *Journal of Education and Development in the Caribbean*, which he edited until his death.

## Analysis of Methodologies

A key area of focus in Craig's work is the specific problem of teaching standard English to speakers of English-lexified creoles, what he calls the "lexifier L2" situation (1998). He notes that former British colonies in the Caribbean are "in a way, trapped within their Standard English traditions" (1971, 375), in that they have adopted English as the official language of government and education. Therefore, a goal of the education system is proficiency in standard English – a goal that has largely not been met. In 1971, the failure rate in English was reported as 60 to 85 per cent (1971, 375), and in 1993–94 it remained at approximately 50 per cent or more for most countries, reaching 75 per cent in Jamaica and 85 per cent in Guyana (2001a, 73). Craig (1983a, 1985) outlines some sociolinguistic reasons for the lack of success in English teaching that are specific to the lexifier L2 situation, such as negative attitudes towards standard English and its speakers, and its lack of relevance to the social needs of most of the students. But in most of his work, he puts the blame mainly on the various teaching methodologies that have been used.

Craig was a longtime critic of the "English-as-the-mother-tongue tradition" (2001a, 66) in the education of speakers of English-lexified creoles in the Caribbean. In this monolingual tradition, students were considered to be merely poor speakers of the standard language. Their creole language was considered typical of the uneducated speech of the lower socio-economic classes, labelled as a "restricted code", according to Bernstein (1964, 1971). This deficit view assumed that creole speech had certain limitations as a form of communication, especially in formal contexts. Therefore, the role of education was seen as compensatory – to make up for creole-speaking students' linguistic disability. Craig (1983a, 1985) was one of the scholars who argued strongly against this point of view. His research (1974) showed that while basilectal creole speakers (members of lower social classes in general) use styles and strategies of communication that differ from those preferred by speakers of a standard variety of language, they achieve the same communicative and cognitive results. He wrote:

> The practice of compensatory education often involves the erroneous perception of lower-social-class children. Such children are normally not linguistically or intellectually deprived in any absolute sense; what happens is that the school system, curricula, and educational methodology of the dominant upper-social culture make no use of the natural linguistic and cultural orientation of the lower social class; instead, they aim from the outset of formal education to remould lower-social-class children into replicas of the upper social class. (1978a, 419)

Similar findings concerning other types of marginalized vernaculars were reported by sociolinguists in the 1960s and 1970s (e.g., Labov 1969).

At the same time, extensive research into pidgins and creoles showed that they are legitimate, rule-governed varieties of language that differ extensively from their lexifiers. Thus, Caribbean students were generally not really native speakers of English. Stewart (1964) used the term "quasi-foreign language situations" to refer to the learning of standard English by speakers of English-lexified creoles and "radically nonstandard" dialects of English. Although these learners have native or near-native command of some aspects of the standard dialect, there are other areas in which the learner's first language or dialect differs markedly from that of the standard. These were thought to warrant the use of methods of foreign language teaching (FLT) and teaching English to speakers of other languages (TESOL), in what became known as teaching standard English as a second dialect (TSESD). Following the audio-lingual approach popular at that time, the emphasis was on habit formation and oral fluency, with teaching focused on particular grammatical structures. Contrastive analysis of the L1 and L2 (in this case, the creole and the standard) was done to determine which structures should be taught, and pattern practice and drills were used to teach them.

However, Craig (1971, 376) observed that for students who speak English-lexified creoles, "English is neither a native nor a foreign language." He was among the first scholars to criticize the use of FLT/TESOL methodologies in the Caribbean. For example, Craig (1966, 57) pointed out that in most foreign- or second language learning situations where English is the target, learners initially are not able to recognize or produce any aspects of the language. But in situations where standard English is the target for speakers of English-lexified creoles, learners already recognize and produce some aspects of it as part of their repertoires.

In several publications, Craig (1966, 1971, 1976, 1983a) proposed that standard English features are divided into four classes with respect to creole speakers:

(A)   those actively known (used spontaneously in informal speech)
(B)   those known but used only under stress (in formal situations – but not habitual)
(C)   those known passively (could be understood according to context, but not produced)
(D)   those not yet known

Because of classes A, B and C, many creole speakers are under the illusion that they already know the standard (Craig 1971, 377), and this affects motivation in the classroom. This has also been pointed out by Fischer (1992) and Nero (1997) with regard to Caribbean immigrants in the United States. Also, because the target patterns of classes C and D above are often very closely linked to those of classes A and B, "the learner often fails to perceive the new target element in the teaching situation" (Craig 1966, 58).

Another difference pointed out by Craig is that in foreign or second language learning situations where English is the target, English does not form part of learner's native language repertoires and therefore remains separate and distinct. But in the lexifier L2 situations in the Caribbean (and with immigrants in North America), there is an "area of interaction" between the learner's familiar speech and standard English – that is, intermediate varieties in a creole continuum (1966, 1971). Because of this interaction, as well as the close links between known and target features, separating the two varieties is often a problem.

Furthermore, in FLT and TESOL situations, two different autonomous linguistic systems are easily recognized. The learner's L1 often has its own dictionaries and grammars, just like the L2. But in TSESD, because of the similarities with the standard, the learner's previous knowledge and the interaction between the L1 and L2 as just described, the learner's creole vernacular is often not recognized as a separate variety of language, despite research to the contrary. This leads to both teachers and students thinking that there is only one legitimate language involved, and just as in the "English-as-the-mother-tongue" tradition, students are discouraged from using their own ways of speaking in the classroom. Thus, students are clearly disadvantaged by not being allowed to express themselves in their own variety of language, a factor which has a negative effect on cognitive development (UNESCO 1968; Thomas and Collier 2002).

Craig referred to such adverse effects on students if their home language is not used in the school, and if it is also restricted in use by the community at large – a situation that was frequently found in the Caribbean. He believed that students' use of their vernacular language should not be inhibited in the classroom in early years of formal education: "The integrity of the self-concept and the balanced development of the creole speaker demand that at least the first part of his/her formal education should utilize the home language" (1977, 320). Craig (1967, 134) also expressed the view that in general, "the teacher has to accept the natural speech of the child without the inhibiting practice of intermittent 'correction'" – except in specific pattern practice exercises.

Craig was also critical of another FLT/TESOL methodology that became popular after the audio-lingual approach: communicative language teaching (CLT). This methodology emphasizes language function and use in real-life situations. Craig (1966, 1983a) observed that unlike learners of a foreign language, creole-speaking learners of a standard variety have no communicative reason to keep using the target (that is, the standard) in the classroom. It is too easy for them to slip back into their own vernacular and still be understood. He noted that in such situations, "learners can all retain their normal language usage for performing communicative tasks, and there is no need to learn anything new" (1998, 12).

## Practical Solutions

Craig (1980, 247–48) outlined six educational policy alternatives or models for the lexifier L2 situations found in the Caribbean, where the standard form of lexifier was socially dominant.

1. Monolingualism in school in the dominant language. In this alternative the home language of the child is completely ignored.
2. Monoliterate bilingualism, in which the home language of the child is used in school only to the extent necessary to allow the child to adjust to school and learn enough of the school language to permit it to become the medium of education.
3. Monoliterate bilingualism, in which both languages are developed for aural-oral skills, but literacy is aimed at only in the one language that happens to be socially dominant in the community.
4. Partial bilingualism, in which aural-oral fluency and literacy are developed in the home language only in relation to certain types of subject matter that have to do with the immediate society and culture, while aural-oral fluency and literacy in the school language are developed for a wider range of purposes.
5. Full bilingualism, in which the educational aim is for the child to develop all skills in both languages in all domains.
6. Monolingualism in the home language, in which the aim of the school is to develop literacy only in the home language of the child.

Craig discussed the constraints on the choice of alternatives, and the practical advantages and disadvantages of each one. While partial bilingualism or even full bilingualism (as proposed by Devonish [1986]) would clearly have cultural and educational benefits, for either of these to become policy, social attitudes toward the two languages would first need to change radically so that the languages were on a more equal footing. The requirement for implementing such alternatives would be "an acceptance by policy makers that the total functional roles of the home language and the formerly more dominant language are equal and the same" (1980, 260). Considering the state of affairs at the time, Craig (1980, 258) concluded that a model of monoliterate bilingualism might be the best compromise.

Therefore, Craig believed that standard English should be taught to creole speakers as a second language (ESL) or second dialect (ESD), but with sweeping modifications taking into account his criticisms of the FLT/TESOL method-ologies, as outlined in the preceding section. He also promoted using a bilingual or bidialectal approach that would develop the students' first language as well.

With regard to teaching the standard, some of the modifications that Craig (1971, 379) proposed were to focus only on the unknown features (class D above) and to focus on those features that are relevant to "the maturity, interests and experiences of specific learners". Furthermore, he stated, the standard should be taught only for use in situations in which it is normally required and used. In addition, Craig proposed methods that went beyond the ESL/ESD approaches. The most important were those aimed at promoting consciousness-raising and language awareness in students – awareness about varieties of language in gen-eral and variation in use according to context, and awareness of the specific differences between home and school varieties. This is done through class dis-cussion and student input, rather than being "taught" by the teacher. According to Craig (2001a, 71), these methods "induce vernacular speakers to perceive contrasts between their own and the targeted standard which they would be unlikely to perceive through mere communicative interaction".

Finally, Craig (2001b, 4) advocated an overall eclectic methodology: "The best policy is to select strategies that are effective, and that satisfy the specific needs of learners, irrespective of the language-teaching approach in which those strat-egies historically originated."

In order to promote these ways of teaching for the benefit of Caribbean students, Craig (2001b, 5–6) believed there should be teacher training and in-service courses that would do the following:

1. create or improve in teachers an understanding of the local language situation and its influence on language education in schools;
2. develop in teachers an orientation to language and literacy teaching which would be guided by their understanding under (1) preceding;
3. acquaint teachers with the salient, though varying, perspectives and approaches that have influenced language and literacy teaching in con-temporary times;
4. equip teachers to select relevant principles from the perspectives and approaches under (3) preceding, so as to provide for the specific language-education needs of vernacular speakers;
5. improve the capacity of teachers to apply the selected principles for a more effective teaching of language and literacy at primary, inadequately achieving post-primary or secondary levels; and

6. provide language and literacy teachers with tools that may increase their ability to be constructive in improving existing syllabuses and schemes of work in their schools.

Significantly, Craig's work was not limited to writing academic papers about the issues. Rather, he himself developed resource materials and wrote textbooks, and he personally conducted training courses and workshops for teachers. Some of Craig's earlier ideas on modified ESL/ESD methodologies are incorporated into the *New World English* series of school textbooks he authored in the 1980s (Craig and Walker Gordon 1981; Craig 1983b). His later book, *Teaching Language and Literacy: Policies and Procedures for Vernacular Situations* (1999), was written especially to accomplish the six goals in teacher training listed above. In this book, he provides a theoretical framework for classroom procedures in language and literacy teaching, consolidating his earlier proposals for teaching methodologies and expanding them to include language awareness and other new aspects. He also presents many useful, practical and detailed suggestions for teachers regarding curricula and classroom activities.

In 2001, Craig himself ran special training workshops based on his book for forty senior teachers and administrators in Grenada, and for eighty final-year teacher trainees in Barbados. In 2002, he conducted a similar seminar at the University of the West Indies for language educators in all Jamaican colleges. These followed more than thirty years of previous experience in conducting educational workshops throughout the Caribbean and serving as a consultant for various educational programs.

## Wider Implications

In the 1960s, applied linguists began to point out the similarities between teaching a standard language to speakers of creoles lexified by that language (the L2 lexifier situation) and teaching the standard dialect to speakers of non-standard dialects of the same language, such as African American English (e.g., Stewart 1964). But it was Craig (e.g., 1976) who continued to highlight the educational issues that concern both speakers of creole languages and speakers of marginalized non-standard dialects. In his article in the US *Journal of Negro Education* (1983a), he explicitly demonstrated how his own views on ESL/ESD methodologies in the Caribbean context were relevant to the teaching of African American students.

Unfortunately, Craig's work has not received the recognition it deserves in writing on standard dialect teaching, but it is interesting to note that later researchers have independently come to some similar conclusions. For example, as referred to above, Craig (1966, 58) observed that when speakers of non-standard varieties are being taught standard English, "the learner often fails to perceive the new target element in the teaching situation". Cheshire (1982, 55) later noted that children in British schools who speak non-standard dialects are unaware of specific differences between their speech and standard English: "They may simply recognise that school teachers and newsreaders, for example, do not speak in quite the same way as their family and friends." Similarly, in the Netherlands, van den Hoogen and Kuijper (1992, 223) observe that speakers of non-standard Dutch dialects learning standard Dutch often cannot detect errors in their speech caused by linguistic differences between the varieties.

Nevertheless, Craig kept a wider focus in his later work, such that it is relevant to teachers in both creole and non-standard dialect contexts. For example, in his 1999 textbook for teachers, he writes: "This book is concerned with situations where a vernacular coexists with an official language with which the vernacular shares a common vocabulary base", and that it "presents a case study of the interplay between the sociolinguistic characteristics of the population, goals for language education, and necessary pedagogical approaches in the schools". Although the case study concerns the Caribbean, he writes, "the book is very relevant to the parallel African-American vernacular situation in the USA" (p. ix). Throughout the book, Craig calls this situation "Teaching English to Speakers of a Related Vernacular", or TESORV.

From my own experience, I have found Craig's work to be extremely valuable in my research on pidgins, creoles and non-standard dialects in education and second dialect acquisition, and have referred to him extensively in many of my publications (e.g., Siegel 1999a, 1999b, 2002, 2003, 2006).

## Conclusion

Devonish (2007, 214–19) indicates that attitudes have recently changed significantly in Jamaica, with a greater number of people wanting Jamaican Creole to be used in more formal contexts, including education. As a result, a Bilingual Education Project was approved by the government and implemented in two pilot schools in 2004, the year that Dennis Craig passed away. The project involves equal use of Jamaican Creole alongside standard Jamaican English in all aspects of formal education from grades 1 to 4 (Devonish and Carpenter 2007), and thus follows the full bilingualism model (see above). However, in other places where teaching standard English to speakers of a related vernacular (Craig's TESORV) is occurring, models of monolingualism in standard English or monoliterate bilingualism are still being followed. Therefore, the methodologies, curricula and classroom activities developed by Craig for such situations still remain relevant, and will remain so for many years to come.

## References

Bernstein, Basil. 1964. Elaborated and Restricted Codes: Their Social Origins and some Consequences. *American Anthropologist* 66: 55–69.

———. 1971. *Class, Codes and Control*. Vol. 1. London: Routledge and Kegan Paul.

Cheshire, Jenny. 1982. Dialect Features and Linguistic Conflict in Schools. *Educational Review* 14 (1): 53–67.

Craig, Dennis R. 1966. Teaching English to Jamaican Creole Speakers: A Model of a Multi-Dialect Situation. *Language Learning* 16 (1–2): 49–61.

———. 1967. Some Early Indications of Learning a Second Dialect. *Language Learning* 17 (3–4): 133–40.

———. 1971. Education and Creole English in the West Indies: Some Sociolinguistic Factors. In *Pidginization and Creolization of Languages*, edited by D. Hymes, 371–91. Cambridge: Cambridge University Press.

———. 1974. Developmental and Social Class Differences in Language. *Caribbean Journal of Education* 1: 5–23.

———. 1976. Bidialectal Education: Creole and Standard in the West Indies. *International Journal of the Sociology of Language* 8: 93–134.

———. 1977. Creole Languages and Primary Education. In *Pidgin and Creole Linguistics*, edited by A. Valdman, 313–32. Bloomington: Indiana University Press.

———. 1978a. Language Education in a Post-Creole Society. In *Case Studies in Bilingual Education*, edited by B. Spolsky and R.L. Cooper, 404–26. Rowley, MA: Newbury House.

———. 1978b. Creole and Standard: Partial Learning, Base Grammar, and the Mesolect. In *International Dimensions of Bilingual Education*, edited by J.E. Alatis, 602–20. Washington, DC: Georgetown University Press.

———. 1980. Models for Educational Policy in Creole-Speaking Communities. In *Theoretical Orientations in Creole Studies*, edited by A. Valdman and A. Highfield, 245–65. New York: Academic Press.

———. 1983a. Teaching Standard English to Nonstandard Speakers: Some Methodological Issues. *Journal of Negro Education* 52 (1): 65–74.

———. 1983b. *New World English*. Books 3–4. London: Longman.

———. 1984. Communication, Creole, and Conceptualization. *International Journal of the Sociology of Language* 45: 21–37.

———. 1985. The Sociology of Language Learning and Teaching in a Creole Situation. In *Language of Inequality*, edited by N. Wolfson and J. Manes, 273–84. Berlin: Mouton.

———. 1986. Social Class and the Use of Language: A Case Study of Jamaican Children. In *Focus on the Caribbean: Varieties of English Around the World*, edited by M. Görlach and J.A. Holm, 71–116. Amsterdam: John Benjamins.

———. 1988a. Creole English and Education in Jamaica. In *International Handbook of Bilingualism and Bilingual Education*, edited by C. Bratt Paulston, 297–312. New York: Greenwood.

———. 1988b. Cognition and Situational Context: Explanations from English-Lexicon Creole. *International Journal of the Sociology of Language* 71: 11–23.

———. 1997. The English of West Indian University Students. In *Englishes Around the World: Studies in Honour of Manfred Görlach*. Vol. 2, *Caribbean, Africa, Asia, Australasia*, edited by E.W. Schneider, 11–24. Amsterdam: John Benjamins.

———. 1998. "Afta yu laan dem fi riid an rait dem Kriiyol, den wa muo?" Creole and the Teaching of the Lexifier Language. Paper presented at the Third International Creole Workshop, Miami.

———. 1999. *Teaching Language and Literacy: Policies and Procedures for Vernacular Situations*. Georgetown, Guyana: Education and Development Services.

———. 2001a. Language Education Revisited in the Commonwealth Caribbean. In *Due Respect: Papers on English and English-Related Creoles in the Caribbean in Honour of Professor Robert Le Page*, edited by P. Christie, 61–76. Kingston: University of the West Indies Press.

———. 2001b. Teaching Language and Literacy in Vernacular Situations: Participant Evaluation of an In-Service Teachers' Workshop. *Pidgins and Creoles in Education (PACE) Newsletter* 12: 4–11.

———. 2008. Pidgins/Creoles and Education. In *The Handbook of Pidgin and Creole Studies*, edited by S. Kouwenberg and J.V. Singler, 593–614. Oxford: Blackwell.

Craig, Dennis R., and Grace Walker Gordon. 1981. *New World English*. Books 1–2. London: Longman.

Devonish, Hubert S. 1986. *Language and Liberation: Creole Language and Politics in the Caribbean*. London: Karia.

———. 2007. *Language and Liberation: Creole Language and Politics in the Caribbean*. Expanded edition. Kingston: Arawak.

Devonish, Hubert S., and Karen Carpenter. 2007. *Full Bilingual Education in a Creole Language Situation: The Jamaican Bilingual Primary Education Project*. St Augustine: Society for Caribbean Linguistics (Occasional Paper No. 35).

Fischer, Katherine. 1992. Educating Speakers of Caribbean English in the United States. In *Pidgins, Creoles and Nonstandard Dialects in Education*, edited by J. Siegel,

99–123. Melbourne: Applied Linguistics Association of Australia (Occasional Paper no. 12).

Labov, William. 1969. The Logic of Nonstandard English. In *Linguistics and the Teaching of Standard English*, edited by J.E. Alatis, 1–24. Washington, DC: Georgetown University Press.

Nero, Shondel J. 1997. English Is My Native Language . . . or So I Believe. *TESOL Quarterly* 31: 585–92.

Siegel, Jeff. 1999a. Creole and Minority Dialects in Education: An Overview. *Journal of Multilingual and Multicultural Development* 20 (6): 508–31.

———. 1999b. Stigmatized and Standardized Varieties in the Classroom: Interference or Separation? *TESOL Quarterly* 33: 701–28.

———. 2002. Pidgins and Creoles. In *Handbook of Applied Linguistics*, edited by R.B. Kaplan, 335–51. New York: Oxford University Press.

———. 2003. Social Context. In *Handbook of Second Language Acquisition*, edited by C.J. Doughty and M.H. Long, 178–223. Oxford: Blackwell.

———. 2006. Keeping Creoles and Dialects out of the Classroom: Is it Justified? In *Dialects, Englishes, Creoles, and Education*, edited by S.J. Nero, 39–67. Mahwah, NJ: Erlbaum.

Stewart, William A. 1964. Foreign Language Teaching Methods in Quasi-Foreign Language Situations. In *Non-standard Speech and the Teaching of English*, edited by W.A. Stewart, 1–15. Washington, DC: Center for Applied Linguistics.

Thomas, Wayne P., and Virginia P. Collier. 2002. *A National Study of School Effectiveness for Language Minority Students' Long-Term Academic Achievement*. Santa Cruz, CA: Center for Research on Education, Diversity and Excellence.

UNESCO. 1968. The Use of Vernacular Languages in Education: The Report of the UNESCO Meeting of Specialists, 1951. In *Readings in the Sociology of Language*, edited by J.A. Fishman, 688–716. The Hague: Mouton.

van den Hoogen, Jos, and Henk Kuijper. 1992. The Development Phase of the Kerkrade Project. In *Dialect and Education: Some European Perspectives*, edited by J. Cheshire, V. Edwards, H. Münstermann and B. Weltens, 219–33. Clevedon, UK: Multilingual Matters.

# 2 | Dennis Craig and Language Education

BEVERLEY BRYAN
*University of the West Indies, Mona*

D ennis Craig's professional life, as a creole linguist, was consistently focused on the development goal of delivering high levels of language teaching to the children of the Caribbean. His research was thus instructive and instrumental. The purpose of this chapter is to (a) examine the nature and significance of the key ideas Dennis Craig presented over the decades of research which he carried out and (b) consider the impact of these ideas on generations of Caribbean language and literacy teachers and their institutions.

## Defining Language Education

The chapter is entitled "Craig and Language Education" because this concept is an important starting point, as Craig played a central role in bringing attention to linguistic content into the educational sphere, to shape a Caribbean version of that discipline described as language education. This term refers to the teaching and learning of languages. Language education is a wide area that might include descriptions of language but also the application of theories of acquisition and can be differentiated from theories of language learning.

One direction in language education, underscored by the creole environment, is taken by Robertson (1999). He notes the difficulties that both disciplines have encountered in gaining recognition from the academe: one area is deemed too hard and irrelevant (linguistics); the other is deemed too mundane and familiar for serious study (education). He suggests an exploration of their symbiotic relationship, and he uses the term "educational linguistics" to refer to that intersection of the two disciplines, in the service of important societal goals. The emphasis is also on society and understanding the macro, the context of the education system and the importance of language in all aspects of schooling. In the intersection of the two disciplines, they become what might seem to be the most powerful and important area of study for those concerned with language teaching. This was the area of Craig's work, with the subject of his research being the languages of the Caribbean.

## Craig's Ideas

In Craig's development of a particular domain that could be called Caribbean language education, a number of concepts seemed particularly important to him. All of them cannot be discussed in this chapter, but some of his ideas, which I see as key to understanding his contribution to education in the region and especially Jamaica, can be examined here. The areas to be considered are

- the specificity of the creole-speaking environment in the concept of the interaction area;
- the notion of the creole-influenced vernacular;
- the needs of Caribbean learners; and
- the search for an appropriate methodology.

## The Interaction Area

Craig took very seriously the specificity of the creole environment and introduced the term *interaction area*. This was a development of Bailey's (1971) and DeCamp's (1971) use of the "continuum" in their characterizations of the Caribbean language environment, which Craig acknowledged. As Holm (1988, 55) has indicated, DeCamp was the first to apply the word "continuum" to the "gradation of varieties between creole and standard English", although the notion of the linkages between the vernacular and the official or source language had been available for some time. In one of Craig's (1971a) earliest and clearest analyses of these distinct varieties, he sought to dissect standard West Indian English and delineate that component part between the extremes of the continuum that is dependent on the bi-directional influences of both creole and standard West Indian English (see figure 2.1). In making his distinct contribution, he used the term *interaction area* to emphasize the bi-directional influences or "mutual interference" between two linguistic systems as speakers combine structures from both. The dynamic mixing consists of (1) all the non-English features of standard West Indian English (represented as *p*) and (2) all the varieties that exist towards the creole extreme.

The psychological connotation of this "interaction" labelling was significant, as Craig wanted to convey how performance and the attempt to move towards the standard helped to create those varieties between the two linguistic systems. He was particularly interested in how children produced these varieties in careful and spontaneous speech, through socialization, schooling and the influence

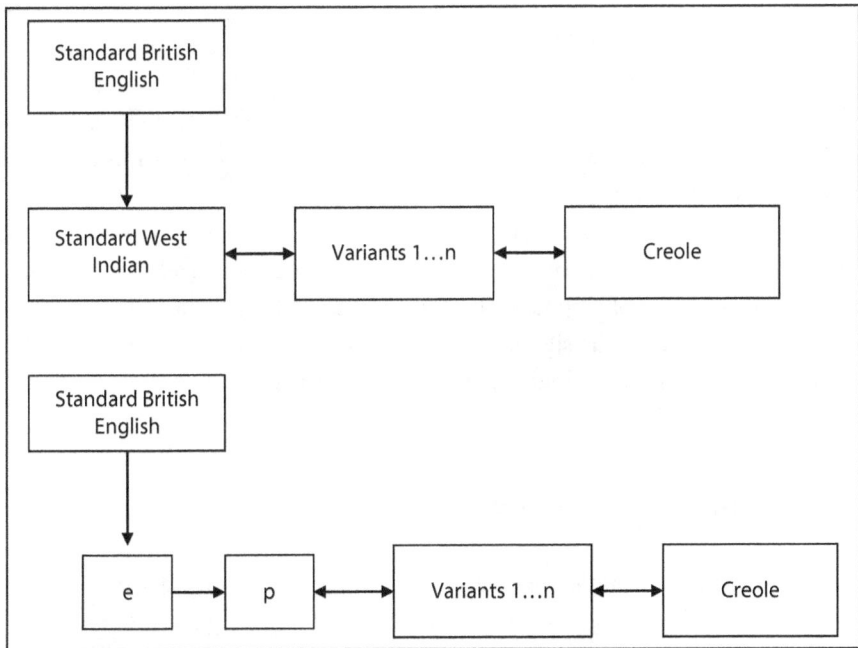

**Figure 2.1:** The interaction area between creole and standard (Craig 1971a, 372)

of the mass media (1971a). His focus was on children's language production both in and out of classrooms. His data on primary-school children shows their flexibility with language and the varieties they produced:

| *Spontaneous utterance and attempts* of the same child at "careful" standard language replacement | Creole and Standard versions not heard |
|---|---|
| /a mi buk dat/ | /a fi mi buk dat/ |
| /iz mi buk/ | 'It's my book.' |
| /iz mai buk/ | |
| (Craig 1971a, 374) | |

For Craig, it was a paradox that this ability to shift into the interaction area did not develop far enough to allow the children to develop a facility with English. At this early stage, he was discussing "fossilization" without naming it, recognizing the interlanguage produced by young children who remain within the "interaction area", resisting typical foreign language techniques. In subsequent work, Craig (1978, 106) used the term *mesolect* and acknowledged early references by Bickerton and Rickford. By this time, the intermediate language was being characterized by reference to Selinker's "fossilization of an interlanguage" (p. 106). For Craig, the development of the intermediate language was the result of social-class mobility, an important variable in his accounts of language behaviour and of elementary educational opportunities, the consistent focus of his work. Craig (1978) illustrates the importance of the former in a study concentrating on the sociology of language learning, and he emphasizes that language planners must take into account a range of social factors, including the correlation between social class and type of language, the consequences of diglossia and the impact of language attitudes. The significance of the latter is continually reinforced by Craig and taken up in his final paper (2006), published posthumously.

## Creole-Influenced Vernacular

The term *creole-influenced vernacular* (CIV) was a later formulation used to describe the folk language or the generic creole-based language of the Caribbean region. Craig exhibited positive attitudes towards the vernacular, which he described as the mother tongue of the children he was most interested in studying. He regarded their language as "historically linked with the African diaspora" (1999, 1). The labelling of that vernacular did not seem to preoccupy him. The names changed as he looked at "creole" in "bidialectal education" (1976) and, later, "creole-influenced vernacular (CIV)" (1999). His concern was CIV, or the "English-based creole", and its varieties (1999, 2). In this last book, first published in 1999 and republished posthumously in 2006, he took on the universalist position of the pidgin-to-creole cycle, emphasizing the influence of the relevant European vocabulary and the importance of language contact. Nevertheless, most of his writing indicated that he saw the close relationship between the vernacular and English as the most salient and altogether the most problematic area of his research in education. It was this aspect of the language situation that guided his work.

Craig (1971(a) 375) took what the children brought to school and was centrally concerned to underscore that academic interest in these matters was "essential to the provision of guidelines for social action, specifically educational action in respect of language". In this way, his research was of the greatest significance to educators, as his insights from research always focused on what was most socially useful for teachers and what was essential for learners.

## Learners' Needs

Craig has seemed first and foremost to be a linguist who put the needs of Caribbean children at the centre of his work. He recognized that children's language was different because of the impact of schooling. As indicated above, he noted that their language had a certain dynamic structure and grammar (1971b), which could be illustrated by supporting research, often involving cross-cultural populations from the wider Caribbean, the United States and the United Kingdom (1965, 1994, 1999). Much of this research was among children in primary schools (1971a, 1971b). This learner-centred work helped him to articulate some of the specific requirements of children in a creole-speaking environment. The requirements explicate the four levels of stratification of the English-language repertoire of West Indian/Jamaican children. These were articulated as follows:

1. patterns actively known and used by creole speakers;
2. patterns used only under stress and learned through school or intermittent contact with native speakers;

3. patterns known passively that would be understood in context but not produced accurately by creole speakers; and
4. patterns that are not known.

According to Craig, the problem here was that the CIV learner failed to notice the level-four patterns – those that were unknown – because of the available access, limited or otherwise, to the other levels. This difficulty, and the psychological consequences of a lack of motivation, were considerable issues for Craig.

Additional to delineation of the levels, Craig presented an important concept that has endured by shaping his prescriptions on language-teaching methodology for creole speakers. The concept of the *continuity of cognitive growth* is not new, and Craig (1999, 58) himself pointed to its antecedents in cognitive learning theory. However, he emphasized its relevance for his "CIV speakers" as much as for "native foreign-language" speakers. The claim was that as young learners progress in their acquisition of the home language, there is a matching progression in the linguistic aspects of their cognitive development. The challenge of schooling in a second language is that there are insufficient opportunities for the continued development of higher-level cognitive abilities in the language they know best, their mother tongue. This language is relegated to less rigorous out-of-school activities. At the same time, children struggle to process at the higher level in the second language, with inadequate linguistic resources. Recognition of the detrimental effects of this situation in Caribbean schools has been an important contribution by Craig, and continues to be an issue in Jamaican schools as educators strive to understand fully how the deficiency in teaching can be corrected.

## In Search of an Appropriate Methodology

Craig's concern in pursuing transitional bilingualism was to find an *appropriate methodology* to use in the teaching of English. This began in his early articles, in which the sociolinguistic examination always turned to the implications for language teaching. His aim was always to improve the teaching of English, but his research indicated that neither a native language nor a strictly foreign language approach was appropriate. His earliest sustained attempt began in 1965 and he delineated it as a distinct methodology in subsequent work (1969), drawing on audio-lingualism but providing a decidedly Caribbean context. This programme aimed at the gradual incorporation of new linguistic items, which would be mixed with old forms as the learner gradually moved along the continuum.

Early on, Craig (1976) revealed his conclusions on the nature of the language situation in the Caribbean and proposed a move to "bidialectal education". This showed the influence of the work being carried out in the United States by linguists and language educators around African American Vernacular English (AAVE). Craig drew significant comparisons from their studies, but he felt that the Caribbean situation had some special features. Because of his sense of the uniqueness of the bidialectal or creole-influenced environment, he had a particular opposition to mother-tongue methodologies such as communicative language teaching (CLT), which he saw as lacking the necessary structured linguistic input that would ensure efficacy. Craig (1999) reviews this method in detail, especially the impact of its extreme forms, which he labels as "whole language". He felt that teachers had insufficient discourse knowledge to structure the learning experience to ensure true communicative competence and that because of this inadequacy, little target language learning took place.

## Vernacular Education

Craig's interest in schooling and his research into teaching meant that he had a profound interest in the potential of policies of ministries of education and governments to deal with the problems he encountered. His delineation of these policy options is set out in a number of his works (1976, 1978, 1980, 1999, 2006). They include

- *transitional bilingualism*: the use of the learner's mother tongue in the earliest period of school until the child is able to handle the target language;
- *monoliterate bilingualism*: oral-aural skills in both the mother tongue and the target language and literacy in the target;
- *partial bilingualism*: oral and literacy skills developed in one set of subjects in the vernacular and in another set of subjects in the target; and
- *full bilingualism*: all skills developed in both the vernacular and the target language.

The latter option has provoked an ongoing debate about the use of creole as the medium of instruction, as a position strongly advocated by Devonish (1986).

This is a not a new debate; Craig (1976) also articulated some of the arguments for and against its use as the medium of instruction. In later works, Craig (2002, 2006) underscores the sociological argument for focusing on English. The earlier paper focuses trenchantly on parents' attitudes and their support for the target language. The posthumous work is presented as a "re-examination" (2006, 99), indicating the positive changes in attitudes to creole and the extended use of the vernacular, and suggesting a level of cultural well-being that makes language as consciousness-raising unnecessary. Nevertheless, Craig (2006, 104) could articulate dual language concerns in the debate about vernacular pedagogy. On one hand, he notes that "social justice demands that goals in relation to [standard English] be made accessible to all vernacular speakers within whatever is the chosen national policy." And at the same time, he asserts that "the absence of an explicitly formulated language policy in any country cannot absolve educators from paying systematic and principled attention to the implications of a child's first language" (p. 105).

This is a reminder that Craig had long pursued the notion of *transitional bilingualism* and emphasized that such a programme had to be carefully planned, with timetabled sessions for both the vernacular (free talk) and English. He linked this programme more carefully with the idea of language awareness in later work (Craig 1999).

The term *language awareness* has many meanings and a long history in language teaching that links it to conscious knowledge of language behaviour (James 1999). Craig was concerned with linking that understanding to his prescription for the provision of the necessary linguistic content within the creole context. For him, the languages were so close that perceptions had to be guided towards recognizing the contrasts, as the problems with noticing mentioned above would indicate. To motivate students, to draw contrasts and to affirm the culture, Craig outlined a sociolinguistic programme of language study that integrated "free talk" around a range of culturally relevant and familiar topics.

In order to be able to carry out this work, teachers themselves needed to know the language they were using and to be able to monitor their own code-shifting behaviour. In focusing on the content of language awareness and emphasizing the critical role of teachers' knowledge, Craig began to touch on a concept that has been explicated as "teacher language awareness" by Andrews (2003). Teachers need to have explicit knowledge of both the language they are required to teach and the related vernaculars – as well as to be able to distinguish between them and carry out contrastive analysis activities. By the end of his career, Craig was moving closer to the post-method positions now clearly being espoused

(Kumaravadivelu 2006). This shift is towards theorizing and effecting a practice that addresses "the parameters of particularity, practicality and possibility" (p. 69). Craig, however, felt that Kumaravadivelu did not address the inadequacies of CLT concerning its linguistic base and the pedagogical treatment of linguistic forms (Craig 1999, 80). Craig's eclectic formulation, which he named TESORV (teaching English to speakers of a related vernacular), was meant to address this problem, combining the variety of approaches advocated over his long career of research in language education.

## The Impact

Craig's ideas have had a profound impact on teachers in the Caribbean, especially in Jamaica. This impact was felt through his influence on the Ministry of Education's approach to language and literacy teaching. In a time when there was little professional help available (except for a few works, such as that of Carrington et al. [1972], which was based on investigations in the Trinidadian education system), Craig's research was directed towards the support of language and literacy in Jamaica. One of his earliest pieces of large-scale research, which he referred to as "an experiment", yielded results that were later directly routed towards an institutionalized reading programme in the Ministry of Education. This experiment in teaching English was an intervention across Jamaica that began in 1965 and which Craig (1969) reported on in detail. It drew on the audio-lingual approach which was being advocated by linguists at the time. This approach was based on the twin foundations of structuralism in language and Skinnerian behaviourism in psychology, with emphasis on new-habit formation and the over-learning of linguistic items. Craig's intervention in Jamaica consisted of a very structured series of activities built on the students' partial knowledge of, and competence in, English. It required a mixing of newly learned linguistic items with older items still being used. The aim was not to teach a completely new system and replace the students' own language. The new and the already established existed side by side as the students learned new forms that moved them further and further along the continuum, producing such forms as *is* for copula use and the AUX + *-ing* form – structures not previously available. The intervention relied on audio-lingual procedures such as substitution tables and pattern practice to reinforce the structures being learned.

The insights from the experiment were fed into the Language Materials Workshop series, which formed the backbone of the reading and language arts material that was available to Jamaican primary-school children for over twenty years. The programme, designed and directed in conjunction with colleagues Don Wilson and Hyacinth Campbell, encapsulated Craig's main ideas on language teaching and was the first example of a Ministry of Education initiative that used locally developed materials (Jennings 1996, 20). Apart from the modified foreign language techniques of the experiment, the series drew on the notion of transitional bilingualism with the procedure of free talk and controlled talk. There was language input in the students' language (free talk) and input in the target language (controlled talk). The series provided graded readers, workbooks and storybooks, along with very detailed and careful instructions in the teachers' guides. The latter texts explained the three-pronged approach to teaching reading, which was in effect an implication of transitional bilingualism. The approach promoted

- the "avoidance strategy" to ensure that the child meets only those words and grammatical structures that are already in the first language;
- the gradual introduction of the structures of written English; and
- the preparation of the learner so that the new English words encountered are already heard and practised in controlled talk sessions.

Pollard and Taube (1995) provide a review of some of the reading material that was offered to young learners entering schools. They note that the material takes account of the linguistic background of the Jamaican children and that this could be seen in many ways (p. 31). There is a rigorous attention to the phased introduction of linguistic input based on a good understanding of Jamaican children's language and the likely creole-influenced difficulties they might encounter. They also note the targeting of the creole adjective with predicate value; the related attention in the reading material to the verb *to be* that is quickly followed by the present continuous form; and the later but necessary attention paid to the verb *to have* in recognition of its invariability in the creole system. Again drawing on the transitional bilingualism orientation, there is the very significant practice of beginning the earliest readers with English-like sentences which are similar to creole in all but one significant way, such as "See my name here, Roy" or "Look here."

Although the Language Materials Workshop series was responsive to linguistic needs, it was not utilized to its fullest potential in the primary schools. The programme was certainly well used, but the training was not in place to maximize the opportunities offered by the texts. Additionally, an analysis of the programme's texts and activities shows that they required sound linguistic understanding of the child's mother tongue in addition to the target language. This was not the situation that obtained with respect to Jamaican primary-school teachers, and Craig was to return to that theme of the importance of teachers' linguistic competence on a number of occasions (see, for example, Craig 1999), as it underscored and reinforced his interest in rigorous teacher training.

It was fortunate, therefore, that Craig could indirectly influence policy, such as that of the Joint Board for Teacher Education (JBTE), which emanated from the draft language education policy of the Ministry of Education (2001). The latter was a project recommended by the Literacy Improvement Initiative (Bryan and Mitchell 1999). In constructing and delivering the policy, the committee was heavily influenced by Craig (Bryan 2004) in several ways. First, Craig's (1980) policy recommendations guided the discussions presented and led to the move, which had already been discussed as Craig's recommendation for Jamaica, to "maintain [standard Jamaican English] as the official language and promote basic communication through the oral use of the home language in the early years (for example, K–3) while facilitating the development of literacy in English" (Ministry of Education 2001, 20).

Second, Craig's repeated demand for teachers' linguistic competence to be seen as a priority was finally acknowledged in the language education policy's recommendation that teachers should be trained through discrete courses in the grammar of both the child's first language and the target language. The JBTE, which is the quality-assurance body for teacher education in the Western Caribbean, took up this recommendation and instituted it as part of their own policy (Lambert 2006). Their concern was with professional language competence, with an emphasis on oral communication, high levels of language awareness, the maintenance of standards across institutions and the promotion of teachers as lifelong language learners. Craig would have approved of these developments, because one of his final tasks was working as consultant and advisor towards this JBTE language policy and towards improving the language programme being used in the teachers' colleges (Lambert 2006).

In other ways, as well, Craig continues to have direct and indirect influence. Devonish (2006) emulates Craig's linguistic activism and acknowledges his indirect influence in emboldening him to go a step further in the bilingual education debate: to explore the modalities by which full bilingual education at the elementary-school level can be realized in Jamaica. The Bilingual Education Project (BEP) coming out of the Jamaican Language Unit of the Department of Language, Linguistics and Philosophy at the University of the West Indies,

Mona, moved beyond the respect for the language that Craig brought to the classroom and went further by designing activities that would allow that language to be the central mode of instruction, with writing activities included. In this way, Devonish (2006) might argue, Craig's inclination to privilege the vernacular is being taken to its logical conclusion. The BEP was instituted in two Jamaican Corporate Area schools as an experiment designed to show whether a truly more concerted bilingual policy option was possible – namely, the comprehensive use of the mother tongue as the language of instruction in the early years, cultivating a strong form of bilingualism for students in grades 1 to 4. The programme has sparked interest and debate, especially about the level of support needed for success and the preparation required, including recruitment of the right kinds of teachers (Taylor 2007).

Feraria (2005) also indicates the way in which Craig is influencing another generation of language educators. Her investigation begins with a recollected interrogation by her language methods teachers, questioning her as to the "other" methods that could be used to teach children who did not speak English. The response was a lecture on how to discourage "broken English" and really an admission that there was no "other" that could be offered. For young teachers being trained, Craig's inquiry and interventions gave permission to explore, research and question in an environment where such topics were not widely researched. A foundation in Craig's ideas allowed Feraria to make a sustained investigation into the treatment of Jamaican Creole by curriculum writers and policy makers, which culminated in a call to empower teachers with an emancipatory pedagogy of indigenous praxis. This is new: independent and reflexive practice being encouraged in the teacher of language and literacy. The aim is to work with teachers, encouraging them to listen to their own impulses towards change (the teacher within) and through reflection trust their own intuitions to teach against the grain, with a focus on innovation and experimentation. Feraria is developing a teacher education philosophy that counteracts her own early training, which took place at a time when Craig's ideas could not find fertile ground in her institution. In the end, Craig's work is inspiring departures.

The discussion above shows that Craig's work is to be marked and celebrated for many different reasons and in many different ways. This chapter honours the man who, more than any other Caribbean linguist, underscored that vital connection between academic research and the field application of his findings (Simon 2006). He was a scholar who saw his work as a seamless continuation of scholarship for social action.

# References

Andrews, Stephen. 2003. Teacher Language Awareness and the Professional Knowledge Base of the L2 Teacher. *Language Awareness* 12 (2): 81–95.

Bailey, Beryl Loftman. 1971. Jamaican Creole: Can Dialect Boundaries Be Defined? In *Pidginization and Creolization of Languages,* edited by D. Hymes, 341–48. Cambridge: Cambridge University Press.

Bryan, Beverley. 2004. Reconciling Contradictions and Moving for Change: Towards a language Education Policy for Jamaica. In *Transforming the Educational Landscape through Curriculum Change.* Kingston: University of the West Indies Press.

Bryan, Beverley, and Ivy Mitchell. 1999. Literacy Improvement Initiative: Background Paper and Plan of Action for Jamaica. Kingston: Ministry of Education.

Carrington, Lawrence D., C. Borely, and H.E. Knight. 1972. *Away Robin Run! A Critical Description of the Teaching of the Language Arts in the Primary Schools of Trinidad and Tobago.* St Augustine: Institute of Education, University of the West Indies.

Craig, Dennis R. 1965. The Written English of Some 14-Year-Old Jamaican and English Children. In *Language Teaching, Linguistics and the Teaching of English in a Multilingual Society.* Kingston: Faculty of Education, University of the West Indies.

———. 1969. *An Experiment in Teaching English.* Kingston: Caribbean Universities Press.

———. 1971a. Education and Creole English in the West Indies. In *Pidginization and Creolization of Languages,* edited by D. Hymes, 371–91. Cambridge: Cambridge University Press.

———. 1971b. The Use of Language by 7-Year-Old Jamaican Children Living in Contrasting Socio-Economic Environments. PhD thesis, Institute of Education, University of London.

———. 1976. Bidialectal Education: Creole and Standard in the West Indies. *International Journal of Sociology of Education* 9: 93–134.

———. 1978. The Sociology of Language Learning and Teaching in a Creole Situation. In *Caribbean Journal of Education* 5 (3): 101–16.

———. 1980. Models for Educational Policy in Creole-Speaking Communities. In *Theoretical Orientations in Creole Studies,* edited by A. Valdman and A. Highfield, 245–65. New York: Academic Press.

———. 1994. Putative Absurdity in Student Writing. Paper presented at the Eleventh Biennial Conference of the Society for Caribbean Linguistics, St Maarten.

———. 1999. *Teaching Language and Literacy: Policies and Procedures for Vernacular Situations.* Georgetown, Guyana: Education and Development Services.

———. 2002. /laik yu nu waan mi pikni fi laan di waitmaan langwij!/ Paper presented at the Fourteenth Biennial Conference of the Society for Caribbean Linguistics, University of the West Indies, St Augustine.

———. 2006. The Use of the Vernacular in West Indian Education. In *Exploring the Boundaries of Caribbean Creole Languages*, edited by H. Simmons-McDonald and I. Robertson, 99–117. Kingston: University of the West Indies Press.

DeCamp, David. 1971. Toward a Generative Analysis of a Post-Creole Speech Continuum. In *Pidginization and Creolization of Languages*, edited by D. Hymes, 349–70. Cambridge: Cambridge University Press.

Devonish, Hubert. 1986. *Language and Liberation: Creole Language Politics in the Caribbean*. London: Karia.

———. 2006. Implementing the Craig Proposal for the Teaching of Language: A Bilingual and Biliterate Approach. Paper presented at the Seminar on Language Education: A Tribute to Professor Dennis Craig, School of Education, University of the West Indies, Mona.

Holm, John. 1988. *Pidgins and Creoles*, volume 1: *Theory and Structure*. Cambridge: Cambridge University Press.

James, Carl. 1999. Language Awareness: Implications for the Language Curriculum. *Language, Culture and Curriculum* 12 (1): 94–115.

Jennings, Zellynne. 1996. Curriculum Change Strategies: The Impact on West Indian Education. In *Education in the West Indies: Development and Perspectives, 1948–1988*, edited by D.R. Craig, 136–56. Kingston: Institute of Social and Economic Research, University of the West Indies.

Kumaravadivelu, B. 2006. TESOL Methods: Changing Tracks, Challenging Trends. *TESOL Quarterly* 40 (1): 59–81.

Lambert, Clement. 2006. Joint Board of Teacher Education's Language Policy and the Language Milieu in Teachers' College. Paper presented at the Seminar on Language Education: A Tribute to Professor Dennis Craig, School of Education, University of the West Indies, Mona.

Ministry of Education. 2001. Draft Language Education Policy. Kingston.

Pollard, Velma, and K. Taube. 1995. Review of Language Arts Teaching Material. Working paper for GOJ/IDB/PEIP II Project. Kingston.

Robertson, Ian E. 1999. Educational Linguistics for the Caribbean: Some Considerations. *Caribbean Journal of Education* 21 (1–2): 75–86.

Simon, D. 2006. Can I Help You Teachers? Paper presented at the Seminar on Language Education: A Tribute to Professor Dennis Craig, School of Education, University of the West Indies, Mona.

Taylor, Monica. 2007. The Experience of Teaching and learning in Jamaican (Creole): A phenomenological account. *Caribbean Journal of Education* 29 (2): 222–42.

Wilson, Don, Dennis R. Craig, and Hyacinth Campbell. 1978. Language Materials Workshop (LMW): Primary Language Arts series. Kingston: Ministry of Education.

# PART 2

# THE BACKGROUND TO CARIBBEAN LANGUAGE

# 3 | The Niger-Congo Languages as a Linguistic Source of Caribbean English

RICHARD ALLSOPP

*University of the West Indies, Cave Hill*

The ultimate ancestor of English, its Germanic sisters and its multiple cousinhood of languages stretching across Europe, the Middle East and into the Indic subcontinent is conveniently called Proto-Indo-European, but its identity has only hypothetically been determined by astute linguistic detective work (starting with the observation of William Jones in 1786), while the possible location of its earliest and evidently semi-nomadic speakers some five thousand years ago remains speculative, placed, we are told, somewhere to the north and west of India. Yet the historic roots of the Indo-European family of languages have ceased to be questioned since the nineteenth century, even though answers to the questions of where and when are patently unestablished.

When this situation is compared with the theories of origin of the Caribbean and Atlantic creoles out of which creolized European languages, including Caribbean English, have come, we know the three-million-square-mile sub-Saharan "slave basin" from which the creators of those creoles came, and we know the period of roughly two centuries – mid-seventeenth to mid- to late nineteenth – when they came. In short, the answers to the questions of where and when are well established.

Yet it is a curious fact that from the first scholarly interest taken in the speech of West Atlantic black people in the United States nearly a century ago by Professor George Krapp, through the most serious development of creole linguistics over the last four decades, there has persisted a scholarly resistance – with the signal exception of Lorenzo Turner (1949) in regard to Gullah – to claims made for the aboriginal input of sub-Saharan African languages to the structure and texture of creole talk in the Caribbean and North America. Such origination I first independently called Afrogenesis (Allsopp 1976), whereas the latest of the "Africa-free" – and it seems to me Eurocentric – set of origin theories is Professor Derek Bickerton's language bioprogram hypothesis (1984), later modified and renamed, according to which it was first-generation *children* in the New World who, mainly out of innate human language universals, created similar talk-ways out of similar circumstances, whence the similarities of all creoles are supposed to be accounted for. This theory, in other words, denies that the creators of West Atlantic creoles were aboriginal Africans.

It is only out of amazement at the reception of the language bioprogram hypothesis by respectable creolists and other linguists that I can merely say it is wholly unsatisfactory to load students with such matter, restraining my preference to dismiss it as romantic nonsense.

However, it is against such academic persistence in seeking other than African sources of, in our case, the anglophone creoles which produced today's Caribbean creolized English, that I find it necessary to demonstrate unequivocally that what enslaved Africans did to express themselves in the anglophone medium came as a matter of fact out of the character of their African languages.

Although this chapter will focus on the anglophone Caribbean, my material can be extended to African American Vernacular English (AAVE), as well as to francophone and other New World creolized languages.

## Africa's Geography and Languages

When one talks of Africa, let it be remembered that it is a land mass of unimaginable size, covering more than three times that of the continental United States. Even the island of Madagascar off its southeast coast is larger than France, which once owned it. There are well over one thousand languages in sub-Saharan Africa; some of these are spoken in several dialect-distinct pockets with different names, so some estimates would put the total number of languages at two or three times that figure. Accordingly, the first error in considering African linguistic influence in transatlantic language products, such as the Caribbean creoles, is to argue that there were too many different languages for any of them to have had a sufficient number of speakers grouped among the slaves at any one time and place to have survived, let alone to have provided sufficient impact to influence the shape of the product in the way that say, French, after 1066, influenced English, or even in the way that Irish speakers influenced American English.

However, the linguistic facts are of a different order. The missionary Sigismund Koelle, in Freetown, Sierra Leone (1850–52), interviewed in English 210 Africans, of whom 179 were ex-slaves (the rest were traders) and who spoke 120 different African languages and 80 dialects. The speakers were all, except two, middle-aged men who were able to give their places of origin. He made a list therefrom of two hundred vocabularies located on a map of Africa that showed that the tongues of these over two hundred informants spread throughout West and Central Africa from Senegal to Mozambique, covering the vast basins of the Niger and Congo rivers. The map may be seen in Koelle's (1963) *Polyglotta Africana*.

In 1966, over a century later, Joseph Greenberg, an American linguist, showed quite independently of Koelle's work that the languages of the Niger and Congo basins (in fact, Koelle's immense slave catchment "basin"), of which he examined some seven hundred, were of one great language family, which he appropriately named the "Niger-Congo languages" (see Greenberg 1966, 177). The immense implication of this linguistic discovery, coinciding geographically with Koelle's historical evidence, is that the languages of the vast majority of all New World slaves – there were some exceptions – had a common ancestry.

Consider first what this means for authenticating the genetic linkage of a great number of superficially disparate languages, as a linguistic map of West Africa would illustrate.[1] Note second that the Euro-political division of West Africa into twelve coastal states of West Africa alone from Senegal to Cameroun (not counting Mali and Niger) indiscriminately overlay these language boundaries with mostly English and French after the Berlin Conference and Treaty of 1885. Then you may begin to understand why European scholars since then have been unable to come to terms with the underlying conceptual similarities – actual semantic sameness in many cases – of superficially different-looking and -sounding African languages which were also politically separated and under different European administrative hegemonies.

Imagine then how much there is to discover of the conceptual linkages that relate many sub-Saharan African languages to one another, and how these would operate to reflect a strong similarity of African world-views – broadly speaking, an African way of looking at things.

To give some examples of what I mean, take the fact that the common Indo-European ancestry of European languages genetically generates a greeting conceptualized in relation to time of day using the same word-frame: *Good morning, Bonjour, Buenos días, Buon giorno* and so on; and compare the fact that in African languages the greeting is characteristically conceptualized in relation to place and person: "Fellow-man/woman" or "Greetings by the river", for example. Compare also the West Atlantic African diasporal greeting: "Hi. How yo' doin? How the children?" or "Hi, cousin" (not implying an actual family relationship, but still typical today of almost any place in the Caribbean countryside).

In my etymological inquiries leading to the production of the *Dictionary of Caribbean English Usage* (Allsopp 1996), I have found phrases or lexical items in sixty-one Niger-Congo and/or sub-Saharan African languages (as pinpointed on a map on the inside backcover of that book, which could underlie a number of Caribbean English idiomatic frames – that is, which are not British or American) by a means of systemic transfer better known as *calquing*. I will explain the process later in the chapter, but let us first step back a little and look at the communicative systems that the Africans brought with them to the New World, in our particular case the Caribbean.

## What Did Africans Bring?

Africans brought to the New World an organization of a way of life, or culture, which we might say consisted of an external structure and an internal structure. Although this organization was destroyed, in that the *external structure* (their social and kinship systems) disappeared with the enslavement experience, all was not lost in the *internal structure* (their belief systems and expression systems remained embedded in the brain). In this chapter I address only the expression systems. By *expression system*, I mean that system of grammatical principles and conventions in the brain which engenders the purposeful exchange of meanings between living human beings. You may call it, more briefly, *communication*, provided you understand that term to embrace art, music and language, of which unfortunately we can here focus only on the last named.

Remembering that language is a network or system through which a human generates meaning in any given situation, it is critical to note that African slaves, like all other humans, had systems which they brought with them in their brains, and we must be clear on what we mean when we acknowledge that.

First, the operation of a system in the brain entails intelligence, a factor that has always been questioned in regard to black people (even by black people themselves). Second, when languages bear a family relationship to each other, they share common systemic properties; consequently, the Niger-Congo language family, sharing such properties, formed one composite network of sub-Saharan languages used by all African slaves (with negligible exceptions).

This meant (a) the sharing of a basically common life-view (which was markedly different from the standard European life-view – observe the little example of greeting behaviour given above); (b) common ways of conceptualizing thought, leading to similar patterns of idiomatic deep structure (as I shall soon illustrate); and (c) similar kinesic or gestural behaviour and body language. Of these, the most easily illustrated is (c). African kinesic behaviour involves a marked, dynamic use of eyes, face, head, hands and body – laughter is dance! – and all of these survive as distinctive features in their Caribbean American environment. Phono-kinesic gestures, such as "sucking the teeth" as a mark of contempt or disgust (Yoruba *pòse*, Hausa *tsaki*, Kikongo *tsiona* and so on) or "cutting the eye", a (usually woman's) gesture of scorn (Efik *ekep . . . enyin*), are common and widespread in the Caribbean territories.

Ideophones, a marked and distinctive feature of sub-Saharan languages, are also a marked feature of Caribbean English, although, mostly restricted to the domains of sound, violence and speed, they cover a narrower range than in homeland African languages.

Pitch-differentiated homonyms, evident descendants of the tonemic character of West African languages, are noticeable in many Caribbean Englishes. Examples are:

1. *farmer, butcher, mason, tailor,* representing professions with the pitch-pattern /2–1/, vs. Farmer, Butcher, Mason, Taylor as family names with the pitch-pattern /1–2/
2. similarly, *brother, father, sister, mother,* representing kinship with the pitch-pattern /2–1/, vs. these same words used to describe members of a religious order with the pitch-pattern /1–2/
3. the active conversion of an adjective into a noun (often jocular) by similar pitch changes: *stupid, ugly, wicked.*

## Syllable Structure

More difficult to illustrate briefly is the syllabic structure that the sub-Saharan speakers brought to their new English-speaking world. The canonical form of syllable structure in the bulk of West African languages is CV(N) or CCV(N) – that is, beginning with a consonant or consonant cluster and ending with a vowel or nasal. This is called an open syllable. The below example is taken from Mende. The sentence means 'He told me that your mother is ill.'

| Mende | i | ndei | lo | nya | ma | ke | bi | nje | ni.ngbe | ngo |
|---|---|---|---|---|---|---|---|---|---|---|
| | v | ccvv | cv | cvv | cv | cv | cv | ccv | cv.cccv | ccv |
| | he | say | (past) | | me | on | that | you | mother | sick | all |
| English | tek | ↔ni | \ng.l\š | s↔n. t↔ns | | s ℘ č | —z | ∂\s | w ℘ n | |
| | cvc | vcv | vcc.v cvc.cvcc | | cvc | vc | cvc | vvc | | |

You will be struck by the opposite feature – that is, the dominance of closed syllables – in the syllable structure of the second example. On encountering this difficulty in language acquisition, sub-Saharan speakers were obliged to keep their own syllable pattern, and as illustrated in the following examples, their Caribbean descendants do so to this day.

/mo po/           'more poor'
/gi i da/          'give him that'
/do le de ge we/   'don't let them get wet'

At the more educated level, there are occurrences such as:

reco(g)nize        ta(c)tics
ge(ntle)men        accounk ('account')
as(k)              correc(t)

In these cases, the consonant clusters are reduced or disappear.

## Word Formation

The sub-Saharan conceptualization of an event leading to labelling that may be briefly illustrated with an example of word formation. The word for *tears* in many Niger-Congo languages literally translates as "water of the eye" (saliva is "water of the mouth", and so on). In Caribbean creolized English there emerge parallel structures: "eye-water", "mouth-water". This is the simple operation of *calquing* or *systemic transfer*, the copying in English of structures patterned from morphs in other languages, in this case a number of different Niger-Congo languages. Note that different African structures (such as those meaning *tears*) simply translate the same way in creolized English – "eye-water" or "water-eye" (and here also in creolized French – *glo-zyé*), giving rise to nearly identical word formations in non-contiguous Caribbean creoles. Thus:

'tears'

| | | | |
|---|---|---|---|
| Mandingo | *na-giyo* "eye-water" | Guyana Cr. | *eye-water* |
| Mende | *ngayei* < *ngamei-nyei* "face (eyes) water" | Jamaica Cr. | *eye-water* |
| Fante | *nyinsuwa* < *enyima-nsu* "eye-water" | Barbadian | *cry-water* |
| Yoruba | *omi-oju* "water-eye" | | |
| Igbo | *anya-mmili* "eye-water" | | |
| Efik | *mmong-eyet* "water of eye" | Fr. Guyana Cr. | *dlo-ouei* |
| Luo | *pi-wang* "water-eye" | St Lucia Fr. Cr. | *glo-zyé* |

This fact eliminates the contention that in order for an African language to survive, there needed to be large groupings of speakers of that language at the same place and time. Also, systemic transfer, remembering Bickerton, cannot be the work of children in any possible way.

More complicated conceptual examples, persisting as indispensable at the more educated level of Caribbean English today, are found in such cases as "hard-ears", "own-way" and "cut-eye", among others.

## Pronouns

Africans also brought with them a pronominal system strongly characterized by minimal to no case or gender distinction. Systemic transfer into Caribbean

Creole and, later, creolized English produced, for example, one form, *(h)e*, for all cases: "gie 'e 'e book", or, in Jamaican Creole, "(h)im tek (h)im book". This form is often used, at the more conservative level, for both genders in the third person, as in this example from (conservative) Guyanese Creole:

> S1: How yo wife?
> S2: 'E get baby soon. ('She is soon to give birth.')

In one particular pronoun, however, Niger-Congo languages differed: there was in those languages always a plural *you* (which English had lost). So the African invented a plural *you-all*, *all-you*, or in one very striking case preserved the Igbo *unu* in Barbados, and by diffusion also in Jamaica and Belize, where it is usually written *oonoo* in narrative dialogue, as in this example from Jamaican H. Orlando Patterson (1964, 85): "But Lawd, oonoo Rasta seem to 'ave somet'ing up oonoo sleeve."

## Phrase Structure

In the structuring of the phrase, economy is a strong determining principle in African languages, and the African speaker brought the same characteristic to Caribbean English, as exemplified in the following specific ways:

1. possession marked by juxtaposition
2. question signalling without sentence transformation
3. situational time signalling (minimizing tense differentiation)
4. concreteness of subject matter
5. active subject replacing passive voice + passivity indicated semantically only (e.g., *the food eat* 'the food has been eaten'), not syntactically, as in standard English

## Multi-usage

Economy of phrasing was accompanied in Niger-Congo languages by deepening and sharpening the connotation of simple "concrete" words to accommodate abstract conceptualization. The resulting idiomatic system was calqued into Caribbean creoles, and lives today in Caribbean English with dramatic effect. Dipping again into the etymological work for my *Dictionary of Caribbean English Usage*, I offer connotations relative to the word *mouth*. Look first at how the calquing worked in the Yoruba rendering of "You cannot (be trusted to) keep a secret" or "You talk too much to be trustworthy":

| Yoruba | enu | è | ko | ni | kọkọrọ |
|---|---|---|---|---|---|
| | mouth | your | not | have | key |
| Caribbean translation | | 'Yo mouth en got no cover' | | | |

Following are other examples of using the same concrete item to serve many abstract connotations.

| Creolized Caribbean English Idiom | Comparisons in African Languages | English |
|---|---|---|
| *be/got have two-mouth* | Nupe | be deceitful |
| *give mouth* | Yoruba, Nupe, Kikongo, Shona | be impertinent |
| | Yoruba | |
| *got/have bad-mouth* | Nupe | be capable of bewitching by pessimistic talk |
| *got/have (too much) mouth/ big-mouth* | Wolof | boast without being able to back your boast |
| *got/have sweet-mouth* | Twi | be an able flatterer |

## African Vocabulary Survivals

It is rather by the means illustrated above than by the few vocabulary remainders and exceptional survivals (usually derogatory) of African names that Niger-Congo language influence may be determined. But unfortunately, it is at the few items such as those below – all typical of low social status – that some investigators have pointed to make their superficial case that African linguistic influence is negligible.

| *akara* | (Yoruba) |
|---|---|
| *Ananse* | (Twi) |

| | |
|---|---|
| *baikra* | (Efik) |
| *baku* | (Proto Niger-Congo) |
| *basa-basa* | (Twi, Gã) |
| *comfo dance* | (Twi) |
| *comkie* | (Fante) |
| *congatay* | (Gã-Adangme) |
| *Congo* | (Congo) |
| *dokunu* | (Twi) |
| *eh-eh!* | (Akan, etc.) |
| *fufu* | (Gã, Akan) |
| *jook* | (Mende, Fulani, Hausa, Tsonga, Nembe) |
| *jumbie* | (Kikongo) |
| *kaiso* | (Efik) |
| *kokobeh* | (Twi) |
| *konkonsa* | (Twi) |
| *mm-hm* | (Krio) |
| *obeah* | (Twi) |
| *putta-putta* | (Twi, etc.) |
| *senseh-fowl* | (Twi) |
| *shak-shak* | (Hausa) |
| *soukouyan* | (Soninke) |
| *susu* | (Yoruba) |
| *warri* | (Twi) |

## Akan Day Names

| Male | Female | Day |
|---|---|---|
| *Cudjoe* | *Juba* | Monday |
| *Cubbenah* | *Beneba* | Tuesday |
| *Quaco* | *Cuba* | Wednesday |
| *Quao* | *Abba* | Thursday |
| *Cuffee* | *Phibba* | Friday |
| *Quamin* | *Mimba* | Saturday |
| *Quashee* | *Quasheba* | Sunday |

(Cassidy and Le Page 1967, 144)

## Proverbs

If there was ever justification for the cliché "last but not least", it is in this domain. There is a very large body of creole/creolized proverbs which, because they are pan-Caribbean, non-British and non-North American, must, on that ground alone, be credited as African survivals even though the search for actual correlates remains to be done on a large scale. One such effort is David and Jardel's *Les proverbes créoles de la Martinique* (1969), in which one may find many African–Caribbean correlated proverbs, one of the best examples being "One finger can't catch louse" (p. 101), which is identified in twenty-two Niger-Congo languages and reflected (allowing for slight modifications on both sides of the Atlantic) in nine Caribbean territories. It could be that the study of proverbs alone as a sociolinguistic and anthropological discipline would establish beyond doubt that the sub-Saharan Africans brought with them to the Caribbean, centuries ago, an expression system which slavery did not kill, but which in fact remains vibrant today, giving colour and difference to the structure of Caribbean English and bringing credit, even acclaim, to Caribbean literature.

## Acknowledgement

This paper was originally presented at the Slave Route Conference held at York University, Toronto, 22 July 1997, and revised in January 1998.

## Note

1. See, for example, the end papers of Ajayi and Espie's (1965) work, after Murdock and Greenberg.

## References

Ajayi, J.F.A., and Ian Espie, eds. 1965. *A Thousand Years of West African History*. Ibadan: Ibadan University Press.
Allsopp, Richard. 1976. The Case for Afrogenesis. In *New Directions in Creole Studies,*

(conference preprints, Proceedings of the First Biennial Conference of the Society for Caribbean Linguistics, 11–14 August), compiled by G.N. Cave. Georgetown: University of Guyana.

———, ed. 1996. *Dictionary of Caribbean English Usage*. With French and Spanish supplement edited by J. Allsopp. Oxford: Oxford University Press.

Cassidy, Frederic, and Robert Le Page. 1967. *Dictionary of Jamaican English*. Cambridge: Cambridge University Press.

David, Bernard, and Jean-Pierre Jardel. 1969. *Les Proverbes créoles de la Martinique*. Fort-de-France, Martinique: CERAG.

Greenberg, Joseph H. 1966. *The Languages of Africa*. Bloomington: Indiana University Press.

Koelle, Sigismund. 1963. *Polyglotta Africana*. Edited by P.E.H. Hair and D. Dalby. Graz, Austria: Graz University Press. (First published in 1854.)

Patterson, H. Orlando. 1964. *The Children of Sisyphus*. London: New Authors.

# 4 | Revisiting Notions of "Deficiency" and "Inadequacy" in Creoles from an Applied Linguistics Perspective

*University of the West Indies, Open Campus*

Since the paper on linguistic hybridization was presented by Keith Whinnom at a conference in Jamaica in 1968 and the published version appeared in *Pidginization and Creolization of Languages* (Hymes 1971), much has been written either in support of or against several of the following statements about creoles found in that paper:

1. "It is clear that pidgins are 'defective' languages of inferior flexibility and adaptability. . . . The further question is whether creoles derived from them are also in some way deficient." (Whinnom 1971, 108)
2. "Any pidgin or creole (or 'primitive' language) can repair its referential inadequacy when it is a question of naming *objects*, and does so when the pressure of its inadequacy is felt. And the third criterion often mentioned is the use of a creole for 'literature'. Literature, and most especially lyric poetry, can be produced in languages adequate for day-to-day intercourse and quite inadequate for literacy criticism (or linguistics)." (p. 109)
3. "There may be some reason to suspect that the creole-speaker is handicapped by his language. Creolists have had a hard enough struggle to justify the respectability of their discipline. . . . I feel that someone should venture the suggestion that modern linguists may

have been dangerously sentimental about creole languages, which, with only a few notable exceptions, constitute in most communities a distinct handicap to the social mobility of the individual and *may* also constitute a handicap to the creole-speaker's personal intellectual development." (pp. 109–10)

A question set for the PhD qualifying examination at Stanford several years ago focused on the third statement and required candidates to either support or defend the statement. From the perspective of a bilingual who had acquired a French Creole simultaneously with English as a first language in childhood, this assertion seemed preposterous, and my response to the question argued that notions of handicap or deficiency are not necessarily inherent in the speakers of creoles per se but derived from and were perpetuated by several factors: first, the inheritance of an ascription of inferiority emerging from the unequal contact situations in which they developed; second, an educational system or systems that remained heavily influenced by a relationship of domination in colonial contexts in which creoles were either ignored or labelled substandard and inferior; and third, a lack of initiative in education to test hypotheses of adequacy. The response had not taken into consideration the issue of language dominance or use for academic proficiency purposes, which is critical in any discussion of the purposes for which a language may be used and it made no comment on its adequacy with regard to these purposes. In the intervening years since the publication of Whinnom's paper, creolists (for instance, Alleyne 1982; DeGraff 2001, 2005; Sebba 1997; and Todd 1974), have refuted his claims, using evidence from selected creoles in some instances to do so. This chapter revisits some of Whinnom's statements and selected commentaries, and it offers some comments from an applied linguistics perspective.

## Deficiency and Defectiveness

Whinnom's statement posits that pidgins "are 'defective' languages of inferior flexibility". He raises the "further question" as to whether "creoles derived from them are also in some way deficient" (1971, 108). In developing this point, Whinnom refers to Chinese Pidgin, which he notes was a dying language in Hong Kong. He argues that Chinese Pidgin, like "many creoles", "are unintelligible to the speakers of the superstrate languages from which they derive their lexicon ... and pidgin, like French Creole, has been stabilized at an extraordinarily low level of intelligibility". He further states, "Where the superstrate is a transient or socially superior minority to which the substrate speakers do not aspire to assimilate themselves, there is (a) reduced motivation for improved performance, and (b) simultaneously, a more limited area of mutual interest in which a defective language can be functionally adequate" (p. 102). While conceding that "no one pidginizes his own language without very considerable linguistic awareness", Whinnom states that one must "account satisfactorily for the stability, the grammaticality, the stabilization at such a low level of intelligibility to the superstrate speaker" (p. 107).

Whinnom's use of the terms *superstrate* and *substrate* emphasizes concepts of superiority and inferiority. DeGraff (2001, 55) refers to traits attributed by some linguists to "older or more advanced" or "sophisticated" languages, where these terms are used generally for "non-creole" languages, which are contrasted with "younger" or "less advanced" or creole languages.[1] Whinnom ascribes to the "superstrates" labels such as "complex", "developed", "advanced", "regular", "sophisticated" and "expressively and culturally rich". Collectively, these terms present implications that ignore the fact that speakers of both the so-called superstratum and the substratum contributed jointly in contact to the formation of the pidgin that they used for communication. Historical usage of *superstratum* and *substratum* acknowledges the dual influence of both in the creation of the language formed through contact.[2]

To concede on the one hand that "considerable linguistic awareness" is a factor in the process of pidginization is to acknowledge the creative capabilities of the speakers jointly engaged in this process; yet, to speak in almost the same breath of stabilization at a "low level of intelligibility to the superstrate speaker" is to suggest somehow that the latter in no wise contributed to the level of intelligibility at which the language stabilized and also to suggest (ambiguously) stabilization at a level of incomprehensibility to the "superstrate speaker".

The idea of a low level of stabilization might be explained almost in the same terms as that of fossilization at a rudimentary level of competence determined primarily by the second language learner's attitude towards the target language and culture. In the same way that the second language learner who may have a strong sense of loyalty to the first or native language and very little motivation to integrate with the target language and its speakers can have a high affective filter that blocks input and limits intake so that the learning of the L2 is limited, I would say resisted, leading to fossilization at an early interlanguage stage, similar factors can most likely influence either or both groups of speakers in a contact situation, thereby determining the level of stabilization of the pidgin. One thinks of the subject Alberto in Schumann's (1978) study as a classic example of a learner with such a high affective filter and such resistance to the learning of the L2 (in this case, English) that, unlike his counterparts in the study, his second language was pidginized at what Schumann might have termed a "low level of intelligibility". The other subjects in the study progressed through the following stages of acquisition of English negation: *no V*, *don't V*, *aux-neg* and *analysed don't*. Schumann reported that Alberto remained at the first stage throughout the study, using mainly *no V* negation. The other subjects progressed to the stage of *analysed don't*. Schumann suggested that Alberto's English resembled pidgin languages in that it was reduced and simplified in comparison with standard English. The "reduced motivation for improved performance" to which Whinnom refers is not necessarily a one-sided affair in which the "substrate speaker" is the sole actor in determining the level of stabilization of the pidgin. To admit on the one hand that a speaker must have "very considerable linguistic awareness" to "pidginize his own language" and then suggest on the other hand that "stabilization at such a low level of intelligibility to the superstrate speaker" is to ignore factors extraneous to the language per se that may exert influence in a contact situation. One may well be the resistance of the speakers to acquire the language for anything more than the most rudimentary of communicative purposes. The variable outcomes of the subjects in the Schuman study would indicate that plausible explanations can be found in the affective domain that exerts a very strong influence on language learning outcomes.

In a contact situation, level of stabilization is more likely determined on the basis of the extent to which both groups are motivated to extend the communicative interaction, and the functional adequacy of the pidgin will itself be determined by the parameters set jointly by both groups in that context. If both groups resist learning the other's language (L2) and that resistance manifests itself in high affective filters, then they both contribute to the low level of stabilization of the pidgin that develops. Whinnom does concede that lack of aspiration by the "substrate speaker" to assimilate (in cases where the superstrate speaker is a "transient or socially superior minority") results in "reduced motivation for improved performance". The question is, why must the motivation to improve rest solely with the so-called substrate speaker? A high valuation of the L1 by the latter in a situation in which the "superstrate" speaker's language is not valued as highly will determine the level of motivation to learn the L2. The same would be true of the substrate speaker's attitude to the languages in question. The level of intelligibility should not therefore be assessed solely on the language acquisition or learning capacity of one group of speakers but also on other important affective factors that can be manifested in contact situations. Situations of social inequality and the exercise of power by one group over another will inevitably influence the attitudes and motivation for assimilation and integration. Language learning is deeply affected in such situations. Alleyne (1982, 3) views descriptions of the sort presented in Whinnom as being "permeated with conceptual bias" that present the "world in a certain way". He explains:

> The same conceptual bias which organizes the physical map of the earth in such a way that certain countries always appear at the top or at the centre, when applied to the relationship between standard and so-called non-standard forms, always somehow derives the latter from the former. Languages, those that are the interest of our study, are "simple" or "shallow", features of syntax such as coordination are not qualified by descriptive adjectives but by metaphorical terms such as "simple". And in all of this there is the implication that something is wrong, or at least not normal, not a product of normal individuals in normal cultures but of special individuals in "sub-cultures".

To speak of a low level of stabilization with respect to a creole would be to deny the species-specific gift of creativity that enables humans to generate languages that are marked for complexity in different ways. Mühlhaüsler (1997, 287) makes the point that "to regard pidgins or creoles as imperfect versions of a target standard language is to miss important aspects of their linguistic nature." Viewed from a universal grammar perspective, notions of inferiority and inequality with respect to language are illogical. As DeGraff (2001, 83) reminds us, "Creole languages are natural languages acquired by children like any other natural languages." Referring to Haitian Creole (HC) as an example, he argues that "there is no reliable empirical or theoretical basis to support the claim that Creole languages (for example, HC) are 'degenerate' (i.e. radically impoverished, thus uniformly less complex) versions of their European ancestors. On the contrary, it can be documented quite straightforwardly that CERTAIN properties of HC grammar, a bona fide Caribbean Creole, signal an INCREASE in complexity over French" (2005, 551). DeGraff provides examples to illustrate the point. Later in the same article, he writes, "The myth that Creole languages are 'simplest' to analyse shunts into oblivion any data set that attests to the complexity of Creole languages as full-fledged languages and that may further contribute to our understanding of Universal Grammar, and thus to our understanding of the cognitive underpinnings of language" (2005, 577).

A child acquiring a creole as a first language would be like any other human being acquiring a first language. A universal-grammar explanation views this process as moving from a stage of being predisposed or hardwired for language but having none at birth; that is, being in a state of zero ($S_0$) for language. The process of acquiring the first language would mean moving "from a genetically determined initial state $S_0$ through a sequence of stages $S_1, S_2 \ldots$, finally arriving at a 'steady state' $S_s$ which then seems to change only marginally" (Chomsky 1980, 37). The process of acquisition involves the setting of "parameters" for the language (or languages, in the case of simultaneous acquisition of two languages in childhood) which is being acquired. The principles would be the state of what I am simply describing as the genetic readiness of the human for language. Cook (1988, 57) explains Chomsky's universal grammar in the following way: "Universal Grammar is present in the child's mind as a system of principles and parameters. In response to evidence from the environment the child creates a core grammar that assigns values to all the parameters, yielding one of the allowable human languages. . . . The principles of [universal grammar] are principles of the initial state."

The steady state is one which Chomsky (1965, 4), in an earlier work, described as "competence", a "speaker/hearer's knowledge of his language". Acquisition of a first language means that the speaker has knowledge of the grammar of the language, of its rules, and can use that language to communicate. In social interaction, the speaker would also be acquiring communicative competence, learning the rules for use and contexts of appropriateness for language in communication. What the speaker does not have is the proficiency aspect, that is, the use and development of the first language for literacy. That aspect is developed through a learning process of engagement and use of the language in education (formal or non-formal) for school or academic purposes and for cognitive development in that particular context. Until then, and unless a creole is used and allowed to develop for these purposes, it is pointless to make claims about the level of intelligibility of its stabilization.

In second language acquisition, a speaker already has an L1 and is moving towards what is generally termed the target language. There is variability among learners in L2 acquisition; the desired end state, what Cook refers to as the terminal state $S_t$, varies for different learners and balanced bilingualism is achieved by a minority. The emergence of a pidgin can be likened to L2 acquisition in the sense that both sets of speakers already have an L1 on which they depend to some extent as they try to learn or understand the L2 of the other group in order to communicate. Second language learners may persist in their efforts to learn the L2 depending on whether their motivation is instrumental or integrative. Affective factors, such as their motivation, attitude and the learning context, will most likely influence their level of success. In contact situations that gave rise to pidgins, mutual intelligibility was a primary objective and to the extent that the speakers achieved that objective, they continued to use the forms that they had mutually created. The level of stability of the pidgin was therefore mutually determined by the speakers involved in the communicative context that gave rise to the pidgin, and its maintenance would have depended on the level of comfort and ease of communication with the pidgin that the groups would have accepted. This is a plausible reason for the longevity and maintenance of some pidgins that still flourish. The point is that in such a situation, level of intelligibility of the stabilization of the pidgin cannot be attributed solely to one group and not the other. The colonizer was as instrumental in the creation and use of the pidgin as those who were colonized.

## Inadequacy

The second statement by Whinnom which I will discuss briefly is statement 2 cited earlier in this chapter, which questions the adequacy of pidgins or creoles for purposes such as literary criticism. The statement points to a pervasive problem related to the way in which creoles have been perceived and discussed within the field by some. How can one determine whether a language is "inadequate" for particular functions unless that language has been put to the test by being used for these functions? Traditionally, creoles have been excluded from the very educational contexts in which they might be utilized and tested for adequacy with respect to literary analysis or other academic functions. DeGraff (2005, 533) uses the term "Creole Exceptionalism", which he describes as a "sociohistorically rooted 'regime of truth' in the Foucauldian sense of the term" and argues that it "obstructs scientific and social progress in and about Creole communities". Alleyne and Garvin (1982, 20), developing concepts first presented by scholars from the Prague School – Mathesius on "flexibile stability" and Havranek on "intellectualization", both in 1932 – make a strong case for standardization as a process of "intellectualizing" the creole, noting that it is a cumulative process that would have the effect of "creating the capacity of allowing translations into the creole languages, the translation of literary and scientific works of other nations being a means by which the participatory function might be achieved" (p. 27). In the same text, they report that the international conference on creole languages which took place in Saint Thomas, Virgin Islands (March 1979), marked a historic moment in the intellectualization of the process as the Haitian academics and colleagues presented their papers in the creole language. Alleyne and Garvin note that this also represents the "internationalization of the language", which they consider to be "a very important step towards total standardization" (p. 26).

Elsewhere, Alleyne (1994, 8) makes the point that the issue of adequacy is bound up with a problem of creole genesis, which "continue[s] to link creole languages definitionally to pidgins and thereby . . . account for them fundamentally through the process of simplification". He goes on to explain that

> the simplification assigned to creoles is not the form sometimes inferred in the process of change from Anglo-Saxon to English or from Latin to French, but some kind of drastic, extreme, extraordinary, or unnatural simplification. Thus the teleological model on which Indo-European language families are based ignores linguistic convergence as a natural development or the possibility that fundamental change may occur through language contact situations typical of creole languages.

Alleyne concludes that ideological assumptions such as these about natural language change "have come to support and fuel those social psychological attitudes that are based on the perception that creole languages are corrupt, deviant derivatives within the Western linguistic tradition and, concomitantly, on the notion of their adequacy" (p. 9). The use and development of a language for purposes of literary criticism or linguistics can only be determined when efforts are made to use the language or the creole in this case for these purposes. The context of development of countries in the Caribbean, for example, has privileged the use of the language of the colonizer, what Whinnom would call "superstrate", over the indigenous languages and the creoles that would have developed in these contexts. The valuation of one over the other led to the exclusion of the creole from formal and educational use, although a high variety of creole (and I refer specifically to French Creole in the St Lucian context) was used by its speakers in a range of formal social contexts. It is the exclusion of the creole from the education context that denied several intelligent individuals from realizing the achievement and fulfilment that can be derived from bilingual literacy.

I refer briefly to the experience of a native speaker of French Creole (Kwéyòl), an informant to whom I will refer as Mr B., who was in his late sixties when I interviewed him. Kwéyòl was his first language and he spoke it almost exclusively. He had never learned English at school and had dropped out in frustration. He nevertheless had built a very successful construction firm, of which he was the CEO and chief architect and designer. Fortunately, Mr B. had two sons who had learned English at school and had done well enough to pass the series of examinations and get certification up to O-levels. He would explain his design concepts and measurements to his sons in Kwéyòl and they would do the necessary calculations and apply them to the designs that Mr B. would sketch and describe. At the construction site, Mr B.'s knowledge, experience and practical intervention would influence the product. Mr B. showed me many of the edifices he had built in and around the community. One day, he said to me, "Mwen ennteligan; mwen ennteligan menm si m'a sa li ek ma ka pale Anglé" ('I am intelligent; I am intelligent, even if I can't read and I don't speak English'). He need not have said this, because from the conversations in Kwéyòl, the logic, conceptualization and reasoning about issues and political affairs in the St Lucian context, one could tell that Mr B. was a person of fine intelligence. The sad part of his story is that second language instruction was not (and still is not) a methodology that is used in education in St Lucia, and neither is instruction in Kwéyòl. I have often wondered what Mr B. could have achieved had he been given an opportunity to develop literacy in his first language and learned English as an L2.

That same thought has continued to haunt me, since the students who were exclusive Kwéyòl speakers in kindergarten when I did the field work for my PhD thesis seem to have fared less well with careers than Mr B. Most of them lagged in the school system without acquiring the L2, then dropped out and got involved in activities that did not advance their personal situations in a positive way. Writing about the Haitian situation, which is comparable to the education situation in St Lucia in some ways, DeGraff (2005, 577) notes:

> The most powerful tool of domination, both actual and symbolic, is the school system, which in much of the Caribbean still devalues Creole languages – even in Haiti, where the vast majority of Haitians speak only Haitian Creole, where all Haitians speak Haitian Creole, and where Haitian Creole is an official language on a par with French. The non-use or limited use of Haitian Creole in Haitian schools violates the pedagogically sound principle that "education is best carried on through the mother tongue of the pupil" (UNESCO 1953, 6, 47). Such de facto stigmatization and/or exclusion of Haitian Creole in the schools and in other formal spheres effectively makes monolingual Haitian Creole speakers second-class citizens.

This is true of the speakers of Kwéyòl: Mr B. and the students in my study. In these cases it was not the intellectual capacity of the speakers nor the language they spoke, but the lack of opportunity for them to use and develop that language for literacy purposes and the absence of use of a reasonable methodology to foster the learning of another language as a second language that resulted in their being casualties of the education system.

Before the acceptance and sanctioning of the use of Jamaican Creole by Devonish, Carpenter and the group at the University of the West Indies, Mona (see chapter 9 of this volume), as a language of instruction in schools in Jamaica, Cooper (2003, 4–5) addressed the issue of the alleged "inadequacy" of creoles to handle literary criticism by electing to deliver her inaugural professorial lecture in Jamaican Creole to make the point that the language was adequate for literary analysis. In her introduction, she provides the justification for her choice of language: "Mi a go shuo unu se me kyan yuuz Jamiekan fi taak bout aal kain a big sobjek. . . . But some a wi jus cyan get it inna we hed seh we can use Jamiekan fi reason. . . . An we a use language; a no language a use we. So fi wi language can do whatsoever wi want it fi do."

She then proceeds to explain how she dealt with the analysis of *Lionheart Gal* by Sistren.

> So hear how mi build up fi mi drum an bass version outa mi owna side argument bout Sistren *Lionheart Gal*. Or if you rather, hear how mi carry over di meaning from English pon di Jamaican ferry. Di first part a di sentence alone woulda did sink di boat: "Recognizing the dialogic nature of oral/scribal and Jamaican/English discourse in the story/text *Lionheart Gal* . . ." So mi stop braps and start from scratch. "Dialogic": Latin again. An di root a disya Latin word, "dialogic", a Greek. Corruption pon top a corruption. Anyhow, all "dialogic" mean, a couple people a talk. So wa mi do, fi start off mi answer to Eddie B exam question, a fi *show* unu di different-different class a people a gi dem story inna *Lionheart Gal*; an mi point finger pon who a talk, who a write, who a write English and who a talk Jamaican, an a so mi carry over di meaning a di word "dialogic".
>
> So wi reach di next part a di carry over: "I wish to engage in an experimental Jamaican subversion of the authority of English as our exclusive voice of scholarship." Fi "experimental" mi seh, "Mi a go chrai a ting." An di "subversion of the authority of English as our exclusive voice of scholarship"? A it dis: "Mi a go shuo unu se wi kyan yuuz Jamiekan fi taak bout aal kain a big sobjek. A no suoso Ingglish wi ha fi yuuz." An a so di reasoning build up lickle lickle.
>
> Den di part bout "seeking to narrow the social distance between the language of the stories and the language of textual analysis". . . . An a so mi come up wid di

next part a di argument bout "the language of the stories and the language of text-
ual analysis". A so mi put it: "An den mi si se, if mi no main shaap, mi a go en op a
pap stail ina Ingglish pon di uman dem uu a tel fi dem stuori ina Jamiekan." Now,
when mi seh "pap stail" mi mean "show off". But mi also a talk bout how yu *dress
up* wa yu a seh. Di style a yu language. Mi step-mother she know weh mi mean an
mi like how she put it. She seh "English come een like dress up clothes and patwa
a yard clothes." So weh mi do, mi tek fi mi yard clothes turn fashion an dress up mi
language inna pretty-pretty bashment stylee fi go out a street an up a university.

Den dis a di last part a di crossing over now: "My analysis of the testimo-
nies of the women of Sistren – their verbal acts of introspective self-disclosure
– will now proceed in Jamaican." Fi "analysis" mi seh "wa mii tink bout dat". Den
"verbal acts" mi change dat up to "dem tel wi". An "introspective" – "dem luk ina
dem laif"; an "self-disclosure" – "dem tel wi di huol a fi dem porsnal an pravit
bizniz". An last-last "will now proceed in Jamaican" tun inna "an mi a go tel unu
ina Jamiekan. Siit ya." (p. 8)

In this paper, Cooper illustrates a point Craig (1997, 327) had made when
he said:

All signalling systems would not necessarily give the same alternatives, but it
is wrong to conclude from this that speakers themselves differ in terms of the
meanings they can or cannot process in any given, naturally evolving, signalling
system or in terms of their own innate capacities. There is no point, for example,
in assuming that the Standard English speaker who says:

(1)   He has no sincerity

is doing anything different from the creole-influenced speaker who does not
possess the term sincerity in his lexicon, but would say instead (in one creole
language):

(2)   /im neva du wa im se/
      He never does what he says

He concludes by pointing out that if a creole language is used in education,
"there is no reason to believe that the creole language will be in any way inadequate as a vehicle for thought and expression; the human being seems to have a
universal capacity to make all languages equivalent in this respect" (p. 328). In
her exposition, Cooper is in fact using the means of expression, like periphrasis,
to interpret abstract messages in the original text.

Although Whinnom (1971, 109) concedes that a pidgin or creole "can repair
its referential inadequacy when it is a question of naming *objects*, and does so

when the pressure of its inadequacy is felt", he does refer to the inadequacy of creoles as a perceived deficiency in coining words, abstract words in particular. He writes:

> One feature which appears to be seriously impaired by pidginization is the capacity for word-coinage from within the resources of the language . . . what cannot be generated very successfully by the combination of concrete words is abstract terms in which it is notorious that pidgins and creoles are deficient.

If we use Antillean French Creole – specifically, St Lucian Kwéyòl – as an example, an examination will quickly disprove Whinnom's claim by showing that the language is not deficient in abstract words. In fact, it abounds with common simplex abstractions such as the following:

| | |
|---|---|
| *lanmou* | love |
| *pasyens* | patience |
| *shagwen* | misery, sorrow |
| *pinitid* | deprivation |
| *lapenn* | grief |
| *bèl* | beautiful |
| *bèlté* | beauty |
| *adowasyon* | adoration |
| *kouway* | strength, force |
| *kouwaj* | fortitude |

Many other examples can be found in the Mondesir (1992) or Frank et al. (2001) dictionaries.

DeGraff (2001, 89) deals extensively with the issue of morphology to refute the claim that creole (using Haitian Creole as an example) derivational morphology has few productive affixes. He presents several examples to show the productive and regular nature of the process of affixation in Haitian French Creole, and he argues that

> it is not clear why Creoles could not express abstract concepts via morphologically simplex terms and periphrases built from such terms. . . . Periphrases may thus be considered the syntactic analogues of morphologically complex words. As with affixed words, it is pieces (and/or processes) from the mental lexicon that enter into the composition of periphrases. The difference is that periphrases are put together with "syntactic glue" whereas complex words are put together with "morphological glue".

In contexts like the Seychelles, French Creole is used in education: it is taught in the first four years of primary school (P1 to P4) as part of an integrated curriculum, then it is taught as a subject from P5 to P7, and it is used as the language medium for "political education, creative arts, family life education and extracurricular activities" in P9 and up. Bollée (1993, 89) notes that extension of the lexicon is one of the tasks faced by educators in creating materials for use in schools. In the case of the Seychelles, we understand that the concern of protecting the Kreol from foreign influences was a factor in the creation of new "motivated" words. Preservation of the identity of words led to the replacement of Anglicisms that had crept into the Kreol, for example:

## Replacement of English Words

| | | |
|---|---|---|
| switch on | > | *alimen* |
| postman | > | *fakter* |
| practice | > | *egzerse* |

## Borrowings from French

| | | |
|---|---|---|
| librarian | > | *biblyoteker* |
| stapler | > | *agrafer* |
| file | > | *dosye* |

## Newly Coined Creole Words

| | | |
|---|---|---|
| dustbin | > | *bwat salte* |
| sugar icing | > | *disik dekorasyon* |
| space shuttle | > | *navet lespas* |
| typewriter | > | *masin tipe* |

Perceptions of creoles as "inadequate" for certain functions have no doubt led to their exclusion from education and consequently to the exclusion of generations of native speakers of creoles from full participation in the economic and political affairs of their countries, resulting in what I refer to elsewhere as "cognitive waste" (Simmons-McDonald 1996). The inadequacy lies in the failure of educational institutions to provide adequate instruction for all people, which has in turn perpetuated a culture of deprivation of opportunity in education for creole speakers, which, rather than their language or necessarily their intellect, is the source of the problem.

## Is Creole a Handicap to the Creole Speaker?

The third statement from Whinnom which I consider is related to the notion that the speaker of a creole is handicapped by the language. The following are statements from Whinnom (1971).

> There may be some reason to suspect that the creole-speaker is handicapped by his language. Creolists have had a hard enough struggle to justify the respectability of their discipline. . . . I feel that someone should venture the suggestion that modern linguists may have been dangerously sentimental about creole languages, which, with only a few notable exceptions, constitute in most communities a distinct handicap to the social mobility of the individual and *may* also constitute a handicap to the creole-speaker's personal intellectual development. (pp. 109–110)

> From what we know of the role of language in intellectual development, one would expect the speakers of these primitive creoles to be intellectually handicapped. (p. 110)

> Linguists do not have the evidence to assert with confidence that speakers of creole-languages are not handicapped by their language, and should not, while any doubt remains, make unsupported assertions to the contrary. (p. 110)

In fairness to Whinnom, at the time he made these statements – the last one above, at least – research had not been done to refute them with evidence. Since then, studies have been done – for example, Devonish and Carpenter as reported in this volume and elsewhere and Simmons-McDonald (2006) in the Caribbean context – and research in this particular field continues to be undertaken. The unfortunate point in the statements, however, is the attribution of handicap not only to the language of the creole speaker but also to the speaker's intellectual development, thereby speculating about the existence of a link between the structure of a particular language variety and the cognitive capacity and development of the speaker of that language. Whinnom's (1971, 110) argument moves from positing a hunch to making an assertion: "one would expect the speakers of these primitive creoles to be intellectually handicapped." Inherent in that argument is the belief that a language like creole is not "good for" nor appropriate to intellectual development. The assumption is that creole is an inadequate language and therefore is not suitable for purposes of education and cannot contribute to the cognitive development of the creole speaker.

The question that has to be asked is whether it is the language itself or the exclusion of the language from certain domains that results in the handicap. The evidence available at this time suggests that it is not the language per se. If it is not, then one supposes that exclusion of the language from certain domains may have something to do with it. An affirmative response to the question will reveal that the matter of a handicap is not something inherent to the individual, but rather a condition imposed from without (through the policies that are adopted and the prevailing attitudes that some languages are better than others for certain purposes). English, at one time, was thought to be crude and lacking in resources to convey the ideas, philosophies and erudition expressed in Greek and Latin. But today it is an international language, and it keeps reinventing itself and expanding to accommodate developments in technology, for example.

What makes it possible for a language to make such accommodation? It is the intellectualization of the language – as proposed by Havranek and elucidated by Alleyne and Garvin – that becomes possible through the process of standardization. Intellectualization is accelerated by the use of the language for purposes of education, literacy and literary purposes. To state categorically that a creole is deficient or inadequate and therefore constitutes a handicap to its speakers is unfounded unless it can be proved that use of the creole for such purposes results in failure. Further, as Todd (1974, 87) points out, it would be difficult to measure an abstraction such as "the detriment to a creole speaker's intellectual development", and she asks, assuming one could measure it, "from whose point of view would it be considered a handicap?"

Modern educational instruments provide us with the means of measuring IQ and EI (emotional intelligence) and assigning a range of other tests to the individual. Inevitably, the IQ tests that have been designed to determine issues like placement of the individual are not designed with the creole speaker or the relevant creole culture in mind, and creole speakers may come out with scores much lower than their English-speaking counterparts who have been using that language for intellectual purposes in formal and informal settings.

Since these assertions were made by Whinnom, we have gathered sound evidence of the benefits to the creole speaker when the creole language is used in education. In such contexts, it is clear that cognitive or intellectual development proceeds in much the same way that it does in the case of monolingual speakers of English. There is evidence to show further that use of the creole, the language with which the child comes to school, promotes the acquisition of literacy in the second language and this bilingualism leads to cognitive flexibility.

The following provide some evidence from creole as well as other contexts on the benefits to learners when their native language – regardless of whether that language is a creole or not – is used for literacy development and in education.

1. If the conceptual foundation of a child's first language (L1) is well developed, he or she is more likely to develop "similarly high levels of conceptual abilities in an L2" (Cummins 1994, 38).

2. Skills basic to academic progress are most easily learned in L1 (Swain, quoted in Walker 1984, 165).

3. It is easier to learn to read in L1 and then apply this skill to L2 rather than learn to read and learn L2 simultaneously (Walker 1984, 165). (Note: This is normally what we ask of native speakers of creole when they come to school for the first time. Before they have any basic communication skills in English, we introduce them to learning literacy in English, which they do not understand.) Walker also notes that "vernacular education will instill children with a sense of pride in their native tongue and culture which counteracts the sense of inferiority long conn ected with minority languages . . . vernacular education serves to develop a child's command of the language in an attempt to make it a viable medium in the modern world" (p. 166).

4. Appropriate teaching methodology incorporating students' vernaculars may well help them acquire the standard (Siegel 1999, 721).

5. The use of Tok Pisin resulted in greater gains for literacy development among children who were native speakers of the pidgin than for children who had not been exposed to programmes in which the pidgin had been used. In this context, it was concluded that the use of the pidgin had been a help and not a hindrance in the children's acquisition of literacy (Siegel 1997).

6. Educational reform in the Seychelles which led to the use of creole in education enabled "a high percentage of pupils to read, write and understand in Creole . . . and improved performance in English" (*Seychelles Nation*, 26 April 1985, 2).

An experiment in St Lucia with creole-speaking children in primary school who at ages eleven and up had not learned to read and write after seven years in school showed that these children made considerable gains in reading and writing in both Kwéyòl and English after only six weeks of intensive instruction (Simmons-McDonald 2006). In this study, the children not only developed phonological awareness in Kwéyòl but they also learned to read and write in Kwéyòl. Their proficiency in English also improved. The following are samples from one of the subjects, Ado, a male learner, who learned to read in both Kwéyòl and English through participation in the study (the errors are the forms in boldface, followed by the correct forms in parentheses):

Kwéyòl sample: Zanndoli andjélé Konpè Chyen pas (lè) i **to** (té) vlé Konpè Lapin poté yo wèspé. Konpè Zanndoli **to** (té) faché piscè Konpè Lapin pa té ni **pus** (pyès) wèspé pou li.

Translation: 'Lizard called out to Comrade Dog because he wanted Comrade Rabbit to respect them. Comrade Lizard was angry because Comrade Rabbit did not respect them at all.'

English sample (same learner): Lester and Joe was going to catch crabs. Lester was having fun on his own. There was no need for flashlight because the moon was shining **britly** (brightly).

The grade 3 pupils speak in the poem. The word that best describes the children is hard-working. I like the way they **exprest** (express) **there filing** (their feelings). They do not fight, steal, or cheat. The best part of the poem I like is we look smart from head to feet.

The issue of bias in testing and materials is one that has to be considered in the preparation of materials for use with creole speakers. In the ongoing experiment, some texts are being developed to provide the best opportunities for learners and to test the hypothesis that use of Kwéyòl in education does not constitute a handicap to creole speakers but rather contributes to bilingual proficiency and cognitive flexibility among native speakers of Kwéyòl. The samples presented indicate progress made by a group subjected to an intensive bilingual programme over a six-week period. One could expect that an extended programme would most likely further development of the learners' ability to comment on the literature they read, that is, to begin to do literary criticism from an early age in Kwéyòl and in English.

Considering what we know about the detrimental effects suffered by children whose first language is not used in education, and considering also the very high failure rates on minimum standards tests, common entrance exams and Caribbean Examinations Council (CXC) school-leaving exams (as indicated by Ministry of Education and CXC reports), and considering further the cognitive waste in our countries over the last few decades and weighing this against the positive outcomes reported for experiments in which creole is used in education, there should be no doubt that we need to set aside negative comments such as those made by Whinnom and begin to implement in a systematic way programmes that are intended to promote literacy and the cognitive development of our children. We can accomplish this through the variety of approaches suggested by Craig as well as through bilingual programmes that will prepare them for life in their communities and the wider world.

## Notes

1. DeGraff cites McWhorter (1998), Seuren and Wekker (1986) and Seuren (1998).
2. *Superstratum*: "A language spoken by a dominant group which has influenced that of a population subordinate to it. For example, speakers of English were dominated after the Norman conquest by speakers whose native language was Anglo-French; hence, Anglo-French became a superstratum that has influenced the history of English." *Substratum*: "A language spoken by (a given) population which has influenced that of a group by which they were dominated." Examples include "English as a possible influence on the evolution of Anglo-French after the Norman conquest, and any of several West African languages as a factor in the formation of pidgin spoken in the West Indies" (Matthews 1997, 361, 362, 363).

## References

Alleyne, Mervyn. 1994. Problems of Standardization of Creole Languages. In *Language and the Social Construction of Identity in Creole Situations*, edited by M. Morgan, 7–18. Los Angeles: Center for Afro-American Studies, University of California.

Alleyne, Mervyn, and Paul L. Garvin. 1982. Standard language Theory with Special Reference to Creole Languages. In *Theoretical Issues in Caribbean Linguistics*, edited by M.C. Alleyne, 19–35. Kingston: Language Laboratory, University of the West Indies.

Bollée, Annegret. 1993. Language Policy in the Seychelles and Its Consequences. *International Journal of the Sociology of Language* 102: 85–99.

Chomsky, Noam. 1965. *Aspects of the Theory of Syntax*. Cambridge, MA: MIT Press.

———. 1980. On Cognitive Structures and Their Development. In *Language and Learning: The Debate between Jean Piaget and Noam Chomsky*, edited by M. Piattelli-Palmarini, 35–52. London: Routledge and Kegan Paul.

Cook, Vivian J. 1988. *Chomsky's Universal Grammar: An Introduction*. Cambridge, MA: Blackwell.

Cooper, Carolyn. 2003. Professing Slackness: Language, Authority and Power Within the Academy and Without. Inaugural professorial lecture, University of the West Indies, Mona, 25 September.

Cummins, Jim. 1994. Knowledge, Power and Identity in Teaching English as a Second Language. In *Educating Second Language Children: The Whole Child, the Whole Curriculum, the Whole Community*, edited by F. Genesee, 33–58. Cambridge: Cambridge University Press.

DeGraff, Michel. 2001. Morphology in Creole Genesis: Linguistics and Ideology. In *Ken Hale: A Life in Language*, edited by M. Kenstowicz, 53–121. Cambridge, MA: MIT Press.

———. 2005. Linguists' Most Dangerous Myth: The Fallacy of Creole Exceptionalism. *Language in Society* 34: 533–91.

Frank, David, et al. 2001. *Kwéyòl Dictionary*. Castries: Ministry of Education, Government of St Lucia.

Hymes, Dell. 1971. *Pidginization and Creolization of Languages*. Cambridge: Cambridge University Press.

Matthews, P.H. 1997. *Oxford Dictionary of Linguistics*. Oxford: Oxford University Press.

Mondesir, Jones E. 1992. *Dictionary of St Lucian Creole*. Berlin: Mouton de Gruyter.

Mühlhäusler, Peter. 1997. *Pidgin and Creole Linguistics*. London: University of Westminster Press.

Schumann, John. 1978. *The Pidginization Process: A Model for Second Language Acquisition*. Rowley, MA: Newbury House.

Sebba, Mark. 1997. *Contact Languages: Pidgins and Creoles*. London: Macmillan.

Siegel, Jeff. 1997. Using a Pidgin Language in Formal Education: Help or Hindrance? *Applied Linguistics* 18: 86–100.

———. 1999. Stigmatized and Standardized Varieties in the Classroom: Interference or Separation? *TESOL Quarterly* 33 (4): 701–28.

Simmons-McDonald, Hazel. 1996. Language Education Policy: The Case for Creole in Formal Education in St Lucia. In *Caribbean Language Issues, Old and New*, edited by P. Christie, 120–42. Kingston: University of the West Indies Press.

————. 2006. Vernacular Instruction and Bi-Literacy Development in French Creole Speakers. In *Exploring the Boundaries of Caribbean Creole Languages*, edited by H. Simmons-McDonald and I. Robertson, 118–43. Kingston: University of the West Indies Press.

Todd, Loreto. 1974. *Pidgins and Creoles*. London: Routledge and Kegan Paul.

Walker, Alastair. 1984. Applied Sociology of Language: Vernacular Languages and Education. In *Applied Sociolinguistics*, edited by P. Trudgill, 160–220. New York: Academic Press.

Whinnom, Keith. 1971. Linguistic Hybridization and the "Special Case" of Pidgins and Creoles. In *Pidginization and Creolization of Languages*, edited by D. Hymes, 91–117. Cambridge: Cambridge University Press.

# 5 | English in Today's World: New Challenges for Caribbean Educators

PAULINE CHRISTIE

*Retired Senior Lecturer, University of the West Indies, Mona*

The general sociopolitical climate in which English is being taught in the Commonwealth Caribbean today is very different from the one which existed when that language was officially introduced into schools during the nineteenth century. It is different, too, in some respects, from that of even approximately fifty years ago, when Dennis Craig began his search for an appropriate methodology for teaching it. The main problems which confronted him throughout his long professional career are still with us, but the immediate environments in which English is taught have become more complex, a development which has important implications for classroom teachers of English.

Our educators in the Caribbean need to be cognizant of certain important developments which have provided grounds for reconsideration of the concept of English that has traditionally been the goal of classroom teaching. These have to do with (1) the increased role of English as a world language; (2) the dominance of the United States since approximately the mid–twentieth century and the concomitant spread of US English; (3) the growing recognition, beyond national boundaries, of local varieties of English which have arisen in former British colonies in different parts of the world; and (4) trends affecting British English, the traditional model in the Caribbean.

The demand for English is ever increasing worldwide. The language is now used in several countries which have had no colonial ties to Britain, its birthplace, and by people with many different mother tongues. More and more of the activities for which English is regularly used take place on the international stage. For example, although official policy recognizes other languages as well for international organizations such as the European Union, in practice the usual working language is English (Seidlhofer et al. 2006, 5).

The increasing spread of English has also been specifically linked to the process of globalization, which has manifested itself in greater interaction and interdependence among nations, notably in matters concerning technology, scientific research, business, trade, popular culture and even politics. Some of the functions with which English is associated today were not even heard of half a century ago. For example, it is the language mostly used with reference to the new advances in information technology which now allow the speedy transmission of messages across the globe.

The varieties of English used on the international stage have been largely influenced by US English, the importance of which has spread, especially since World War II, as a consequence of the military, economic, scientific and technological dominance of the United States and its major role in the spread of popular culture via electronic media. Because of the geographical proximity of the Caribbean to the United States, this region is particularly susceptible to relatively informal contacts as well, through, for example, mass tourism and mass migration in search of work, leading to regular contact with relatives who live in the United States.

Not surprisingly, the functions of English on the world stage vary widely. In some cases, it is the language regularly used by the educated élite in countries where other languages are spoken by the masses. In others, it is used only informally, as a lingua franca in casual conversation between persons who have no other common language. Within these groups, too, communicative competence varies among individuals. There is, of course, far more uniformity across the world in written language – particularly in the language of edited books, newspapers and journals – than in spoken language, especially when the latter is used at the informal level.

The spread of English in recent years has implications for the Caribbean in view of increasing interaction on the part of local and regional governments, business executives, academics and popular entertainers, for example, with non-traditional partners from across the globe, many of whom rely on English as a lingua franca.

Other fairly recent developments with regard to English prompt reconsideration of the language situation in the Caribbean itself. The dismantling of the British Empire in the latter half of the twentieth century and the concomitant political and socio-economic changes in its former colonies in Africa, South-East and South Asia, and the Caribbean have led to a modification of attitudes towards British English and the emergence, in all these countries, of varieties of English which are less dependent on the traditional British model. The greater consciousness of a national identity which followed political independence in the former colonies has also contributed to the functional expansion and greater acceptance of local vernaculars by persons in the society. In many of these countries, English has nevertheless remained the language of the élite, the language of secondary and higher education at least, the language of administration and business, and a lingua franca for different ethnic groups. In the Caribbean, as Dennis Craig (2006, 105–6) reported, significant expansion of the functional roles of Caribbean creoles, liberalization of social attitudes and the evident decline of traditional linguistic prejudices and inhibitions were also accompanied by the absorption of several vernacular forms into local standard varieties of English.

American English was, of course, the first of the varieties from former British colonies to achieve international status. Australian English and Canadian English followed. The term "new Englishes" does not refer to any of these. The speakers of these varieties belong to what Kachru (1985) has defined as the "inner circle" of speakers of English – that is, the varieties developed in places where massive numbers of the initial settlers were native speakers of that language. The term "new Englishes" is applied instead to varieties which (1) are developed through the education system by virtue of being taught as a school subject and in many cases used as a medium of education where the main language is not English, (2) are used for a range of functions and (3) have become "localized" or "nativized" through the adoption of some language features of their own (Platt et al. 1984, 2). These varieties, which include Indian English, Nigerian English and Singapore English, belong to Kachru's "outer circle"; that is, they are used in countries in which the majority of the population uses another language for private interaction but public affairs are conducted in English.

The relatively wide range of variation between standard English and basilectal creole in the Caribbean territories makes generalization problematic in their case. Kachru, recognizing this, deliberately omitted Jamaican speakers from the "circles" he identified on the grounds that while the varieties occurring at the upper end of the Caribbean continuum met the given criteria for new Englishes, being clearly English, the co-existing basilectal creole did not. Besides, it is not always clear where the dividing line between the varieties in the Caribbean can be drawn.

The norm for formal written language throughout the Caribbean region, which is assumed in this chapter, is close to internationally accepted standard English, especially with regard to syntax. It also includes, as would be expected in today's world wherever some form of English is used, alternations between some British and US English features in addition to indigenous ones. Deviations from the traditional norm are not unusual in local newspapers, but they are less frequent in literary work, such as published novels, which has usually been subjected to serious editing based on international standards. Some writers, however, deliberately exploit local usage from time to time in their work to give it a "local flavour", even where dialogue is not involved.

Formal spoken English, too, remains fairly close to the traditional British model, despite its greater use of localisms, some of which are illustrated later in this chapter. Scholars from outside the Caribbean, however, have sometimes failed to discriminate between the varieties of spoken language, with the result that what they identify as Jamaican English would never occur in the formal usage that is the main concern of this chapter, although it may not be unusual in other contexts. Examples of such lack of discrimination are the use of *friend* as a verb, as in "She said if he wanted to friend her he would have to go to her mother and ask her", and pronoun copying, as in "The black Americans they speak English", both of which sentences are given by Platt et al. (1984, 99, 120) as examples of Jamaican English, without further explanation.

This chapter discusses some characteristic features of formal spoken and written Jamaican English, problems with its definition and acceptance, and implications of new developments for the teaching of English. Although the Jamaican situation is singled out for special focus here, it is fairly representative of the language situation in the anglophone Caribbean. Despite the fact that different colonial histories and settlement patterns account for some intra-regional differences, the principle on which this chapter is based – that is, the need for reconsideration of the traditional model – applies to all the relevant territories.

Who uses Jamaican English? A retired Jamaican secondary-school teacher, expressing disapproval of what he considered to be the degradation of English, described Jamaican English speakers as "persons who know and should do better, but fail or prefer not to do so" (Burgess 2002). He was evidently referring to persons who were relatively well educated, such as professionals and civil servants, whose formal language might be expected to be more or less identical with the traditional British model of standard English. There seems to be general agreement about using educational level as a working criterion in studies of usage. For example, Irvine (2004) based her study of Jamaican English phonology on white-collar employees of a quasi-government agency, for her a highly educated group. This is comparable to the criterion used by Allsopp for his *Dictionary of Caribbean English Usage* (1996). According to him, his concern was with usage at the middle and upper levels of the educational scale at the regional level (1972a). It is recognized here, however, that the repertoire of even highly educated persons in the Caribbean, including Jamaica, is varied, more widely for some than for others. For this reason, the discussion in this chapter adds another dimension. It focuses on the formal usage of such persons in given situations – specifically, on the language they use when they are assumed to be on their "best behaviour".

In the first place, Jamaicans can be readily identified by social class on the basis of certain aspects of their pronunciation. Some diagnostic features are shared with anglophone Caribbean neighbours, but others are not. A few features also make discrimination among Jamaican English speakers possible, as the occurrence of these often differs appreciably from one individual to another. This is not surprising, as pronunciation within any language group is fairly variable. This is most evident, of course, where there is no strong social pressure towards a common standard. Received Pronunciation, which, since the latter part of the nineteenth century, was deliberately exported from Britain to the colonies as the prestige model, was never widely adopted in Jamaica. Such social pressure as exists is more or less confined to the classroom and is directed at those features which are associated with creole, or stems from a conviction that the pronunciation of a word must closely match its spelling.

Characteristic features of pronunciation which are very obvious in the formal usage of educated persons, among others, include

- the occurrence of a palatal glide following /k/ and /g/ before /a/, and less generally before /e/, in words like *can, gap, care* and *case*;
- variable occurrence of word-final consonant clusters in, for example, *stand, left, lost* and *find*;
- rhoticity, or the pronunciation of the post-vocalic *r* before consonants, in, for example, *part, heart* and *particular*;
- the placement of stress on the penultimate syllable of polysyllabic words, in, for example *character, maintenance, Manchester, Clarendon, Pegasus, interesting, administrative* and *electoral*, and on the initial syllable in

words of two syllables, such as *refer* and *prefer*. The influence of the United States is particularly evident nowadays in the placement of stress on the first syllable of the verb *protest*, for example, resulting in the homophony of noun and verb. This tendency is particularly common among media personnel.

As regards the vocabulary of Jamaican English, since this linguistic level inevitably reflects the environment in which a language is used, there are several words in general use which represent local flora, fauna and culture. Others preserve dialectal usage in Britain, or reflect changes in the grammatical function or the meanings of the original input forms. Still others are Jamaican or Caribbean innovations, some of which are partly traceable to African sources. At the same time, some words which are frequently used elsewhere in the anglophone world are rare in Jamaica and the rest of the Caribbean. Cassidy's *Jamaica Talk*, first published in 1961, and the *Dictionary of Jamaican English* by Cassidy and Le Page, which first appeared in 1967, have both provided useful documentation of Jamaican vocabulary. Since the authors deliberately made no attempt to distinguish between levels of usage, however, they included words usually associated with creole as well as others more generally distributed across the continuum, the category which is of special interest to us here.

Some forms which are spontaneously used in formal speech by Jamaicans are apparently not considered "good enough" to appear in writing. Thus, the plant that is pronounced "skellion" (< English *scallion*) is regularly represented as *scallion* or *escallion* in writing, and the popular dish "scoveitch fish" (< Spanish *escabeche*) becomes *escoveitched fish*. Similarly, *curried goat* or *curried mutton*[1] is often the written equivalent of the dish most usually referred to in speech as "curry goat", and *jerked pork* that of the usual "jerk pork". One even sometimes finds *roasted pork* for "roast pork", the label generally used in both speech and writing outside the Caribbean. In some other instances, the attraction of an external standard in writing has led to false semantic associations, as in the case of the pejorative Jamaican *facety* 'impudent, bold, rude, overbearing' being written as *feisty*, a form commonly used in the United States with positive connotation.

The examples that follow further illustrate general usage in Jamaica. Even where alternative words are available in the traditional external British model, using them does not give the same effect, especially when one is addressing fellow Jamaicans. Writers have sometimes singled out some of these words by using inverted commas, but this practice has almost disappeared. Of course, even some educated Jamaicans are not conscious of what is particularly Jamaican or Caribbean usage and what is not.

## Examples of the Vocabulary of Jamaican English

### A. *Words and phrases referring to local flora, fauna and culture*

| | |
|---|---|
| *garden-egg* | eggplant |
| *john-crow* | carrion crow |
| *brawta* | something given as an extra |
| *duppy* | spirit (of the dead) |
| *chain* | a distance of a few yards |
| *bammy* | cassava cake |
| *baby-mother* | used, often by the father, to refer to a woman who has borne him a child, usually out of wedlock; cf. *baby-father* |
| *best butter* | butter (i.e., not margarine) |
| *Irish potato* | potato (i.e., not sweet potato) |

### B. *Miscellaneous*

| | |
|---|---|
| *grater* (*vb.*) | grate |
| *care* (*trans.*) | take care of, as in "Let's care our children more" (motto for Child Month) |
| *grow* (*trans.*) | 'improve', as in "The station that grows your mind" (slogan of the now defunct Radio Mona) |
| *break* | break into, as in "Three Shops Broken" (newspaper headline) |
| *miserable* | bad-tempered |
| *ignorant* | easily angered |
| *next* | other |
| *police* | policeman |
| *eye-water* | tears |
| *foot-bottom* | sole |
| *hand-middle* | palm |
| *drop asleep* | fall asleep |
| *catch fight* | start fighting |

Jamaican English questions are usually distinguished from corresponding statements only by their rising sentence-final intonation, as in "You like that one?" or "Why you don't buy a new car?" This characteristic is taken for granted in spoken language.

Other characteristics of the syntactic level are repetition of verbs, adjectives and adverbs, and front-focusing, used for emphasis. Still another characteristic is verb serialization, as in the following examples:

1. The woman was tall tall.
2. They sent for the doctor quick quick.
3. We ran and ran until we could not see him again.
4. It's afraid she's afraid.
5. The woman over there, she is Cheryl's sister.
6. The children ran go see what was happening.

The use of *not . . . again* with the meaning 'no longer', as in sentence (3), is another distinguishing feature of Jamaican English.

The attitude of the former school teacher mentioned earlier in this chapter raises the question of acceptability. He strongly objected to departures from the traditional model of standard British English. At least some of these, however, as indicated earlier, reflect a local norm as yet ill-defined. Besides, while the conservatism of many older persons in particular remains strong, casual observation suggests that certain forms and structures which were formerly highly stigmatized are gradually becoming less so. Where pronunciation is concerned, these include "*h*-dropping", resulting in the homophony of *his* and *is*, *hair* and *air*, for example; absence of interdental fricatives so that *thin* and *this*, for example, are pronounced [tin] and [dis], respectively; morpho-phonological examples such as *voilence* 'violence' and *aks* 'ask'; and also possibly the syntactic structures illustrated earlier, among others.

The traditional concept of a monolithic standard English is particularly questionable when one is confronted with situations such as those in the Caribbean. It has, of course, been questioned elsewhere as well (cf. Bex and Watts 1999). Its inappropriateness in today's world is mainly attributed to the following:

1. It ignored variation over time, place and circumstances.
2. It focused on written usage.
3. Its original motivation emphasized prescription as opposed to description of actual usage.

4. It has been closely associated with the spread of English imperialism and culture.

Despite recognition of these as shortcomings and the welcome loosening of the pressures traditionally imposed by standardization, however, the concept as such undoubtedly has some advantages. Teachers everywhere need a systematic model that will enable them to distinguish between what is part of the educated, accepted variety and what is not. They should, however, envisage this standard as a yardstick rather than primarily as an unchanging prescriptive tool.

Interestingly enough, at a conference on language teaching, linguistics and the teaching of English held at the University of the West Indies, Mona, as far back as 1964, the participants acknowledged that a norm had developed inside Jamaica as a result of the "informal standardization" represented by the speech of educated Jamaicans (see Allsopp 1972b, 3). As was characteristic of the time, however, the conference went on to state that the goal of teaching was to produce an identity between educated British English and educated Jamaican at the written level. As has already been indicated in this chapter, however, identity, even at this level, is not a practical goal in the twenty-first century. It must also be noted that British English has itself changed and will continue to change, as will its Caribbean counterparts.

Allsopp's dictionary was intended to provide an authoritative lexicographical account of English usage in the region for the guidance of teachers after the introduction in 1979 of examinations at the secondary level, set and marked in the Caribbean instead of Britain (Allsopp 1972a, 5). However, to date there has been no corresponding grammar. Existing grammars are based on the assumption that Jamaican English or Caribbean English is or should be identical with British English. An authoritative reference grammar is needed here, one that is no longer entirely focused on external norms, and that also distinguishes between registers as far as possible. Based on systematic empirical research, it should aim at documenting characteristically local usage and attitudes to this, while not ignoring the significant core that is shared with internationally accepted standard English, thus accounting for the variation that exists in all languages.

What is being recommended here is neither a free-for-all nor a grammar which makes value judgements about usage. Rather, the recommendation is for a description that makes it clear that English is neither monolithic nor unchanging. It is also suggested here that at least some items that are now confined to spoken language in Jamaica and the rest of the anglophone Caribbean have already been absorbed, or are on the road to being absorbed, into a local standard and therefore deserve acceptance in the written form as well. Examples from the growing body of Caribbean literature could be used to support this. Such a grammar would help clear up the uncertainty about standards that currently exists. Evidence suggests that there are important differences at present between what individual teachers will and will not accept in the classroom. For example, some already take for granted, in speech or in writing, US *gotten* (vs. Br. *got*) and US *different than* (vs. Br. *different from*), or Jamaican *not . . . again* 'no longer', and even use these regularly themselves, whereas others loudly condemn such usage.

At the same time, it is still possible to identify, at all levels, forms and structures sometimes used in formal Jamaican English, for example, which obviously conflict with the local norms and which educated persons on the whole would even now consider mistakes, whether they occur in speech or in writing. The examples provided below illustrate these deviations. They are taken from newspaper headlines and reports, public notices and advertisements, as well as from spoken usage in radio and television news broadcasts.

The use of the term *deviation* here is not driven by direct comparison with a British model, but is instead motivated by contrast with the usually accepted norms for written and spoken formal usage in Jamaica itself. These norms, of course, originally derived to a large extent from the metropolitan norms, but they have also been much influenced by "nativized" usage. However, although Jamaicans and others are likely to agree that such norms exist, mere observation of usage is not a sure guide to identifying them. For one thing, as has been suggested, there is not always consensus as to what they are. Some users are more conservative than others in their attitudes, as we have seen. Indeed, only recently, objections were raised in the media to the use of the word *fording* for a ford, or river crossing, although the word has long since been the one most widely used in Jamaica in writing as well as speech. It is not, however, to be found in the *Oxford English Dictionary*. Similar objections have also been raised in some quarters to the long-established use, at all levels of the society, of *officer* as a general term for a policeman instead of it being reserved for policemen above a certain rank, and of *people* instead of *persons* to refer to a group of individuals. In fact, those who object sometimes find it necessary to "correct" their own spontaneous usage in this regard, sure evidence that the usage they criticize has been absorbed into Jamaican English, at least.

The deviations illustrated here are but a small sample of those that occur from time to time in formal spoken and even written English. They fall into two main categories: (1) those that reflect trends away from the traditional norm, and (2) those that reflect an incomplete grasp of English pronunciations or grammar. The tendency to make a verb agree with a preceding noun which is closer to it than the head noun of the subject phrase, and the tendency to use *whom* instead of *who* in subject position, belong to the first group. In the second group come instances of hypercorrection and malapropisms.

## Examples of Deviation[2]

### Category 1

### A. Attraction of singular/plural modifiers preceding the verb

1. *Some members of staff of the United States Embassy *is* to return home. (radio news broadcast)
2. *Smoking ganja and other illegal drugs *are* not permitted. (public notice)
3. *Work on some roads *are* incomplete. (radio news broadcast)

### B. Use of whom for the subject of a clause

*The school's motto must reflect the core values of all *whom* pass through. (speech by government minister at a public function)

Both sets of examples illustrate usage which is becoming increasingly frequent in formal spoken and written English in Jamaica. These same trends are evident to some extent in the United Kingdom and the United States as well, as illustrated by the following examples:

1. *A fleet of ambulances *were* waiting. (BBC News)
2. *The crew of three boats carrying forty-two cases of whisky included an eighty-four-year-old man *whom* Customs Officers suggested should have his pension docked. (report in the *Times* of London)
3. *. . . another man *whom* the police say should have been questioned. (news report on CBS programme, *48 Hours Mystery*)

## Category 2

## A. Hypercorrected forms

1. a. *[hiz] 'is'
   b. *[hevri] 'every'

2. a. *Pope *Threads* Carefully (newspaper headline)
   b. *Harmond* Barracks (notice in newspaper)

Hypercorrection indicates that the user has a false idea of the relevant English norms. The cases illustrated here also indicate that the users were trying to avoid usage associated with the creole end of the continuum. Thus, in example (1), the users were conscious that English words with initial /h/ often have creole counterparts without the initial aspiration, so they overcompensated by producing it where the standard English words in question begin with vowels. In the second set of examples, it is spelling that is affected by the effort to avoid creole usage. Thus, English *tread* was written *thread*, as the user overcompensated for the fact that creole lacks the interdental fricatives which are represented orthographically in English by *th*. Similarly, the representation of Harmon Barracks as "Harmond Barracks" reflects overcompensation for the lack of word-final consonant clusters in creole by a user who was unsure of the English model.

## B. Malapropisms

1. *Some of the island's leading money dealers are *barking* at government's proposal to tax the interest earned by Jamaicans who hold its global bonds. (newspaper report)
2. *The car travelled a *considerate* distance. (television news report)

Uncertainty as to the relevant standard English norm also accounts for malapropisms. The examples given here illustrate confusion between words which sound alike. In the first example, the less familiar *balk* is confused with *bark*, and in the second, *considerate* is confused with *considerable*.

Other examples of Category 2 deviations are particularly evident nowadays in the spoken and written English of some secondary- and tertiary-level students, some of whom are teachers-in-training. These include absence of inflection on past participles as well as on nouns with plural meaning, as in, for example:

1. *His father was *rob* and *kill.*
2. *thousands of *insect*
3. *one of the *thing*

Hypercorrection occurs here too. It is most often manifested in:

1. double marking (i.e., both the auxiliary and the main verb are inflected), as in:
   *He did not *realized.*
2. inflection of the verb in complements of verbs of perception, as in:
   *I heard someone *called* out to me.

## Conclusion

The issues discussed in this chapter are highly relevant for the teaching of English, not only in Jamaica but also in the rest of the anglophone Caribbean. The Caribbean has had a relatively long association with English, even if formal education in the language officially became general only after emancipation from slavery in the nineteenth century. As Dennis Craig put it more than thirty years ago, "The societies in all the territories are, in a way, trapped within their Standard English tradition" (1971, 375).

The spread of English throughout the world has made it more important than ever for Jamaicans and their Commonwealth neighbours to be able to speak and write English that is understood outside the island and the region so that they can interact usefully with users of other varieties in a range of possible geographical and social environments. At the same time, it is important that indigenous varieties have a place both inside and outside the classroom, since it is these that reflect the learners' personal experience. Instead, the traditional education system has concentrated exclusively on foreign and often archaic models. Even at the time when Craig wrote the words quoted here, the assumption was that only one form of English should be taught. In the intervening years, however, as we have seen, the importance of models defined by native-speaker norms has become clear. The use of models with which they can identify is also likely to prove more interesting to learners, many of whom are currently turned off by what they see as being of little relevance to them. The replacement of traditional foreign examinations by those set and marked in the Caribbean by Caribbean teachers at the secondary level, and the establishment of local and regional universities which are providing graduates for the work force, including teachers, reinforce the principle.

The diversity of English and the significance of this in today's world have also been recognized by teachers of English operating outside the Caribbean, some of whom, with hindsight, admit to earlier misconceptions. Thus, Luke Prodromou (2007, 6), commenting on the attitude of English teachers originating in Britain in the late 1970s and 1980s, and implicitly contrasting this with a more recent one, stated:

> We English language "experts", all emanating from the UK, saw nothing problematic in native-centric models; there was only one standard form of English, and that was indeed – ultimately – the language of Shakespeare. But what we were not fully aware of at the time, in our enthusiasm to teach "authentic English" as defined by native-speaker norms, was that English, itself, was also going forth and multiplying.

By "native" in this context, he meant, of course, native to Britain.

In light of the discussion in this chapter, the expression "English-as-mother-tongue approach", used to refer to the traditional policy to which Craig, among others, was radically opposed, is not sufficiently explicit. A more appropriate, if less elegant, designation for what has long existed would be "the British-Standard-English-as-mother-tongue policy". It is certainly true that the mother tongue of the majority of learners in Jamaica, for example – that is, what is usually identified by Jamaicans as *patwa* or *creole* – has been ignored in the classroom, with serious negative consequences. It is also true, however, that the model of English that has been aimed at by teachers and used in textbooks differs in important ways from the norms applied by educated Jamaicans, among others, in the anglophone world today, including many persons in contemporary Britain itself.

## Notes

1. The word *mutton* is used in Jamaica to refer specifically to goat flesh.
2. * indicates that the sentence in question is considered deviant.

# References

Allsopp, Richard. 1972a. Why a Dictionary of Caribbean English Usage? Circular, University of the West Indies, Cave Hill.

———. 1972b. The Problem of Acceptability in Caribbean Creolized English. Paper presented at UNESCO conference on Creole language and educational development, St Augustine, Trinidad.

———. 1996. *Dictionary of Caribbean English Usage.* Oxford: Oxford University Press.

Bex, Tony, and Richard J. Watts, eds. 1999. *Standard English: The Widening Debate.* London: Routledge.

Burgess, Chester. 2002. Standard English: Prescription for Jamaica. *Gleaner,* 5 February.

Cassidy, Frederic. 1961. *Jamaica Talk.* London: Macmillan.

Cassidy, Frederic, and Robert Le Page. 1967. *Dictionary of Jamaican English.* Cambridge: Cambridge University Press.

Craig, Dennis R. 1971. Education and Creole English in the West Indies: Some Sociolinguistic Factors. In *Pidginization and Creolization of Language,* edited by D. Hymes, 371–91. Cambridge: Cambridge University Press.

———. 2006. The Use of the Vernacular in West Indian Education. In *Exploring the Boundaries of Caribbean Creole Languages,* edited by H. Simmons-McDonald and I. Robertson, 99–117. Kingston: University of the West Indies Press.

Irvine, Alison. 2004. A Good Command of the English Language: Phonological Variation in the Jamaican Acrolect. *Journal of Pidgin and Creole Languages* 19 (1): 41–76.

Kachru, Braj B. 1985. Standards, Codification and Sociolinguistic Realism: The English Language in the Outer Circle. In *English in the World: Teaching and Learning the Language and Literature,* edited by R. Quirk and H. Widdowson, 11–36. Cambridge: Cambridge University Press.

Platt, John Talbot, Heidi Weber and Ho Mian Lian. 1984. *The New Englishes.* London: Routledge and Kegan Paul.

Prodromou, Luke. 2007. Forty Years of Language Teaching. *Language Teaching* 40: 1–15.

Seidlhofer, Barbara, Angelika Breiteneder and Marie-Luise Pitzl. 2006. English as a Lingua Franca in Europe. *Annual Review of Applied Linguistics* 26: 3–34.

# PART 3

## POLICY ISSUES AND PERSPECTIVES ON VERNACULAR EDUCATION IN THE CARIBBEAN

# 6 | Introducing Policies and Procedures for Vernacular Situations

## Peter Roberts

*University of the West Indies, Cave Hill*

**M**y aim in this chapter is to draw greater attention to Dennis Craig's major work *Teaching Language and Literacy* (1999), republished posthumously (2007) as *Teaching Language and Literacy to Caribbean Students*, in which he sets out "policies and procedures for vernacular situations". This chapter is not a critique of the book, but an introductory discussion of factors that should provide a basis for adding to and modifying the detailed organization of syllabus and techniques set out in the book. It can be read in conjunction with Roberts (1994), *Integrating Creole into Caribbean Classrooms*.

## Literacy and Ideology

In the anglophone Caribbean, the prominence given to the English language in school, and in society generally, in part reflects the reality that the educational system is government controlled and that the language of instruction in school is seen as a national unifying force. In other words, language uniformity and a prescriptive intent are regarded as central in a national approach to general formal school education. In addition, the English language is seen as providing access to international resources and facilitating international communication. In this respect, the designation of English as the language of instruction is not just a unilateral political decision, but it also reflects the aspirations of a significant segment of the community. Policymakers in the Caribbean realize that for any language education policy inside or outside the formal schooling process to succeed, its philosophy has to be consistent with the reasonable expectations of the people. Throughout the Caribbean, movement and migration with the goal of poverty alleviation have traditionally been powerful determinants of the culture of the people, and so language education policy in part facilitates the expectations of impoverished people who see migration to North America especially (where there is a perceived standard variety of English) as a way of solving their problems.

Right from the beginning of formal schooling, the road to language proficiency starts with the development of literacy (that is, learning to read and write) and an attendant ideology. Learning to read and write is de facto couched in an ideology, whether it is implicit or explicit and, in any case, literacy as a purely formal exercise in a cultural and political vacuum could not be meaningful or helpful to the individual. Street (1993, 7) makes his position on the matter quite clear when he says: "I use the term 'ideological' . . . because it signals quite explicitly that literacy practices are aspects not only of 'culture' but also of power structures." In an earlier work, Street (1984, 96–97) identifies ideological factors as a matrix for literacy, which he relates to "technology": "Technology, then, is a cultural form, a social product whose shape and influence depend upon prior political and ideological factors." He continues: "But literacy, of course, is more than just the 'technology' in which it is manifest. No one material feature serves to define literacy itself. It is a social process, in which particular socially constructed technologies are used within particular institutional frameworks for specific social purposes."

It should be evident, then, that imposing a purely formal standard and requiring the individual to conform to it would not achieve much, unless there is a sound political and ideological basis for it and unless the power possibilities of the language are apparent or are revealed to the learner.

There is an interdependence of political, economic, cultural and even religious factors in the schooling process; in fact, literacy is often promoted as a medium that allows the individual and the society to break free from the shackles of ignorance and underdevelopment. Indeed, Freire and Macedo (1987, 157) advocate what they call "emancipatory literacy" as a vehicle for the transformation of society:

The new literacy programs must be largely based on the notion of emancipatory literacy, in which literacy is viewed "as one of the major vehicles by which 'oppressed' people are able to participate in the sociohistorical transformation of their society". In this view, literacy programs should be tied not only to mechanical learning of reading skills but, additionally, to a critical understanding of the overall goals for national reconstruction. Thus, the reader's development of a critical comprehension of the text, and the sociohistorical context to which it refers, becomes an important factor in our notion of literacy. The act of learning to read and write, in this instance, is a creative act that involves a critical comprehension of reality.

In this kind of formulation, the tremendous potential of literacy is never divorced from the specific language chosen to enable it.

A contradiction exists, however, in that in the societies of the Caribbean, which have been described as culturally "plural", "syncretic" and other such terms which summarize their history of culture contact and conflict, national policy appears to be advocating cultural and social uniformity through language education, especially in the face of a relatively high degree of language variation. The national motto of Jamaica, "Out of many, one people", which is probably inspired by "E pluribus unum" of the United States, reflects this vision of uniformity, which is pursued principally through formal schooling and language education using English as the language of instruction. The motto of Trinidad and Tobago, a nation which is more ethnically diverse today, also has a suggestion of uniformity in "Together we aspire, together we achieve."

Notwithstanding this drive for uniformity in the Caribbean through English as the language of instruction, there are two contrasting ways in which cultural literacy may become the essence of school education: either by shaping the individual to conform to the norms of the society or by encouraging the individual to express his or her cultural preferences and as a consequence fostering a culturally diverse society. These positions are put forward, in the context of the United States, by McLaren (1991, 288):

> Among the exponents of "cultural literacy", two polar positions seem apparent that reflect both liberal and conservative orientations in the cultural literacy perspective. The "prescriptivists" argue that students' success in the North American marketplace depends upon their successful entrance into the academy. This generally means being taught from a prescribed canon of literary works and acquiring a standard form of English. The "pluralists", on the other hand, argue for the

legitimacy of a broader range of discursive practices which reflect more closely the language practices, values, and interests that students bring into the classroom.

It is because the first of these two approaches, the prescriptive one, is traditional and entrenched not only in the Caribbean but also in most Western societies that the second is seen as problematic. Consequently, multicultural education is today an emotional political issue in developed countries, where there has been a significant amount of recent migration.

A brief look at the development of English teaching in Australia in the last three decades of the twentieth century is informative. English instruction in that period can be seen to be consistent with the notions of multicultural education, according to Davis and Watson (1990, 152). After conceding that Australia is a "society grounded in 'White Australia' mythology", they go on to state that "first and foremost, there is the post-war migration, which has made Australia, after Israel, the most multicultural nation on earth." In their discussion, therefore, they support strongly a move away from national tests and prescriptivism generally and support the recommendation that

> the English language classroom should be . . . a place where pupils meet to share experience of some importance, to talk about people and situations in the world as they know it, gathering experience into new wholes and enjoying the satisfaction and power this gives. But in doing so each individual takes what he can from this shared store of experience and builds it into a world of his own (Dixon 1969, 6–7). (p. 158)

This philosophy is different from the traditional one in that it focuses on the blossoming out of the individual rather than the "melting pot" idea, which is essentially the curtailing of the individual's choices and possibilities.

The relevant question that has to be raised, as far as language teaching in the Caribbean is concerned, is whether there should be a change in the ideology that determines language education in Caribbean schools. Is it time to put more emphasis on truly understanding the vernacular as a first step to getting "graduates" at all levels to be able to master language in literary, religious, legal, political, academic and other spheres? This is much more than one of those facile clichés, such as "using the vernacular to teach the standard", which, as Dennis Craig (1999, 32) says, "are sometimes adopted as guidelines without adequate exploration and clear understanding of what their implications are in practice, and what they mean in terms of a comprehensive language and literacy programme". Another such cliché is "teaching English as a foreign language".

## The Language of Instruction as a Deliberate Development

The choice of language of instruction, especially for beginners in Caribbean schools, has been a major preoccupation of educators, notably Dennis Craig, for a long time and has been a contentious issue in academic circles, even if nowhere else. The fundamental problem which provokes the constant preoccupation with the language of instruction in the Caribbean is the low level of success that has been realized using English as the "sole" language of instruction in a situation where English is not really the home language of the vast majority of school children. One of the crushing statistics that dogs the status quo is that in many Caribbean countries, less than 25 per cent of the children of the relevant age actually take and pass the CXC CSEC (*Caribbean Secondary Education Certificate*) English A examination, which is universally viewed as the standard to be attained.

Serious proposals have been made over the years for varying degrees of use of the home language (as is or standardized) in the formal education system, but since such proposals usually appear to be driven by a revolutionary nationalist ideology or by unconventional minority groups, they usually make little headway. Logical arguments are put forward that development of the vernaculars is just as necessary in the Caribbean today as it was in various European countries centuries ago. Thus, in a look at national development, an analogy may be drawn between the development of English in England then and, as an example, the development of Jamaican Creole in Jamaica now.

To understand such an analogy and to see how instructive it may be for decision-making in the Caribbean, the following comments on the historical process of the standardization of the English language in Britain can be used to show, in part, how English was converted from a low-status vernacular to a prestigious and powerful national language:

> The establishment of a standard language did not take place overnight. In the fourteenth century, while Chaucer was writing in what was to become the standard language, Langland was writing his *Piers Plowman* in a South-West Midland dialect, while in the North-West Midlands there was a school of poets writing in that local dialect. . . . But gradually the prestige of the London language grew, and in the fifteenth century its influence was increased by the introduction of printing. (Barber 1993, 145)

> There were social groups which fought hard for the retention of Latin, because their professional monopoly depended on excluding ordinary people from the mysteries of their art; physicians appear to have been particularly bitter in their

attacks on medical works published in English. This led to fierce controversy about the suitability of English for works of science and scholarship, which raged especially in the second half of the sixteenth century. This controversy was gradually won by the supporters of English, as more and more fields of study were successfully invaded by it. (Barber 1993, 177)

A gentleman scientist like Gilbert wrote in Latin, but there were plenty of Elizabethan treatises on practical subjects like navigational instruments, geometry, and warfare, which were written in English for the plain man, and sometimes by him. Here an important part was played by the spread of literacy and the expansion of the reading-public which followed the introduction of printing in the late fifteenth century. (Barber 1993, 177)

In Middle English and Early Modern English, there had been no standard spelling: spellings varied from writer to writer, and even within the work of one writer. Even proper names were not fixed.... A powerful force for the standardization was the introduction of printing, and by the middle of the sixteenth century, although there was no standard system, there were quite a number of widely accepted conventions. By the end of the Early Modern period, spelling had become standardized in printed books, though there was still considerable variation in people's private writings. (Barber 1993, 201)

The English Reformation had reduced the hold over school-teaching previously enjoyed by the clergy, the group most attached to the academic use of Latin; and from the fifteenth century onwards the well-to-do – nobility, gentry and merchants – had been setting up schools staffed by laymen.
All the new literary activity was fast enriching the English language, and at the same time schoolmasters and others were eagerly compiling *handbooks* to enable it to be learnt more systematically....
    A matter about which schoolmasters ... were especially exercised was *regularization of spelling*. (Bourcier 1981, 181)

As already noted, the introduction of printing, although it had highlighted the need for some standardization, had not yet brought it about. Indeed, sixteenth-century spelling had been further variegated by individual, piecemeal attempts to reform it. Some reformers tried to parade their classical learning by devising spellings based on the ultimate Latin etyma of words borrowed into English from French and in French forms.... Be that as it may, during the later sixteenth century and still more during the early seventeenth, English spelling was gradually becoming more uniform; but the process was slow, and even works printed in the 1650s still showed a fair degree of variation. (Bourcier 1981, 181–82)

These excerpts highlight certain crucial factors or realities in the development of English into the standard language in Britain:

- the length of time it takes;
- the role of printing;
- the role of schoolmasters;
- the participation of the general public in the process and the concomitant increase in literacy;
- the intransigence of certain interest groups, such as professional groups and established teachers; and
- the counterproductiveness of experts, that is, their refusal to agree on common standards.

The critical question is whether history can be repeated or recreated in the Caribbean today.

One fundamental difference between Britain then and the Caribbean today is that printing and the general dissemination of printed material is a reality today and therefore the standardization of a national language cannot be part of a technological revolution, unless somehow development of a standard language today is seen to have some intrinsic link to computer technology. Even then, there would have to be some special nexus established between computer technology and language teaching in the Caribbean. More importantly, one has to consider the prospective role of a new national language in this part of the world and its possibilities for success in the face of the overpowering economic importance of English, which relegates even established national languages to secondary roles. The world is a far different place, as far as communication and global influence are concerned, than when English, French and other European languages were converted into national languages.

A fundamental response to varying levels of competence in the national language or the language of instruction in school, whatever it is, a response that will hardly change today or at any other time, is an attitude of social and academic snobbery. This is manifested in the form of complaints about falling standards and incursions from "lower-class" behaviour. For example, more than two hundred years ago, Thomas Sheridan (1783, xii–xiii) complained bitterly about the general lack of proficiency in English in England, claiming, "Each county in England has its peculiar dialect, which infects not only their speech, but their reading also", and "many pronunciations, which thirty or forty years ago were confined to the vulgar, are gradually gaining ground; and if something be not done to stop this growing evil, and fix a general standard at present, the English is likely to become a mere jargon, which every one may pronounce as he pleases."

Ironically, what this kind of snobbery reveals, more than anything else, is the constant and inevitable influence of the oral on the written, the inevitability of generational changes and consequently the reality that standards are not static. Yet because it is so persistent, it always has to be weighed carefully against reality, that is, against verifiable standards attained across the population, and spurious ideas about superiority, which usually prompt such outbursts, should not be allowed to determine national policy.

## An Evolutionary Consideration in Moves to Involve the Vernacular in the Formal Educational Process

In many, if not most, countries, public education is a mass process in which there is usually at the national or regional level a common language as well as perceptions of common syllabuses and common standards within a framework of primary, secondary and tertiary levels in which practical objectives are transparent. The development of the vernacular for use in the Caribbean school system has to be initiated within such a framework, if it is to make a positive difference in achieving higher levels of literacy and language proficiency. It has to be seen to be serving practical purposes that are important to the people involved. In addition, in the context of the Caribbean, it must be seen as a path and a complement to an international language rather than as being in competition with one. One question that arises in this desire to make the vernacular a positive and more powerful force in the formal educational system is: How does one deliberately create a formal register for a variety that has served the purposes of an informal register for all its life?

Before attempting to answer this question, one has to look at and appreciate the historical role of English as well as creole languages as vernaculars in the colonial context. The following presents in skeleton form the evolution of language communication across social levels in the anglophone Caribbean.

### 1650–1785

This was the period of initial contact which initiated an embryonic or formative period for languages of general communication across various ethnic groups. It was the period during which the different ethnic groups speaking different languages and dialects accommodated themselves to each other's speech, with the African population having to do more accommodation than the others. During this period, the literature speaks of English, Scottish, Irish and Welsh, and of Eboes, Coromantees and several other ethnicities of African and, later, creole slaves. In other words, the ethnic distinctions were sharper and clearly revealed themselves in speech.

At this time there was no single, dominant, normative standard, either in Britain itself or in the colonies. It was only around 1755, with Samuel Johnson and others in England, that the normative and centralizing tendency began to gain momentum. Proficiency in English had no strong social benefits and could not unlock the doors to higher social positions. Among the slave population, language competence was not generally a precondition for selection to superior status (this was usually a matter of colour or behaviour); it was a consequence of such selection.

## 1785–1850

The years 1776 to 1804 were years when revolution was in the air – the Americans had declared independence, the French Revolution affected the French colonies, and also Trinidad and Haiti became independent. This period parallels the Industrial Revolution in Britain, which ushered in urbanization, centralization of government and uniformity in communication. During this period, characteristic national dialects and accents emerged in the West Indies, which means that not only had the speech of the blacks stabilized into varying social dialects but also that white speech had diverged from British speech and had taken on a national character in each respective colony. In the descriptive literature on the Caribbean of this period, samples of black speech began to appear, and disapproving comments were being made that local whites were using features of black speech.

The year 1785 is here identified as the start of a new era because it was the date when a white Barbadian, Anglican priest, plantation and slave owner, and justice of the peace signalled his intention to establish a charity school for black slaves to teach them to read. This formal instruction in English was really for practical purposes: reading was seen in part as a way to give people access to the Bible and other religious material and to tie them to the Church. This was the beginning of a long tradition of education for the maintenance of the status quo and education for only specially selected persons. Those who received formal instruction saw themselves as superior, and through speech (and writing) had to constantly demonstrate this superiority. It was therefore not simply the formal instruction by itself which caused proficiency in English but preferred status and the perceived social responsibility to demonstrate proficiency. However, for the mass of the population, whose lives involved little public formality, the vernacular was the language that had come out of the creolization process.

## 1850–1950, 1950–present

This was the period during which, little by little, proficiency in standard English emerged as a badge of success and a prerequisite for social mobility. In this respect, it established itself in the minds of the populace in a sharp, diametric contrast with the vernacular. Between 1850 and 1950, when education was elitist, the social system absorbed speakers of English into privileged positions, which is what English was for. However, in the period from 1950 to the present, because education has become generally available, its socially distinguishing role has not been so apparent. The corollary of this is that the vernacular has made gains socially, especially in the scenario of national independence.

The creole language developed to facilitate communication between different cultures. Even though Caribbean societies are no longer dominated demographically by large, non-native ethnicities, the role of the creole language has not been completely transformed from its original function, in part because of the historical consequences of these highly stratified societies. In other words, it is the variation or flexibility within creole languages that has provided them with one of their most powerful communicative functions. While the life-cycle theory of the evolution of the vernacular in the Caribbean (creolization followed by decreolization) may have flaws, consistent social and economic development, which is a major determinant of the life cycle concept, is seen by some as gradually limiting the role of creolized varieties of language, leading to their eventual disappearance. With such a scenario in mind, the role of creole in the educational system would at best be viewed only as transitional.

## The Problem of Variation in the Conversion of the Vernacular into Classroom Language

### A. Orthography

The formal educational process at the primary level (or before) normally begins with literacy instruction (referred to as the language arts) which is form-based and prescriptive. At this level, children are taught the writing and spelling systems of a specific language, which are rigidly uniform in nature, primarily because the first step in literacy is seen as requiring simplicity and uniformity. The rigid requirements for this stage present difficulty for the vernacular because the reality of variation in the spoken language, the notion of individual freedom it creates and the illusory need to capture the intricacies of speech in writing are in direct conflict with pedagogical necessities.

The language of instruction in school, in its structure, is intended to correspond to the level of cognitive development of the learner, starting with uniformity and simplicity, and gradually and increasingly becoming more complex and sophisticated. In the teaching/learning process, therefore, mastering language variation is seen as a point towards which one is going and not as a starting point. However, outside the classroom, variation is the reality, and especially in the Caribbean the consciousness of variation, its social functions and its consequences develops early on. Prominent in the early stages of the schooling or pedagogical process, therefore, there is the need for reduction to uniformity and simplicity by selection of a single variety (for example, orthography, dialect, language) to decrease the cognitive challenges of literacy as well as to facilitate economical instruction in a classroom.

Representation of the vernacular in written form, as in novels, short stories, dramatic pieces and verse, is generally idiosyncratic, without any binding need for conformity. Readers therefore have to try to decipher in each case, with varying degrees of success, written versions of the vernacular. Suggestions that artists should use a uniform system are interpreted as attempts to curtail the artists' freedom. In contrast to the artist's view, the fact is that the orthographic system, for classroom use, does not and is not intended to represent either dialectal variation or language change. This is only one of the conflicts that confront those who try to develop a vernacular orthography for use in the classroom.

Since most of those who propose vernacular orthographies for the classroom are aware of this, it is usually other considerations, ideological ones such as separate identity versus historical connections and cognitive ones such as simplicity versus sophistication, which generate heat between orthography designers. What is ironic is that, in the long run, no orthographic system, unless it is woefully complicated and extensive, will prove to be worse than any other.

## B. Focus on Form or Focus on Meaning?

In addition to such challenges faced by orthography designers, the unresolved conflict between form-based instruction and meaning-based instruction at higher levels of the school system seems to set the initial stage apart as different because of its heavy and inevitable concentration on form. However, even at the initial stage, one of the general problems which must confront the classroom teacher in the Caribbean, as well as those who design teaching syllabuses, is how much weight to put on form-focused instruction and how much to put on meaning-focused instruction. A factor which makes this even more signif- icant is that, traditionally, a great number of (lower-working-class) children in the Caribbean are reticent in the classroom and suggestions have been made that since heavy doses of early correction of form only serve to increase this reticence, such correction should be avoided. For the teacher, this is a very real problem, the solution to which has a direct effect on pupils, especially when the area of written work (that is, learning to write and spell) is considered.

If, again, the history of the standardization of the English language is used as a point of reference, it appears that during the period of standardization, form- based instruction was the norm. The newly emerging grammars of the English language used Latin as the model of grammar and the study of English (as a first language) became a study of forms, structures and rules. Modern practice, however, vacillates between form-based and meaning-based instruction. The consequences of this, when several dialectal varieties are involved, can be appre- ciated by reference to teaching practice in England, where a "normal" degree of social and geographical dialectal variation can be said to exist, and where the problem that confronts teachers and advisers remains without a generally agreed solution.

Williams (1989, 197):

> The multiplicity of variables to consider when assessing a piece of writing is reflected in the variety of correcting strategies used by the teachers in the sample. Whereas some teachers simply made a global assessment in the form of a general comment

at the end of the text, others corrected individual features, although in both schools only a relatively small percentage of dialect features were corrected. . . .

Finally, there seems, as yet, to be little in the way of policy for dealing with dialect features that occur in school writing. Teachers appear to deal with such features on an *ad hoc* individual basis.

Williams (1989, 193):

> Expert advice is varied. The Bullock Report (1975) suggests: "Only after responding to what has been said, is it reasonable to turn attention to how."
>
> Stewart Frome in his note of dissent to the Report takes the opposite view: "There is not the rigorous critical marking of spelling, punctuation and grammatical error there needs to be."
>
> Stibbs (1979) stresses the need for teachers to attempt to "assess the qualities of the thought processes" rather than placing emphasis on "accuracy in speech, writing and reading".
>
> Edwards (1979) argues that standard English should be used for all school writing and that consistency of approach in the early school years would make "the ability to produce standard written English where it is required more easily acquired".
>
> Perera (1984), Edwards (1983) and Richmond (1979), however, advise teachers to ignore dialect features until children are able to discuss them with their teachers. In Perera's view, this would take place once the consolidation stage . . . is complete and children are becoming aware of the differences between speech and writing (on average about the age of nine or ten).

It is logical to assume that the same problems which confront first language teaching in situations where the school language and the first language of the children do not differ very greatly are magnified in the Caribbean situation. The additional problem for the Caribbean classroom, one which stems from what is a characteristic in many creole situations, is the degree of variation which exists in the society as a whole, for in some places, such as Jamaica and St Lucia, there are several varieties of languages corresponding to social and geographical spread.

Focus on meaning-based instruction in a Caribbean creole language situation will unquestionably cause differences, subtleties and nuances of meaning to surface and will reveal that variation is more problematic than the initial preoccupation with orthography. It will become much more apparent that a contributory factor to lack of success in the acquisition of the school variety today is the fact that the intricacies of the vernacular are consistently dwarfed by the overpowering effect of the presence of the standard language as the language of instruction in schools. The overpowering effect is in part due to the overlap between the non-standard and the standard, which Craig consistently drew attention to and which pushed him to put more emphasis on the learning of formal language structures in the schooling process. However, teaching literacy with an emphasis on forms and structures is not necessarily going to improve or consolidate communicative competence. On the other hand, teaching the semantic and other subtleties of language as part of communicative competence will not guarantee mastery of language forms and structures, which is seen as fundamental at the primary stage of language education. There must be some degree of balance between these two, but with greater respect for the intricacies of the vernacular.

## Semantic and Formal Intricacies of the Vernacular Considered

The "genius" of creole languages across the Caribbean has long been remarked on, with the view being repeatedly put forward about the ability of these languages to say things that the European language could not say. The reality is that creole speakers are often more satisfied with the way the creole language says what they mean than with the way the standard language does. Thus, the apparent closeness of the creole to the standard in form and structure results in the fact that when creole speakers are required to use the standard variety, they very often do not feel that the standard is saying what they really want to say. In semantic terms, this is a question of whether there are ever "true" synonyms or "true" equivalents within or across languages. It also calls into question the notion of "free variation", as opposed to the notion that all changes in language form within a language correspond to changes in meaning or intention.

One can take an example of this kind of "variation" from a Caribbean country that is not even predominantly creole in its language. In Barbados, vernacular speech marks the habitual in the present tense form – for example, "I does work at the port" ('I work at the port'). When the non-standard speaker is put into a more formal situation requiring some indication of standard English, this is changed to "I works at the port". The presence of the affix -s is not a case of hypercorrection; it is the maintenance of the marking of the habitual. For the non-standard speaker, "I work at the port" not only is unsatisfactory as an expression of the habitual, but it also retains the past-tense meaning which it has when used in informal situations. The simple and basic difficulty for the learner is that the shift from vernacular to standard at times involves what for the individual may be termed *loss of expressiveness*. The problem is initially psychological: it is not that the standard is not saying what is intended, but that the speaker is not satisfied that it is. Furthermore, the variation is not one-dimensional: the speaker also uses the *-s* to say (1) I am speaking properly, or (2) I am distancing myself from you. The affix in the vernacular is thus being used for both semantic and socio-stylistic purposes, which is not characteristic of standard English outside the West Indies.

There are two strong tendencies in developing materials for Caribbean language classrooms that cater to the home language of the children, whether directly or indirectly. One is to match the forms and structures of English with those of the vernacular in a fairly direct and straightforward manner; the other is, in this matching exercise, to reduce the "variation" in the vernacular by elim- inating what seem to be the most deviant forms and structures. The problem is that since some of the vernacular word forms may appear, because of their reduced phonetic shape, to be what people believe to be "corruptions", they seduce teachers and some who construct teaching materials into resorting to the original, full English word as the sole source of the vernacular construction. This inevitably leads to loss of expressiveness, as the following sections will show.

## A. Differences in Meanings of Subordinate Conjunctions and the Implications Thereof

The following sentences, taken from the speech of six-year-old Jamaicans, reveal that already at that age they are expressing subtle differences in meaning, and they are doing this through word forms that derive from English but are not (in some cases) used in English in the same way.

1.    *truu ~ biko ~ ko*

The forms *biko* and *ko*, used in the vernacular in Jamaica, both come from English 'because', and it is easy to assume that there is little or no difference between them in the vernacular. Indeed, Bailey (1966, 58), in her analysis of Jamaican Creole syntax, makes the following statement: "These [causal con- junctions] introduce subordinate clauses of reason, and include *az* 'as', *sins* (*az*) 'since', *bikaaz*, *sieka* and *truu*, all meaning 'because'." A careful study of the sentences shows that establishing equivalence between the vernacular and

standard English is much more difficult than it first appears and that, contrary
to what Bailey suggests, *bikaaz* and *truu* are not straightforward discourse
(pragmatic) equivalents.

> truu Biinii not komin to skuul im stop kom
> an truu Pat neva gi shii pensil, wentaim shii si ya komin, shii run go tek it up
> an truu mi neva di waan . . .
> truu mi di waan waata fi dringk
>
> mi no go fi it biko di chier kyaan kom aut
> biko i no waan ya ier im taak biko i no waan au ya ier au im taak
>
> ye, ko ya duu rong ting
> ko wen dem lik mi, dem aal waan se a mi firs staat it
> ko mi gyet ier
> ko wentaim ya gruo big
> fo aaf die dem musn, mi nuo, fo aaf die dem musn kom ko nabadii no di de ko
> nabadii na di de an tiicha no da ya
> if ya waan eniting tel mi ko mi jus tek up gaan uova Finiks

In English, *through* is used as a preposition (as in "Through his stupidity, we
lost the game") and not as a subordinating conjunction, as in the children's sentences. The children's sentences with *truu*, however, preserve the realis feature
(reference to an actual, past event) of the nominalization (in this case, a noun
formed from a verb) which follows the preposition *through*. In other words, the
children are using *truu* to introduce clauses which refer to actual events in the
past, as opposed to *biko* and *ko*, which are not restricted in this way. The nearest
English equivalent to the children's *truu* is *since*, which has a time reference
element in it that *because*, on face value, does not have.

As far as the difference between *ko* and *biko* is concerned, the latter seems to
put the reason (the point being adduced in the very clause) more in focus than
the former – this may be due to a longer form being used to make the clause
focal rather than pragmatically subordinate.

Currently, with English as the stated language of instruction, in most cases
only one of the alternatives is correct. In other words, since *through* in English functions as a preposition, *because* functions as a conjunction, and *'cause*
is regarded as non-standard, the sentences that do not conform to these rules
of standard English are regarded as incorrect and the subtleties of meaning are
overlooked.

(2)    *if (eva) ~ enitaim*

The same pragmatic relationship that holds between *if* and *when* in English seems to hold between *if (eva)* and *enitaim* in the Jamaican vernacular. In English, *when* suggests or presupposes the likelihood of the event (as in "when there is a fire"), whereas *if* does not (as in "if there is a fire"). Insensitivity to such nuances and hasty assumptions of equivalence lead to a loss of linguistic flexibility.

Bailey (1966, 57) gives the gloss 'whenever' for *enitaim*, which essentially means in this case that *if (ever)* is being contrasted with *whenever*.

> if ya waan eniting tel mi ko mi jus tek up gaan uova Finiks
> an mi wi tun daun pon ya if mi eva si ya
> if ai ad sum muo munii an ai siev dat an if ai gyet muo ai wil siev it
> enitaim pipl ded, if dem dres ina da shirt de . . . an if uman ded, dem no av on shuu an . . .
> iet Tavn Draiv, up dier so, enitaim ya si di iet pon di giet iz dier wii liv

> enitaim Sandra di den in de, moma se mus gyet up auta di chier an lak it aaf
> enitaim da faul de ded, di ruusta ded, a gain iit . . .
> enitaim mii de saida mai mada, ya si, mii riich mai mada rait ier so, up ya so, up ar shuolda
> mi se enitaim mii go bak a taun mi goin bai somting fi ya

What is also abundantly clear in the second set of sentences is that the three-syllable word *enitaim* allows for exaggerated vocal stress that is not characteristic of the monosyllabic word *if*. In other words, *enitaim* differs in two respects from *if*: semantically and stylistically.

(3)    *wen ~ wentaim*

Both *wen* and *wentaim* are used as temporal conjunctions in the vernacular in Jamaica and it is difficult to distinguish between them semantically. Furthermore, if claims can be made about differences between them, it is still difficult to prove that these differences are sustained across a significant section of the population. However, the same kind of distinction seems to hold in this case as between other long and short forms, in that *wentaim* allows for more vocal stress than does *wen*. In addition, the longer form often seems to be said as two words and in no way can be considered to be monomorphemic.

an wen ai gyet nuf ai wil bai lots ov furnicha
ai wud bii sievin it til wen ai redii to kom uova bak
wen im di kom ier aal nau im fuul fuul, ya sii
an wen dat kom dutii, ya sii, dat musii tek ten die fi dun wash aaf
an wan liedii se mus wentaim mii dringk it mi mus tek a litl an wash aut mi maut
wentaim wii gyet wii dina, den wii go plie dolii aus
an wentaim dem gi mi di irb mi neva duuduu aut eni
wentaim shii si ya komin, shii run go tek it up

In the sentences above, *wentaim* seems to be used for events that are more definite prospectively, more likely or when the speaker is highlighting the information in the subordinate clause. It is difficult to confirm these interpretations because they are embedded in the speaker's intention and are quantitatively rather than qualitatively different. The following sentence is interesting because the word *taim* occurs not immediately following *wen* but as a noun in the subordinate clause:

so wen di taim kom fe Brada Anansii an dem fa ries

In this case, the reference is to a real event and not just a prospective one. Yet it seems to give an indication of the development of *wentaim* in the vernacular.

In the preceding sections, (1) to (3), just a few of the innumerable intricacies of the vernacular are illustrated. In any transition to standard English through formal teaching, there must first of all be a recognition of such intricacies; second, an appreciation of the intentions of the speaker of the vernacular; and third, an ability to deal with these intricacies in the development of materials for the classroom.

## B. Differences in Forms of the Plural and the Implications Thereof

Bailey's (1966) study can probably be used as the best-known attempt to construct a formal creole system (Jamaican Creole) without reference to the actual linguistic competence of any speaker. However, what Bailey did was not an aberration of the past, for there is a persistent idea, expressed in linguistic terms such as "basilectal" as well as popular lay terms such as "the real creole", that there is and most certainly was an isolatable variety standing in polar contrast to the standard language. Indeed, Craig (1999, 233) proposes Bailey's study as "a convenient starting point . . . which speaks of 'the principal differences between Jamaican Creole and English syntax' ". In perceptions of such extreme varieties, there is often a notion of uniformity, narrowness and consistency. A description of the plural in Jamaican Creole would therefore claim, in such perceptions, that it is formed by adding the third-person plural pronoun after the noun, as in "di man dem" to give the meaning 'men'. However, since the creole has operated, in many if not most cases, in a colonial and postcolonial situation where the standard language is seen as the polar extreme and where visions of the creole stick to this polar extreme philosophy, the total inescapable consequence is that the creole language is being determined by the European language.

To proceed on this basis belittles the competence of any speaker of the vernacular in Jamaica and everywhere else and gives no idea of the variant forms of the plural used by any one speaker. Bear in mind that the variation in form is not caused by semantic nuances reflecting different concepts of plural – the meaning is constant and the various forms and structures used reflect the historical interaction of the languages in contact.

To give a more graphic idea of the diversity of the vernacular, we will look at examples from Barbados, which has a linguistic situation that is said to be far more decreolized than that of Jamaica. Such a linguistic situation, one that is considered to be closer to standard English, would suggest that development of materials for the classroom should be easier. The examples are taken from a continuous stretch of speech of over twenty minutes produced by an old woman from a rural agricultural area of Barbados which is considered by Barbadians to have the most typically non-standard Barbadian speech. The woman is recounting her experiences as a child in what is essentially a consistent and unbroken monologue (there are only a few short responses, mainly "yes" or "no", from the person she is speaking to). The feature selected is the plural and the focus is on the ways in which it is expressed.

In Barbadian speech, the plural is either zero-marked in the noun or marked as it is in English by suffix (with allomorphs); there is no free-standing pluralizer coming after the noun comparable to the Jamaican *dem*. In the Barbadian woman's monologue, there are 137 occurrences of the plural. Words such as *clothes* and *upstairs* are not counted, the former because it is never given a singular form and the latter because it is not a noun. The word *cow-dung* occurs as a singular count noun in "you put a cow-dung in the fire", but the word without the article is not counted as a plural.

Of the 137 occurrences of the plural, 54 (39 per cent) are marked plural by suffix; the others are zero-marked in the noun itself. Of the 54 that are marked by suffix, 6 are in local idiomatic expressions, for example,

nights enough I sleep in the pen
for weeks and days I . . .
many by the days . . .

Of the 54 that are marked by suffix, 29 are words which (a) most often occur as plural or (b) are strong forms of the plural; for example,

a. *jacks, sea spries,[1] blows, nimbles,[2] sand flies, ants*
b. *children, men, women*

The other 19 occurrences of the suffixal plural are "deliberate" pluralizations. As an overall ratio, this is a matter of 19 out of 137 cases (14 per cent). Of the 19, there are 4 cases of emphatic stress, as in

the people use to walk eighteen mile*s* out and walk back with load on their head you had to walk about three mile*s* for water three mile*s* for water

Of the remaining 15 occurrences, it is not possible to give a clear reason for the marking by suffix in all cases.

Overall usage in this idiolect, which is typical for that age group and rural location, can therefore be characterized in the following way:

- The plural form is often not used when the context clearly indicates plural.
- Some uses of the plural suffix are not immediately explainable.
- Set plural forms occur in idiomatic usage.
- Certain nouns which occur more normally in the plural form in English retain this as the basic form in the vernacular.

Since 39 per cent of the references to the plural are marked, even if one argues that only 14 per cent are "deliberate", it is clear that marking the plural as in standard English is a part of the vernacular. On the other hand, not marking the plural is even more characteristic (61 per cent) of the vernacular. It is therefore imperative to understand why marking is only partial in the vernacular. It would be difficult to argue that this reflects transition or development in the speech of someone who was over seventy years old. This kind of competence is more complex than that in the Bailey-type "creole" construct which clearly and consistently marks plural but in a different way.

## Elements of the Cognitive Processing Involved in the Movement from Vernacular to Standard

The movement from vernacular to standard must be looked at as a dynamic process in which the individual uses all the available data, heard and interpreted, through a system already in place. The individual then forms hypotheses involving generalizations. The result, like early child language, is not an objective reproduction of features of the data but a subjective re-analysis of these features.

In order to demonstrate the kind of processing involved in the movement from the vernacular to the standard, we will use parts of one of the features given to illustrate the intricacies of the vernacular as well as features of the past tense.

### A. The Third-Person Singular -s in Standard English

This section focuses specifically on the use of -s as a third-person singular marker. The grammatical feature -s can be regarded as the most marked in a hierarchical and integrated set of features in the subject–verb relationship in English: it is one that distinguishes automatic production precisely because it is semantically empty (it adds no non-grammatical meaning) and structurally irregular (it occurs only in the third-person singular of the present tense).

A person is exposed from birth to language data, that is, the language that is produced within earshot. The person, as a learner (especially in the first four years after birth), makes sense of this linguistic input, using it together with innate human linguistic abilities to construct a linguistic system which is substantially the same as that of the ambient community. In the case of the anglophone Caribbean, the data on -s to which the learner is exposed is the following:

| Context | Meaning/Function | Example |
| --- | --- | --- |
| 1. after most nouns | plural | *hats* |
| 2. after nouns | possessive | *the children's toy* |
| 3. after pronouns | possessive | *hers, its, ours, yours, theirs* |
| 4. after verbs, third-person singular | present, future, past | *He loves Mary; she goes tomorrow; He scores!* |

| Context | Meaning/Function | Example |
|---------|------------------|---------|
| 5. after third-person pronoun | short for *is* (aux.) durative, future | *he's there* *he's coming* |
| 6. after third-person pronoun | short for *is* (verb) stative/durative | *he's a fool* *she's happy* |
| 7. after third-person pronoun | short for *has* (aux.) present perfect | *she's been found* *she's found it* |

The extent to which each individual is consistently conscious of all occurrences of -*s* depends on native dialect as well as phonetic environment. The fact that the learner does not acquire all the features that are heard is explained graphically in terms of a "filter" in the learner's brain which allows only part of the "input" to become "intake".

Making sense of (1) to (7) means first working out general rules and then moving towards context-sensitive rules. In doing this, the individual uses strategies born of both social and linguistic experience. For example, the learner

- may come to believe that English rules are the opposite of creole/non-standard rules and proceed to change relevant features of the native dialect, or
- may come to realize that standard English requires many suffixes which do not seem to add any meaning.
- The learner also has to resolve specific linguistic difficulties – for example,
- that -*s* marks both singular (the verb) and plural (the noun);
- the relationship between -*s* as a reduced word and as a suffix;
- whether -*s* can be used as a shortened form of any auxiliary which ends in *s*;
- that the noun nearest to the verb on the left side is not always the one which determines whether the -*s* should be used or not;
- that whether the subject is singular or plural is sometimes a matter of meaning and sometimes a matter of form; and
- that a possessive pronoun determines the number of the verb but a possessive adjective does not (for example, "They are awful" but not *"Their grammar are awful").

All of the challenges in relation to -s outlined above, which the learner has to resolve, can be regarded as part of bottom-up processing which keeps the learner far away from the automaticity required. Furthermore, it should be even more evident that the kinds of subject–verb agreement rules given in the formal school context are inadequate in coverage and are often simplistic in that they disregard some of the major difficulties (some of which are mentioned above) faced by the learner.

In the short outline of -s occurrence above, the most common context is third-person singular, which suggests that this should be salient for the learner. However, it is significant that in no case is use for the third person the first and most powerful rule that the learner applies. It seems as if the use of -s as an indicator of "sophisticated" formality is much more important to the learner. It further suggests that person number, noun number and noun possessives are not so sharply contrasted as to make the third person stand out clearly for the learner.

## B. Marking the Plural of Nouns with an Affix

Plurality as a grammatical concept is easy to understand, but the attachment of a suffix to a noun to show that something is not one unit, or not made up of one unit, is arbitrary in English. Thus, unlike the third-person singular -s, the plural -s may initially seem to be motivated and meaningful, but the language data to which the learner is exposed does not prove this to be so. In other words, though the plural may be a clear-cut grammar point for the linguist and teacher, for the learner of English it is not, since there are several common words which have a plural meaning but have no affix to indicate this, for example, *people*, *Man*, *grass*, *food*, *hair*. In addition to these "collective" nouns, there are count nouns which have no marking for the plural, such as *sheep* and *deer*, and, even more confusing, there are nouns that are marked for the plural according to what they are interpreted to mean, such as *fish* vs. *fishes* or *people* vs. *peoples*. There is no rule or set of rules which can be clearly deduced from the language data of English and which can guide the learner into a precise way of establishing a connection between the presence or absence of an affix and the meaning "more than one".

So, one can argue that the vernacular "boils down" the conflict between form and meaning in plural marking into a system in which empty marking caused by redundancy is not characteristic; that is, where plural meaning is provided elsewhere by the context, the plural is not marked on the noun. Movement to the standard therefore involves an increase in "empty" marking, which (in terms of percentage) makes marking more characteristic than non-marking, even creating the impression that it is absolute in standard English.

The problem for the learner is compounded by morphological factors. Some morphological features are not conceptually difficult in themselves, but the accumulation of them is. In addition to -*s*, standard English has a variety of endings which indicate plural (for example, -*a*, -*en*, -*i*) and may not be perceived as endings even by advanced learners. For example, the vowel at the end of *criteria*, *data* and *phenomena* does not seem to be an ending indicating a specific meaning because many English nouns end in -*a*, including place names and medical words.

Transfer from oral to written is popularly believed to be the most influential factor in learners' errors in the classroom. However, this is not as straightforward as it first appears to be in the case of plural marking. In some cases, it is not clear whether the learner perceives or understands the ending of the English word. For instance, in the case of the class of words that end in -*ist* (referring to people, such as *tourist, dentist, artist, scientist*), it is not clear why these words are often not marked for plural even among advanced learners. It cannot simply be that there is an *s* sound at the end of the reduced word in vernacular speech, because there are several words in both English and the vernacular which end with an *s* sound which are pluralized, including [glas] *glass*, [boks] *box* and [taks] *tax*. Short, common words, such as [des] *desk*, [tes] *test* and [lis] *list*, do not seem to have a popular plural form in the vernacular in more "sophisticated" contexts, and this is even more true for longer words. It may be that the learner has some indication from the language data that these words really do not end with -*s* in English, but because no distinct plural ending is ever heard or perceived (because of the consonant cluster), the learner concludes that the word form without an -*s* also serves as plural.

## C. The Past-Tense Marker in Standard English

In the above information on the expression of the plural in the Barbadian woman's speech, it is evident that the plural suffix occurs in and is an integral part of it. On the other hand, the past-tense suffix never occurs. From this evidence, it seems that the suffixal method of past-tense marking is not as powerful or as "intrusive" as the plural suffix for the learner. In English, the past-tense suffix is less prominent phonologically than the plural suffix in that the consonant in the former occurs very often as unreleased, post-consonantal and voiceless. If one takes the sixty-five verbs which occur in the woman's speech and looks at their English past-tense forms, the following is revealed:

- 4 uninflected (*shut, put, cut, beat*)
- 7 suppletive (e.g., *be, do, can, go*)
- 22 replacive (e.g., *run, come, eat*)
- 32 suffixal:
  - 15 with -*t* (e.g., *wash, watch, laugh*)
  - 11 with -*d* (e.g., *live, bathe, tie*)
  - 6 with -*id* (e.g., *want, plant, plait*)

There is clearly no single dominant pattern to impress the learner in these most common verbs, and the only one that can be said to be phonologically prominent is the last one, with -*id*. It is quite significant that the only past-tense forms which occur in the Barbadian woman's speech are those of the suppletive type – *done, gone, was, did, went, could, left, dead* – which, except for the last two, are used exclusively as past-tense forms. It is not because they are suppletive that they occur but because they are among the most frequently used and therefore prominent. In short, it is not the nature of the structure that determines acquisition (for suppletion analytically seems more difficult than the others) but the prominence of it that allows the learner to work out a strategy for marking.

The kind of processing referred to above merely looks at features in standard English which the learner has to consciously come to terms with, as if they are all external to the learner's competence; it is not yet taking into account the fact that some of these features are already entangled in the learner's native system. When the learner is confronted by the kinds of problems posed by the third-person singular, plural and past tense, he or she has to create rules not just to make sense of the language data but also to capture facets of reality. So, in addition to grammatical and discourse rules, the language material has to be processed according to the individual's imagination, intelligence and all those other factors that are captured by the general word *comprehension*. Grammaticizing of experience by the individual is unpredictable, often creative and idiosyncratic. The aim of the teaching process is to remove or reduce this, but until this happens, it affects production. The confusing search by the learner for hypotheses is supposed to be made easier by provision of knowledge, but the problem is determining the details of the information required and the format to bring about a reduction rather than an increase in confusion.

## Standard Acquisition

The term *decreolization* is used to express explicitly the notion of movement away from a creole language system and implicitly the notion of movement towards another language system, one which is in most cases a world language. It is significant that there is no specific term to capture the latter (implicit) notion, and it is not accidental that the process is explicitly labelled as *loss* and, as such, is conceived of as a purging of the undesirable or unsophisticated. Decreolization is usually seen as a gradual, imperceptible, sociohistorical process.

An alternative, graphic picture of the movement from creole/non-standard to standard is captured in the analogy given in Ho's (1986, 41) study: "Cross language interference may be long lasting in the case of closely related languages. . . . It is analogous to the difficulty in disentangling a piece of thread which has been tangled up with another of similar color, thickness, and texture." Craig's (1999, 5) comment on the movement shows that it is even more complicated than that:

> Because the vernacular and IAE [Internationally Accepted English] have certain features in common, it necessarily follows that vernacular speakers targeting English need to acquire only those English features that are absent from the vernacular. This may not be as easy as it sounds however, from a pedagogical perspective, since features linked to each other to form a vernacular may have systematic vernacular relationships that cannot interchange with English substitutes in the performance of speakers.

In developing classroom materials and a procedure for acquisition of the standard which addresses the idea of "disentangling" the vernacular, one comes face to face with the following theoretical issues raised in both first language and second language learning: the acquisition/learning dispute, the innateness/interaction dispute and the validity of the concept "the mature state of the language faculty".

The relevance of the *acquisition/learning dispute* to the matter of achieving fluency and written competence in standard English in the Caribbean is that millions of dollars are spent yearly teaching the standard language in formal education and, equally important, the standard language is expected to be used naturally in formal contexts in the society. In other words, teaching/learning is not seen as distinct from acquisition and spontaneous, fluent production.

The *innatist/behaviourist/interactionist dispute* has many facets, but one which is especially relevant to the acquisition of standard English is the "poverty of environment" notion, raised initially by Noam Chomsky and used by Derek Bickerton to argue for the programmatic creation of creole languages. The specific question here is whether the learner can use a poor model (that is, the teacher and the classroom) to work out and produce the normal rules of the language, or whether there has to be extensive interaction (actual practice in meaningful everyday situations) for the learner to produce the normal rules of the language.

As far as the "mature state of the language faculty" is concerned, if this concept is valid, it means that language learning after the mature state has been reached must be quantitatively and qualitatively different from that of the pre-mature state. Is SA (acquisition of the standard) therefore part of "mature-state" language learning, or is it, on the contrary, a part of a non-discrete birth-to-death process of language learning?

## Acquisition of the Standard from an Innatist Perspective

In contrast to the sociohistorical view of language change in the Caribbean, one can look at SA from the perspective of the individual and try to determine what changes take place in the individual's brain during his or her lifetime. Universal grammar, as proposed by Chomsky, regards language as an organ which grows to maturity like other organs in the human body. Development to maturity is seen to be outside the conscious control of the child – the core of the native language (L1) is seen to be the result of the interaction of received data on a programmable system of parameters. Chomsky (1988, 62) explains this theory as follows:

> The principles of universal grammar have certain *parameters*, which can be fixed by experience in one way or another. We may think of the language faculty as a complex and intricate network of some sort associated with a switch box consisting of an array of switches that can be in one of two positions . . . the switches are the parameters to be fixed by experience. The data presented to the child learning the language must suffice to set the switches one way or another. When these switches are set, the child has command of a particular language.

Using this image of a network with an array of switches, the settings of which are determined by the linguistic data received by the learner, Chomsky (1988, 38–39) comments on the quantity of linguistic data necessary for setting the switches. He writes:

> The language faculty functions in humans even under conditions of severe pathology and deprivation. . . . Such examples illustrate that very limited data suffice for the language faculty of the mind/brain to provide a rich and complex language, with much of the detail and refinement of the language of people not similarly deprived.

He also comments as follows on the quality of the linguistic data: "The environment is far too impoverished and indeterminate to provide this system to the child, in its full richness and applicability" (p. 153). It is important to point out that the foregoing comments refer to the core language, for when referring to non-core/peripheral elements, Chomsky says that in such cases "the linguistic environment must be rich enough to determine the value of the parameter" (p. 17).

Chomsky's comments seem contradictory, and they become more so when one remembers that, as many critics of the theory have pointed out, the distinction between core and non-core elements is hard to establish and may even be imaginary. Such criticisms also seriously undermine Bickerton's theory of creoles as core grammar, a theory already undermined by Goodman (1985), who convincingly argues that the relevant creoles were created by adults rather than children. The important consideration here, however, is not the genesis of creoles but the quality and quantity of data required to set the switches in contexts of SA. In determining this, we have to look at other attendant concepts, the first of which is the "mature state of the faculty".

Chomsky (1988, 35–36) presents the idea that when the switches move into position, the language comes into being in the individual: "When the process is completed, the language constitutes the mature state attained by the language faculty. The person now speaks and understands this language." He does not specify a critical period for acquisition, but the way in which he presents it rules out the idea of language development as a birth-to-death process or a repeatable process. However, the many cases of West Indian children over six years old who have migrated to England, Canada and the United States show that peer group and school cause a major change in their production without this interfering with their comprehension of parents and other close persons. This kind of situation is of course common in all immigrant groups. Since such changes in children of immigrants involve substantial acquisitions and losses in productive competence, it shows that the implication of a once-and-for-all setting of switches is misleading, for from such examples one would have to conclude that "native" production is replaceable and repeatable.

Another attendant concept we have to look at is language as fixed and uniform. The notion of parameters and switch-setting restricts each language within certain boundaries. Although Chomsky (1988, 32) recognizes variation, he does not change his parameterized view of language. He writes, "The extent to which this framework can be modified by experience and varying cultural contexts is a matter of debate, but it is beyond question that acquisition of vocabulary is guided by a rich and invariant conceptual system, which is prior to any experience." This is preceded by, "To the extent that dialects differ, there must be possibilities of variation permitted by the fixed biological endowment, these possibilities being resolved by experience; the same must be true of the variety of languages more generally. But a great deal is constant, determined quite independently of experience" (pp. 23–24). This view is one which makes variation peripheral rather than central.

If one accepts that language evolution is caused principally by modifications to the language by individuals in the acquisition stages, this means that switch-setting is being modified by experience. In a situation characterized by a high degree of variation and which historically evolved quickly, experience will have played a greater role in modifying switch-setting than in "normal" situations, the biological endowment having been less in control rather than more. Furthermore, when Chomsky (1988, 35) says, "The child constructs a language, Spanish, or more properly the variety of Spanish to which it is exposed", to make this observation relevant to the Jamaican child, one would have to say not "the variety of English" or "the variety of creole", but "the varieties of Jamaican", for the child will be exposed to a number of varieties. It is a matter of each individual integrating the varieties heard into a coherent linguistic system, resulting in the kind of variable competence proposed by Tarone (1988), Tarone, Bigelow and Hansen (2009) and others for second language acquisition. This is a dynamic process for each individual, clearly involving an increased use of experience in setting switches.

Part of this dynamic process is maturational in nature. The Piagetian distinction between "egocentric" and "sociocentric" can be extended in a special way for the anglophone Caribbean. The child is at first not aware of social requirements and first produces what for some is identified as a basilectal variety. The child gradually acquires afterwards a set of social and stylistic variants. Dennis Craig makes the point that awareness of the social significance of language is earlier and more pronounced in the maturation of West Indian children. Acquisition of native language competence in such cases means collapsing into a single linguistic competence (that is, making sense of) features which, if viewed externally, do not all belong to the same linguistic system: features referred to by linguists as standard English features and those referred to as creole features.

One also has to look at historical cases in Grenada, which are examples of language shift within the lifetime of an individual. Unlike the cases of immigrants mentioned above, change in functional, everyday language is not restricted to the pre-teenage period and cannot be said to be a dialectal shift. Unlike the cases of immigrants, the shift is gradual in that the individual is operating within the same society. In rural Grenada in the early twentieth century, some individuals were exposed to French Creole with very few accompanying forms of English, and by the 1960s the same individuals were exposed to forms of English with little or no accompanying French Creole. In such cases, competence in French Creole declines because there is no productive use of it and competence in the local variety of English (Creole) is not distinguishable in the final analysis from that of monolinguals. Such situations do not accommodate the notion of a neat, uniform local variety of a language for which switches are set after a small amount of exposure. Such cases involve a birth-to-death process and a greater and undiminished role for experience in determining linguistic competence.

It is clear also that the notion of identity between the individual's linguistic competence and a specific, identifiable language must be revised. Chomsky (1988, 36) himself makes this point clearly and specifically:

> I should mention that I am using the term "language" to refer to an individual phenomenon, a system represented in the mind/brain of a particular individual. If we could investigate in sufficient detail, we would find that no two individuals share exactly the same language in this sense, even identical twins who grow up in the same social environment. Two individuals can communicate to the extent that their languages are sufficiently similar.

The problem is that it is almost impossible in discussions of detail which have a background of monolingualism and ideal speaker-hearer competence that the "social" phenomenon will be dealt with rather than the actual competence of individuals. In the case of the Caribbean, however, what we must look at is how it is possible for an individual to make his or her own language out of the different kinds of linguistic data received, that is, what positions the switches are set in. In addition, one has to determine whether differences between individuals are greater in these situations and whether, as a result, interaction is less satisfactory, that is, whether there is a lesser degree of mutual intelligibility across the society than obtains in "normal" societies.

In spite of differences in social language awareness in maturation, replaceable native language production and the increased role of experience in setting parameters, there is no overall argument to challenge the theory of switch-setting. In fact, there is substantial evidence to support it. The observation made by Hale (1988, 32) is one familiar to many teachers in the West Indies: "Certain L1 parameter settings may be extremely difficult to eradicate from an acquired L2, at least at the level of integrated linguistic competence (as opposed to conscious intellectual understanding of surface grammatical facts)." Implicit in this is that parameters are not modified forever by experience and that after some time they become set. It also implies that SA is not a continuous, undifferentiated process. The "pre-mature" process, with its increased use of experience, is an integrative process; the "mature" process is a matter of "disentangling" the integrated varieties. A common factor, however, is that both make use of experience.

## SA, Automaticity and the Cognitive Perspective

In SA, the individual is motivated to use experience to "disentangle" and add appropriately to a linguistic competence which has been integrated by biological endowment and experience. The major difference between the "pre-mature" process and the "mature" process is automaticity. Automaticity is accurate production without a delay for processing. It would seem as if the biological endowment controls automaticity and correlates it negatively with conscious awareness; when conscious awareness develops and is activated, automaticity in production is obstructed. One could argue that automaticity really has nothing to do with biological endowment or switch-setting but that it is a logical consequence of increase in knowledge – knowledge provides options and options create a delay in processing. One could argue also that it is the same controlling factor which distinguishes between "acquisition" and "learning", as well as between speech and writing. The single variety of early acquisition is complicated by the addition of several varieties in later acquisition. Moreover, the further apart the varieties are and the more pronounced the social significance, the more automaticity is affected.

Another complicating factor is that a distinction has to be made between speech production and other areas of linguistic competence. Speech production requires enactive competence, involving essentially use of the motor cortex in the brain. Not much is known about the transmission of signals from one area of the brain to another, but it is clear that the functioning of the motor cortex is affected by lack of information, or, in computer terms, the information is not in a form that the cortex can process it in. The fact that the motor cortex requires a kind of detail that is beyond conscious analysis can be gleaned from Glass and Holyoak (1986, 426): "When you try to speak, the signals for all the successive, distinct sounds that must be made if you are to speak at a reasonable rate come too fast for the vocal apparatus to react separately to each one. Instead, the movements for the various sounds become jumbled up and compromised." The way in which this detail is actually realized then may be partly transfer, partly idiosyncratic, partly from experience and use of target elements. How this is done is certainly not clear. It seems reasonable to assume that all available, helpful information is used.

Automaticity is actually a twofold problem in SA, for not only does it have to be produced but it also has to be suppressed. Suppression of automaticity is related to both social and non-social factors, the former being mainly conscious and the latter unconscious. In the case of the former, the individual becomes aware that certain features are stigmatized or not appropriate for the context and has to suppress the reflex action to produce them. In the case of the latter, the information being processed is not detailed enough and the brain supplements it with appropriate details which are already there. One can conclude that SA, as a "mature" process, needs a linguistic environment that is rich enough and experience that is adequate to effect automaticity.

Bearing in mind that -s is just one of many features in which the "mature-state" learner has to achieve automaticity and that it is not just a matter of volume of features but also of interdependence, it should be clear that the achievement of automaticity in a formal teaching situation is a major problem. Behaviourists thought that automaticity could be achieved unconsciously by formal training; some innatists clearly discount this by making a distinction between acquisition and learning. Cognitive theory has proposed that automaticity can be achieved by conscious training.

Automaticity is a major area in cognitive theory and explicit statements about it are given by McLaughlin (1987, 139): "The initial stages of learning involve the slow development of skills and the gradual elimination of errors as the learner attempts to automatize aspects of performance. In later phases, there is continual restructuring as learners shift their internal representations." This summary follows upon a more detailed explanation of the restructuring process by Karmiloff-Smith (1986, 173–75).

When we apply this theory to SA, there are two problems with which we are immediately confronted. The first is the idea of adding new features to old ones and the effect of the one on the other; the second is the idea of stages, in which automaticity precedes restructuring. While these are reasonable interpretations of what happens in second language acquisition, in the case of SA, they are not. In SA, features may be regarded as "new" in relation to production, but not in relation to comprehension, since the individual would have been exposed to them from very early (Craig [1999, 6] identifies these as "Class C characteristics"). In fact, a major problem that English teachers in the SA context have to deal with is the belief on the part of learners that they already know what is being taught.

The second problem is that the idea that automaticity precedes restructuring is contrary to the experience of "successful" learners in the SA context. When McLaughlin (1987, 136) says, "Repeated performance of the components of the task through controlled processing leads to the availability of automatized routines", this disregards the unpredictable maintenance of L1 parameters in L2 performance. In fact, this is one of the determining factors in the production of *-s* in subject–verb agreement. Automaticity is possible in simple routines, as seen in the following example:

| | |
|---|---|
| simple third-person singular pronoun + verb | *he runs* |
| simple (unqualified) subject + verb | *Sheila goes* or *the girl plays* |

However, automatic production of *-s* is automaticity in one lower-order feature in the whole tense/aspect/mood system of English, which for the creole speaker amounts to major restructuring. The explanations of cognitive theory, therefore, may be satisfactory for second language acquisition, but they are not for standard acquisition.

## Tailoring a Pedagogical Grammar for the Vernacular in the Classroom

Van Els et al. (1984, 137) regard pedagogical grammar as grammar which contains a reduced set of rules taken from scientific grammar, the selection of these rules having taken place on the basis of considerations of usefulness, frequency and conceptual familiarity. In addition, according to them, the ordering of the material has to be brought into line with the demands of teaching and learning. In the same vein, Stern (1983, 175) writes, "The teacher, the textbook writer, or student should have a selection of linguistic data, derived from the scientific grammar, modified in accordance with the purposes and conditions of language learning."

Right from the start of the development of a pedagogical grammar, one has to recognize that form and meaning are inseparable. In addition, as has been pointed out before, the prescription of form starts at the beginning of literacy with the learning of the orthography and spelling of the language of instruction. Yet for the classroom, one has to set out in a graded way the distinction between the early requirements of literacy and the ultimate objectives of native language proficiency, the former requiring general compliance and the latter facilitating the growth of the individual. In other words, the approach to language teaching implicit in the following is quite sound: "The kind of role I am speaking of would be one which focuses as much attention upon what we use a grammatical construction for as upon how that construction is put together. Such a role would bring to consciousness the necessity for choosing among grammatical alternatives in satisfying the basic principles of information arrangement within discourse" (Rutherford 1988, 182).

Native language teaching is a part of the curriculum in most school systems across the world. Its objectives are seen as different from, and superior to, those in literacy campaigns as well as those where the language is taught as a second or foreign language. The aims of native language teaching reach right up to proficiency in literary appreciation and creative writing as well as familiarity with scientific and technical language. In countries where the native language is the sole official language, the standard form of the language is required in all domains where there are formal activities, such as government, church, school and the media. So not only does the language itself have a range of varieties to cover all domains, but also native language teaching seeks to provide for the attainment of competence in all these areas (excluding very technical areas where special terminology is required). Native language proficiency exams therefore endeavour to test students in objective language, artistic language, persuasive language and argumentative language. The student is usually required to demonstrate proficiency in both comprehension and expression in these different types of language. In most cases, however, it is proficiency in the written language which is the major or exclusive area of concentration in native language proficiency examinations.

To a very great extent, native language teaching is prescriptive and is dominated by a standard form of language. All societies have acceptable and unacceptable behaviour, including language behaviour. Within the formal school system, from the first introduction to language learning, as in the formation of letters of the alphabet and in spelling, the notion of right and wrong language is reinforced. Thus, native language learning involves not just the acquisition of functional skills but the acquisition of the right language behaviour (as determined by the society in general and by teachers in particular).

All of the preceding discussion leads to the conclusion that the following should be kept in mind in developing policies and procedures for SA:

1. Affective (that is, attitudinal and motivational) factors need to be more directly aligned with an explicit ideology which details the advantages of literacy and language skills in the vernacular and the standard.
2. The nature of the individual's competence needs to be more carefully studied.

Assuming that in the vernacular,

- there is integration of features from apparently different linguistic systems into a single individual competence,
- parameter setting is prolonged and changeable as a result of social experience and a greater number of linguistic variables, and
- the individual's parameters are modified into the mature state by non-uniform, variable societal models,

the following questions have to be addressed:

- Does the notion of "disentangling" capture the process of SA or is it a matter of "restructuring" native competence?
- What techniques will best effect movement from an oral system with more kinds of variation to a written system which is more rigidly controlled and tends toward uniformity?
- Is there any relationship between automaticity in writing and automaticity in speech?
- What techniques will effectively achieve automaticity in the standard and at the same time control unwanted automaticity, that is, maintenance of Ll features in L2 production?

3. A greater appreciation of the vernacular should be inculcated through comprehension.

This suggestion is consistent with the following stipulation by Craig (1999, 8): "In order that vernacular speakers may develop the awareness of their own language, already explained as essential, and in order also for them to develop a heightened appreciation of their own self-worth and cultural heritage, they need to be assisted into a deeper perception of the vernacular itself." For instance, the best way to highlight, in the classroom, the kinds of alternatives given earlier (*truu, biko, ko; if, if eva, enitaim*) is to examine their linguistic context and their meanings and identify them as various alternatives, in which case the student in the classroom, as part of the language learning process, has to come to know consciously when each is used and what the differences in meaning are between each one. Accordingly, in setting a native language proficiency test in Jamaica, you may give the sentence

mi se enitaim mii go bak a taun mi goin bai somting fi ya.

with an instruction to select one or more out of a number of possible implied meanings:

a. I am not going back to town soon, so you will have to wait some time.
b. Since I go to town often, you will not have long to wait.
c. The speaker, who has no plans to go back to town, is trying to put off or deceive the hearer.

The student comes to believe that the language used has specific meanings (that is, there are standards), the teacher in the classroom can teach and explain the intricacies of the language, and the examination procedure, especially if it is done on a national scale, can be completed with a high degree of consensus. This kind of focus in this single example (which is just one of a multitude in a battery of native language examinations) puts the emphasis on the capabilities of the language.

Thus, in a situation where a language, in the experience of its native speakers, has a history of being called simple, suitable for simple subjects and appropriate for the simple-minded, it is necessary to get the native speaker to recognize the intricacies of his or her native language. As a result, the language will grow both in the mind and in the valuation of its speakers.

4. Practice, both in speech and writing, in the intricacies of language should be put in train as early as possible in order to cause learners to grow intellectually by being able to express themselves more effectively.

These suggestions, together with Dennis Craig's (2007) *Teaching Language and Literacy to Caribbean Students* and insights and knowledge gained from the Jamaican Language Unit spearheaded by Hubert Devonish, should form the basis of a government-supported project aimed at improving native language education in the anglophone Caribbean.

## Notes

1. This is a conception, as a count-noun plural, of the water from the sea (probably a combination of *spray* and *spry*), which affects coastal things (for example, it causes metallic materials to rust quickly).
2. Very tiny, highly mobile insects that adversely affect the human body.

## References

Bailey, Beryl Loftman. 1966. *Jamaican Creole Syntax: A Transformational Approach.* Cambridge: Cambridge University Press.

Barber, Charles. 1993. *The English Language: A Historical Introduction.* Cambridge: Cambridge University Press.

Bourcier, Georges. 1981. *An Introduction to the History of the English Language.* English adaptation by Cecily Clark. Cheltenham: Stanley Thornes.

Chomsky, Noam. 1988. *Language and Problems of Knowledge: The Managua Lectures.* Cambridge, MA: Massachusetts Institute of Technology.

Craig, Dennis R. 1999. *Teaching Language and Literacy: Policies and Procedures for Vernacular Situations.* Georgetown, Guyana: Education and Development Services.

———. 2007. *Teaching Language and Literacy to Caribbean Students.* Kingston: Ian Randle.

Davis, Diana, and Ken Watson. 1990. Teaching English in Australia: A Personal View. In *Teaching and Learning English Worldwide*, edited by J. Britton, R.E. Shafer and K. Watson, 151–74. Clevedon, UK: Multilingual Matters.

Freire, Paulo, and Donald Macedo. 1987. *Literacy: Reading the Word and the World.* South Hadley, MA: Bergin and Garvey.

Glass, Arnold Lewis, and Keith James Holyoak. 1986. *Cognition*. 2nd ed. New York: Random House.

Goodman, M. 1985. Review of *Roots of Language*, by Derek Bickerton. *International Journal of American Linguistics* 51, 109–37.

Hale, Kenneth. 1988. Linguistic Theory: Generative Grammar. In *Linguistic Theory in Second Language Acquisition*, edited by S. Flynn and W. O'Neil, 26–33. Dordrecht: Kluwer Academic.

Ho, David Y.F. 1986. Two Contrasting Positions on Second-Language Acquisition: A Proposed Solution. *International Review of Applied Linguistics in Language Teaching* 24 (1 February): 35–47.

Karmiloff-Smith, Annette. 1986. Stage/Structure Versus Phase/Process in Modelling Linguistic and Cognitive Development. In *Stage and Structure: Reopening the Debate*, editded by I. Levin, 164–90. Norwood, NJ: Ablex.

McLaren, Peter L. 1991. Culture or Canon? Critical Pedagogy and the Politics of Literacy. In *Language Issues in Literacy and Bilingual/Multicultural Education*, edited by M. Minami and B.P. Kennedy, 286–309. Cambridge, MA: Harvard Educational Review.

McLaughlin, Barry. 1987. *Theories of Second Language Learning*. London: Edward Arnold.

Roberts, Peter. 1994. Integrating Creole into Caribbean Classrooms. *Journal of Multilingual and Multicultural Development* 15 (1): 47–62.

Rutherford, W. 1988. Aspects of Pedagogical Grammar. In *Grammar and Second Language Teaching*, edited by W. Rutherford and M. Sharwood Smith, 171–85. New York: Newbury House.

Sheridan, Thomas. 1783. *A Rhetorical Grammar of the English Language*. Philadelphia.

Stern, H.H. 1983. *Fundamental Concepts of Language Teaching*. Oxford: Oxford University Press.

Street, Brian V. 1984. *Literacy in Theory and Practice*. Cambridge: Cambridge University Press.

Street, Brian V., ed. 1993. *Cross-Cultural Approaches to Literacy*. Cambridge: Cambridge University Press.

Tarone, Elaine. 1988. *Variation in Interlanguage*. London: Edward Arnold.

Tarone, Elaine, Martha Bigelow and Kit Hansen. 2009. *Literacy and Second Language Oracy*. Oxford: Oxford University Press.

Van Els, Theo, Theo Bongaerts, Guus Extra, Charles van Os and Anne-Mieke Janssen-Van Dieten. 1984. *Applied Linguistics and the Learning and Teaching of Foreign Languages*. London: Edward Arnold.

Williams, Ann. 1989. Dialect in School Written Work. In *Dialect and Education: Some European Perspectives*, edited by J. Cheshire, V. Edwards, H. Münstermann and B. Weltens, 182–99. Clevedon, UK: Multilingual Matters.

# 7 | Instructional Models for a Creole-Influenced Vernacular Context: The Case of St Lucia

HAZEL SIMMONS-McDONALD
*University of the West Indies, Open Campus*

## Revisiting Some Pertinent Issues Related to Language and Education

Issues related to vernacular education have been discussed in several works (e.g., Tabouret-Keller et al. 1997; Craig 1999). The main focus in the literature has been on the situations in which vernacular education would be beneficial to selected groups of learners and also on the impact of language policy on the overall development of vernacular speakers. Some other works have examined issues related to pedagogy but, for the most part, these discussions have been primarily theoretical in nature. This chapter revisits some pertinent issues related to language education in St Lucia and discusses a context for the implementation of a language-instruction programme designed to promote literacy in the dominant varieties spoken in St Lucia.

Problems related to inadequate learning outcomes of creole and vernacular speakers at primary and secondary levels have been widely discussed in the literature on education and applied linguistics. Some causes cited for the low achievement of learners range from the relatively benign notion of linguistic interference of one code on the learning of another, to more pernicious ideas about cultural, cognitive and linguistic deficiencies (Bernstein 1961) and the notion of genetic deficiency (Jensen 1968). Although the work of Bernstein and Jensen was not related specifically to the Caribbean, the educational circumstances and issues with which they were concerned have some relevance for populations in that region.

Some St Lucian educators have cited interference from French Creole as a primary cause of low achievement in English by learners in the system. However, the findings of a study done by Winch and Gingell (1994, 177) showed that interference was not the primary factor in the written work of St Lucians. Using comparable samples from primary-school students in St Lucia and the United Kingdom, the authors showed that the error types occurring in the writing of students in these two contexts were similar, even though the students in the United Kingdom had had no exposure to French Creole. Based on their analysis of the writing samples, Winch and Gingell concluded that the errors could be "attributed to misunderstanding of the relationship between speech and writing".

Typically, research findings such as these influence neither pedagogical practice nor policy in St Lucia. Since the island became a British colony in the early 1800s, English has been the official language and the language used for instruction in schools. Generally, St Lucians have been unreceptive towards the use of French Creole for educational purposes, and the monolingual language-education policy has had the effect of marginalizing a significant number of native speakers of French Creole. While the pronouncement in 1999 by the government of St Lucia that St Lucian French Creole (Kwéyòl) could be used in parliament, and the use of this variety by the governor general every year since then to deliver part of her speech at the opening of parliament has led to a resurgence of interest in the functions for which Kwéyòl is used, there has not been marked advancement with respect to a formal review of the policy regarding the language used for instruction in schools.

Scholars such as Le Page and Tabouret-Keller (1985) have suggested that the policy of monolingual English for education has indirectly led to the emergence of the English-lexicon vernacular that is now widely spoken by the majority of St Lucians. They describe the acquisition of this variety as "indirect" in the sense that learners produce it in their attempts to learn English in school. Christie (1983) also suggested that the English vernacular variety that is spoken in Dominica is likely to have developed from attempts to teach children standard English in the classroom. Simmons-McDonald (1988) supported this view based on evidence from the second language acquisition patterns of native speakers of Kwéyòl who learned English within the context of the classroom. In later studies, Simmons-McDonald (1994, 1996) reported that the language-learning process of exclusive speakers of Kwéyòl seemed to become fossilized once they had acquired forms that were common both to interlanguage systems of ESL learners (with different first language [L1] backgrounds) and to the vernacular variety spoken in St Lucia.[1] Garrett (2003) suggested that another way in which the English-lexicon variety developed was from the attempts of native speakers of Kwéyòl to communicate with English speakers in informal contact situations.

The St Lucian English-lexicon vernacular (SLEV)[2] has been described as a creolized form of English consisting of calqued forms from French Creole (Isaac 1986) and other structures that are similar to those found in some other Creole English varieties spoken elsewhere in the Caribbean. There has been some discussion as to whether it is a creole (Garrett 2003), but at this stage it may be best referred to as a creole-influenced vernacular (CIV; see Craig 1999) that embodies features of the languages – namely, English and French Creole – from which it emerged, and has marked structural differences from St Lucian Standard English (SLSE). Some examples of SLEV utterances have been presented by Garrett (2003) and Simmons-McDonald (2001).

The explanations of emergence through contact with SLSE in school settings and that of proliferation through contact in communities are both plausible, but initially they probably applied variously to adults and children. It is reasonable to assume that children (ages four and up) who were exclusive speakers of Kwéyòl when they entered school produced an English vernacular variety in that setting as they tried to learn English (Simmons-McDonald 1988). This was probably reinforced in their communication with members of the community outside school who spoke Kwéyòl primarily, and who may have had limited competence in and production of English. It may well be that in the early stages of emergence, some adults who did not have formal schooling may have developed *minimal* use of a vernacular-like variety from contact with English speakers. Although at present the word on this issue is not definitive, the situation, as it developed, strongly supports the hypothesis of early emergence originating primarily in the school setting.

If one considers the language distribution patterns in the 1940s, when there were no records of a vernacular variety in the census documents, nor was such a variety evident elsewhere in use in communities, and if one also considers that at least 43 per cent of the population were exclusive speakers of Kwéyòl, it hardly seems likely that the vernacular SLEV would have emerged solely through casual contact between speakers of Kwéyòl and English, given the social distance that then existed between these groups of speakers, nor that it could have spread at such a rapid rate as to be so clearly distinguished in several parts of the island by 1961 (Alleyne 1961). Had this been the case, in the 1980s the number of exclusive speakers of Kwéyòl entering school would have been negligible. Based on a calculation of figures for urban and rural enrolments reported by principals of all primary schools in 1983, the figure is 11 per cent; N = 13,057 (Simmons-McDonald 1988).

In a school-based study done in St Lucia, Simmons-McDonald (1988) reported that fourteen previously exclusive speakers of Kwéyòl (out of a class of twenty-five) who were included in the study learned the vernacular through their attempts to learn English at school. This was despite the fact that, in addition to Kwéyòl, the vernacular was being spoken in and around the communities in which the children lived. When they entered school they had very limited comprehension and no production of English, and they did not speak SLEV. Considering this, one could argue that the more likely explanation for the emergence of the vernacular is that attempts to learn English in the formal school setting acted as a catalyst for use of the vernacular, and further contact in the community by those who had learned it led to its more widespread use. If one accepts this explanation as plausible, one will be forced to admit that the formal education system played an active role in the emergence of the vernacular variety. Results from both minimum standards tests and the promotional Common Entrance Examinations support the suggestion that primary-school instructional programmes in English in St Lucia are not resulting in acceptable levels of proficiency in English, particularly for creole and CIV speakers, for success in schoolwork and for certain types of employment in public and private sectors within the society.

Current evidence suggests that the English-lexicon vernacular variety is now widely spoken by the majority of St Lucians in both rural and urban areas, and it appears to have displaced Kwéyòl as the dominant language. Carrington (1988) and Frank (1993) indicated that the number of exclusive native speakers of Kwéyòl has gradually decreased while the number of bilinguals and monolingual English speakers has increased. Similar trends were also reflected in the school population. Enrolment figures submitted by teachers of kindergarten classes (formerly referred to as Stage I in St Lucia) for all primary schools in the system in 1984 revealed that the number of exclusive Kwéyòl speakers entering school in that year was 2 and 3 per cent for Kwéyòl speakers in urban and rural settings respectively, as opposed to 20 and 12 per cent for English speakers in these settings, respectively. The number of bilinguals (English and Kwéyòl) was higher in both settings: 43 per cent in urban districts and 85 per cent in rural. The percentage reported for English speakers was high, at 77 and 86 per cent in rural and urban settings, respectively. There were some slight discrepancies between the figures reported by the teachers and those given by principals. The latter reported a higher figure for Kwéyòl speakers, namely 8 and 6 per cent for urban and rural settings, respectively. They also reported higher numbers for bilinguals in both settings and fewer exclusive English speakers in both (Simmons-McDonald 1988). The difference between the numbers reported by kindergarten teachers and principals probably results from some inaccuracies in recording the language backgrounds of children when they entered school. Nevertheless, in both cases, the trends reflected the estimates given by Carrington and Frank for the wider society.

Reasons for the shift towards English have been presented by both Carrington (1984) and Simmons-McDonald (1988, 1994). One of the principal factors mentioned by Carrington is the increased participation by children in the school system. However, a related factor that may have resulted in lower levels of SLSE proficiency in school and an increase in vernacular speakers is the increased demand for school places by a fast-growing population. This resulted in the concomitant growth of the educational system in the form of more schools, the employment of a larger number of untrained teachers and more stress on the Teachers' College to keep pace with the demand for trained teachers. This situation was exacerbated by the gradual exodus of experienced teachers to the private sector to find better fortunes in other forms of employment.

Regardless of the reasons for the increase in the number of vernacular speakers, the overall effect appears to have been a decline in learning outcomes. Craig (1999, 29) compared learner performance in the CXC English language (English A) examination in 1988–90 and 1994–98. The figure he reported for St Lucia is –7.64 per cent, which represents negative change over a period of nine years, and which also indicates that overall, learner performance in English deteriorated in that period. On the basis of the figures for the anglophone West Indian countries (excluding the Bahamas), Craig concluded that "the Creole-influenced, majority student population of the Caribbean experiences a magnitude of difficulty in acquiring English language and literacy which is at least equivalent to that experienced by the AAVE [African American Vernacular English] student population of the USA" (p. 29).

A conclusion that can be drawn from the Craig study is that language learning outcomes for CIV-speaking populations in formal school settings seem to be similar, as are the language learning difficulties that these speakers experience. This seems to be the case regardless of differences between the varieties themselves or the contact situations that gave rise to them – that is, whether AAVE, Kwéyòl, Jamaican Creole or other CIVs. From a second language acquisition/learning point of view, these issues are straightforward and they should not be confused with or obfuscated by synchronic contemporary linguistic arguments or diachronic perspectives that attempt to attribute the problems to the sources of dialects or creoles.

The important point is that populations of dialect/creole/CIV speakers experience similar problems when they attempt to learn English as a second language or dialect in formal (school) settings. A comparison of findings from selected works would seem to suggest that this is no accident (Rickford 1999; Simmons-McDonald 2001; Winch and Gingell 1994). The comparisons Craig (1999) made with corresponding groups in the United Kingdom led him to conclude that the performance of CIV speakers in the West Indies is significantly lower than that of speakers in equivalent age cohorts in the United Kingdom.

Craig (1999) cited several studies in which the primary-school test scores that were reported indicated deficiencies in the use of English by West Indian children. He concluded that the scores were reflecting a "West Indian language-education problem all relate[d] to the primary-school level" (p. 27). In the case of St Lucia, the 7.64 per cent decline in performance over a nine-year period is a good indication that problems that emerge in the primary school tend to be compounded as students progress to the secondary level. From the available evidence, it seems reasonable to assume that current instructional approaches are not as effective as one might wish, and policy and pedagogical practice should be reviewed, particularly with respect to learners who speak Kwéyòl or a CIV as their first language.

A factor that has to be considered in the St Lucian context is the linguistic heterogeneity of learners in given classrooms. In the early years of primary school, particularly in the rural areas, classroom composition may comprise learners who speak Kwéyòl, SLEV and SLSE as first languages.[3] For example, one can expect to find a range of competence in an English variety that represents what Isaac (1986, 29) referred to as "a cline" from a calqued version of the French Creole towards standard English. There is also considerable variation among learners in terms of competence in the standard. Such heterogeneity presents a challenge for second language learning and the development of literacy.

Unfortunately, current policy and pedagogical practice have not exploited this situation to promote success in learning. The assumption underlying current practice is that children learn in identical ways and the sameness with which language and other content areas are taught leads to what Cummins (1984, quoted in Cloud 1994, 252) termed "pedagogically induced learning disabilities".

In a real sense, creole and CIV speakers who exit the secondary system having achieved only minimal functional literacy can be considered to be "curriculum casualties" (Hargis 1982, quoted in Cloud 1994, 252).

## Learning Contexts

The use of the vernacular as a means of promoting literacy among AAVE speakers received considerable mention from as early as the 1960s (for example, in the works of Baratz and Shuy [1969] and Rickford and Rickford [1995]). Theoretical perspectives and experiments with vernacular literacy in other contexts have been reported by Tabouret-Keller et al. (1997). Some findings in bilingual contexts have revealed that the acquisition of two or more languages has positive effects on the metalinguistic development of the learner (Bialystok 1991). Also, comparisons of children who had acquired literacy in two languages indicated better performance by these children when they attempted to acquire a third language than by monolingual or bilingual children who had not acquired literacy in their home language (Swain and Lapkin 1991).

Siegel (1997, 94) reported that the use of Tok Pisin to develop literacy in pre-school children resulted in greater gains for them than for others who had not been exposed to the programmes in which Tok Pisin had been used. He stated, "Overall, children who had been involved in the prep-school programme scored significantly higher, not lower, in term tests than those who had not been involved. Importantly, the higher achievements were in English, as well as in Maths and general subjects." Siegel concluded that the use of the pidgin did not hinder the learning of English. His findings are similar to those reported by Bollée (1993) for Seychellois children who were taught literacy in French Creole first, before French and English.

Cummins (1994, 38) reviewed studies which showed that "the better developed children's L1 conceptual foundation, the more likely they are to develop similarly high levels of conceptual abilities in their L2." He made the additional point that the "positive results of programmes that continue to promote literacy in L1 throughout elementary school can be attributed to the combined effects of reinforcing students' cultural identity and their conceptual growth" (p. 39). In an earlier work, Cummins (1979) had proposed the notion of the interdependence of first and second language proficiency in bilingual children. He had also proposed the distinction between basic interpersonal communication skills (BICS) and cognitive academic language proficiency (CALP) and explained that the latter is needed for successful functioning in academic work. CALP has to do with the learner's ability to master the use of school language which is "highly explicit, context free, logical and expository" (Calfee and Freedman, 1980). Swain (1981, 5) made the point that tasks that require students to use language to explain, classify, generalize, gain knowledge and "apply that knowledge" in all academic subjects in the curriculum result in the development of CALP or academic language.

The CALP and BICS distinction has been considered to be problematic in the sense that the dimensions do not necessarily present a sharp dichotomy. Ovando and Collier (1998, 93), for example, prefer the term *academic language* to refer to the same types of skills and abilities that the notion of CALP embodies. They explain that "this dimension of language proficiency is an extension of social language development" and that "social and academic language development represent a continuum; they are not separate, unrelated aspects of proficiency." They also indicate that "academic language extends into more and more cognitively demanding uses of language, with fewer contextual clues to meaning provided other than language itself, as students move into more academically demanding work with each succeeding grade level." Despite possible reservations about BICS and CALP, this construct provides a useful context for examining the processes that CIV learners, particularly speakers of Kwéyòl (as L1), go through in their attempts to become literate and successful in school.

When children who speak Kwéyòl enter school, they are immediately exposed to activities that are designed to develop literacy in English. They are introduced to the names and symbols of the English alphabet, and they repeat them in an effort to learn them. The problem is that the children have difficulty following proceedings in the classroom because they are unable to communicate in English. They must therefore jump through several hoops in order to function at the same level as their classmates who speak English. They must try to understand English, communicate in it and follow the more abstract structures of materials that are written in English and the stories and poems that are read to them, even as they are trying to acquire the language for communicative purposes. Classroom observations have shown that a fundamental problem is that the instructional activities are not designed to foster acquisition of English. The focus is primarily on teaching literacy in English, and the acquisition of English is a by-product of this. It is no wonder that speakers of Kwéyòl in the study reported by Simmons-McDonald (1988) ended up speaking the CIV, SLEV, at the end of two years of instruction at school. The latter study also reported that speakers of Kwéyòl as L1 do not progress as well as their English-speaking peers in their understanding and use of academic language in English, and some of them are held back in kindergarten and grade 1, with the result that they fall behind by two years.

The challenges for speakers of SLEV may be less daunting because they have varying levels of English comprehension. Yet the variability in phonology – to use the example of a fundamental building block that they need for literacy – between English and SLEV requires a special focus on the development of phonological awareness in English. Ongoing literacy studies show that this is one of the most challenging areas for both Kwéyòl and CIV speakers.

The point made by Cummins (1994, 39) is relevant in this context. Reiterating a suggestion he had made in an earlier work, he noted that children require different time periods to attain peer-appropriate levels in conversational skills in English as compared to academic skills. He cited some studies that showed that learners approach native-like levels of conversational skills within two years of exposure to English, whereas they require a period of five to seven years of school exposure to achieve as well as native speakers in academic aspects of English. This observation applies to the learning profiles of both Kwéyòl and CIV speakers in the St Lucian context. When one considers this in relation to the type of instruction in English that creole and CIV speakers are exposed to in the early years, it helps to explain why many of these speakers do not acquire acceptable levels of literacy by the end of primary school.

The figures presented by Craig (1999) also support the notion that vernacular speakers in the West Indies need a longer time than native speakers of English to become proficient in the academic aspects of English. He cites test scores suggesting that learners had inadequate development of academic English. The finding that second language learners require at least five to seven years to acquire academic language proficiency points to the need for a strong support system throughout primary and secondary school (in all the subject areas) to foster the development of proficiency. Teaching language in isolated time-tabled slots that separate language domains and restricting academic language instruction only to language arts lessons will not result in acceptable levels of proficiency in academic English by the end of the primary level. One way of providing adequate language exposure for the development of academic language proficiency is through a language-driven curriculum, which provides a variety of contexts for language learning and which allows students to be active participants who take ownership for their learning. Through the use of cross-curricular content in integrated activities that allow for the appropriate use of the home language, students who are creole or vernacular speakers can be helped to maximize opportunities for developing cognitive proficiency in the L1 and also to become proficient in the language of the school.

The shift to an integrated, language-driven curriculum would require all teachers at all levels to pay close attention to the language of the students. This means that the English language lesson would not be the only context in which teachers would focus on correctness of language. Rather, the same principles that operate in comprehension and explaining language concepts would be emphasized in all the subjects across the curriculum, and students would have increased opportunities to develop proficiency in English.[4] In addition to this, the primary-school teacher needs to have a healthy attitude towards language and should not convey the impression that creole and creole-influenced varieties are inferior to the standard English variety that is used for instruction in the classroom.

The teaching programmes that are offered in creole and CIV settings also need to present varied ways for helping learners to construct meaning from print in the languages available to them, even as they acquire an L2 and develop cognitively through the use of both the L1 and the L2. An analysis of videotapes of lessons conducted in randomly selected kindergarten to grade 2 classes in St Lucia indicates that the procedures used in current practice are limited and cannot achieve these ends. The videotapes were collected as part of an ongoing study on language teaching, interaction patterns and teacher talk in language arts lessons. Teachers were aware of the purpose of the study and a random sample was selected from those who had expressed a willingness to participate in it.

The equipment was set up at the back of the classroom and more than one session was taped. The analysis was based on the last taped session, during which the teacher and students were no longer focused on the presence of the equipment and the observer. Handwritten notes were also made to document any interesting interactions and these were used to provide further clarification of taped material where necessary. However, the transcripts of the tapes provided the main database for the study.

A positive feature of most classrooms was the genuinely caring attitudes of the teachers towards the children. However, the management procedures, specifically the interaction patterns and teaching style, did not allow teachers to maximize opportunities for the students to practise using the language. In all the classrooms, teachers controlled the proceedings from a dominant fronted position. Even in instances where some teachers had physically arranged the desks into small group configurations, the interaction pattern was predominantly one-to-many, with the initiation and flow of communication coming primarily from teacher to students. As high as 80 per cent, and in some cases 90 per cent, of the discourse in the classroom was teacher talk for purposes of explaining concepts and regulating behaviour. Student talk involved mostly short turns, often of monosyllabic length or short sentences in response to questions posed by the teacher. This pattern resulted in students having too few opportunities for long turns in which they could formulate longer sentences.

The delivery of information was another area that showed little variation in the majority of classrooms. There was a shortage of the use of key visuals for presenting content. Teacher explanation supplemented by illustration on the chalkboard was the most frequent method of delivery.[5] The sameness in the style of delivery did not cater to variation in the learning styles of students, so one would expect those students who relied more on visuals to do less well than those who learned best by listening. These observations suggest the need for greater variation in learning activities and tasks, to encourage more interaction among peers, more one-on-one teacher–student interaction and more initiation and participation by students in activities. A change that incorporated these management procedures would help to foster greater confidence among learners in their use of language for school purposes.

The acquisition of language and the development of cognitive academic language proficiency are both viewed as "active, constructive processes whereby children generate their knowledge of the world and their linguistic knowledge within a matrix of social interaction" (Cummins, 1994, 45; Wells 1986). The video data showed that the structure of lessons provided few opportunities for the exploitation of Vygotsky's (1962) notion of the zone of proximal development (ZPD), which Cummins (1994, 45) explains as being "the distance between children's developmental level as determined by individual problem solving without adult guidance and the level of potential development under the influence of, or in collaboration with, more capable adults or peers". Exploitation of the ZPD would require varied interaction patterns between teacher and learners and among the learners themselves and less reliance on exclusive, one-directional transmission of information and knowledge from teacher to learner. This formulation of the teaching/learning context would point to a more learner-centred approach in which children play a more active role in their learning. The classroom contexts that were observed did not reflect such an orientation.

Tharp and Gallimore (1991, 1) proposed the feature "instructional conversations", which are dialogues "between teachers and learners in which the teacher listens carefully to grasp the students' communicative intent, and tailors the dialogue to meet the emerging understanding of the learners". This notion is not unlike the strategy of responsive elaborations proposed by Duffy and Roehler

(1987) for improving the reading competence of learners. As teachers monitor their students' reading and observe blocks in their comprehension, they use queries in conversation with the students to teach them strategies they can use first to recognize that they have a difficulty and then to illustrate how they can overcome their misunderstandings. Ovando and Collier (1998, 226) observed that the instructional conversations proposed by Tharp and Gallimore are used to work with children in the ZPD and that these "serve to work with both linguistic and content-area zones of proximal development".

From the concept of working within the zone of proximal development of learners, one can deduce that a focus of the teaching and learning programme should be to make use of the language and abilities with which learners come to school, in order to help them generate knowledge of their world and also to construct their cultural identities and realities. This is likely to make learning interesting and relevant to learners, particularly those who speak a first language that is different from that used for school purposes. One might imagine that such a focus would help them to see the relationships between the subjects they learn, and to understand the relevance of the latter to the world outside school. An integrated language-driven curriculum is one that is more likely to make the relationships between different content areas clear to learners.

An approach based on the transmission model – that is, one-directional transmission from teacher to students – by its very nature prevents the outcomes referred to at the end of the foregoing paragraph and can result in "under-educated" children, a term used by Cloud (1994). The instructional model proposed in this chapter explores alternatives within the context of an intervention programme that incorporates the following:

1. a focus on the learner as an active participant in the construction of meaning in oral exchanges and for varied purposes, through interaction with text, teacher, peer and content;
2. the integration of content in a way that helps the learner to see the relationship between the concepts presented within language and across content areas; and
3. activities that foster the development of academic language in both the second language and the child's first language, Kwéyòl.

Programmes intended for creole and CIV speakers are likely to be more effective if they incorporate these principles which provide the basis for the instructional model presented in the following section. Another important factor, which has been taken into account in designing the model and the related instruc-

learners who speak Kwéyòl exclusively as their first language. The latter situation is probably rare, considering the changes in language distribution that have been reported.[7] The treatments proposed in the model are therefore designed to cater to varying contexts, and they will also allow for comparisons of outcomes for native speakers of Kwéyòl who are instructed in homogeneous and heterogeneous situations.

In a homogeneous classroom situation, speakers of Kwéyòl would be instructed as an exclusive group. The model would be applied from the earliest stage of schooling (kindergarten) to grade 6, which is the level at which learners write the Common Entrance Examination. In a heterogeneous classroom, the model would be applied across the same grades, but in actual instruction the teacher would have flexibility and would use discretion in configuring groups for specific tasks. In both situations, the model allows for treatments that will expose learners to at least one and a half hours of instruction in Kwéyòl and three and a half hours in standard English on a daily basis. The length of the school day at the primary level is six hours. Fifteen minutes are devoted to a morning break, another ten or fifteen minutes are spent on morning devotions and administrative matters at the start of the day, and lunch time lasts for one hour. This means that the time available for learning activities in the classroom is four hours and thirty minutes. If the early-morning devotions, roll call and other administrative matters are skipped, then the time for learning is four hours and forty-five minutes. In both heterogeneous and homogeneous situations, the model allows for treatments that would expose learners to one hour and thirty minutes to two hours maximum in Kwéyòl and two hours and forty-five minutes to three hours in English on a daily basis. This is different from a phased programme – for example, of the type used in the Seychelles – in which students are exposed to instruction in the creole for one to two years and then to instruction in English. The concurrent bilingual approach is preferred for the St Lucian situation, since it allows for the development of early literacy in Kwéyòl even as learners are acquiring communicative competence in SLSE. Research findings support early exposure to the L2 for more complete acquisition (Cummins 1994; Craig 1999). The approach suggested for the St Lucian context is likely to foster early acquisition of communicative competence in SLSE and the acquisition of academic language in both Kwéyòl and English. This model partially embraces a recommendation by Craig (1977): use of the home language in the early education of children whose L1 is not English.

During the time devoted to Kwéyòl instruction, learners will be exposed to a programme which in the early grades (K–1) will focus on emergent literacy in Kwéyòl. As learners become more literate in Kwéyòl and acquire increasing communicative competence in English, literacy in the latter will be given increasing focus from grades 2 to 6. The emphasis in reading will be on the development of critical literacy in the two dominant language varieties. An integrated programme is suggested, and it will incorporate rich reading selections, including material in which characters express themselves through Kwéyòl, SLEV and English, and which will allow for judicious comparisons between structures in Kwéyòl, the CIV and SLSE. Texts that use SLEV are mainly narratives in which characters express themselves in that variety. Because of the closeness of SLEV to SLSE in some respects, its use for instruction is not likely to lead to the desired goal of academic-language proficiency in English but is more likely to reinforce the use of SLEV. On the other hand, the introduction of texts in which it is used will allow learners to appreciate its use in literature and compare its structures with those of the standard. The SLEV-speaking group constitutes a special case in this context, and issues specific to their case will be explored further below.

The emphasis in teaching language through activities in the language arts and other subject areas will be on the use of strategies that teach learners *how* to learn. The instructional programmes recommended within the model will therefore be designed to promote strategic learning, collaborative group activities and focused, age-appropriate language-learning activities that will help learners to construct the grammars of the languages in question and learn to take ownership of their learning as well. The models and outlines of treatments are presented in figures 7.1, 7.2 and 7.3. Figure 7.1 presents the model for Kwéyòl speakers.

The models for SLEV and SLSE speakers are similar since they both emphasize early literacy in English and raise learners' awareness of the differences between the varieties. It is therefore the selection of texts and the types of tasks designed for the programme that will help SLEV speakers to effect shifts between the varieties when appropriate and to attain proficiency in SLSE.

Language education and instructional approaches have remained relatively the same despite changing trends in language-distribution patterns in St Lucia. In former years, SLEV speakers and Kwéyòl speakers were taught English as though it was their mother tongue or first language. Yet the fact that many more St Lucian children speak SLEV as a first language than they did fifteen or even ten years ago complicates the issue of language education. As noted earlier in this chapter, classrooms are more heterogeneous, comprising children with language backgrounds that are either SLSE, SLEV or Kwéyòl, and instructional approaches more often than not do not accommodate these differences. Factors

| Kwéyòl Instruction (1½ to 2 hours ) Allows Kwéyòl speakers to: | SLSE Instruction (2 hours 45 mins. to 3 hours) Allows Kwéyòl speakers to: |
|---|---|
| • develop literacy in Kwéyòl • use Kwéyòl for creative expression • develop academic-language proficiency in Kwéyòl | • acquire oral proficiency/communicative competence in SLSE • acquire literacy and academic-language proficiency in SLSE |

OUTCOMES

• Literacy in Kwéyòl
• Literacy in SLSE
• Academic-language proficiency in Kwéyòl and SLSE
• Communicative competence in SLSE

**Figure 7.1:** Kwéyòl intervention

| SLSE Instruction (3 hours 15 mins.) Allows speakers of SLEV to: | Kwéyòl Instruction (1½ hours) Allows speakers of SLEV to: |
|---|---|
| Allows Kwéyòl speakers to: • acquire communicative competence and oral proficiency in SLSE and use it in appropriate situations • develop academic-language proficiency in SLSE • use SLSE and SLEV for creative purposes | • learn Kwéyòl as a subject and become literate in it • acquire communicative competence and oral proficiency in Kwéyòl • have Kwéyòl available as a choice for communication and creative purposes |

OUTCOMES

• Academic-language proficiency in SLSE
• Communicative competence in SLSE
• Oral fluency and literacy in Kwéyòl

**Figure 7.2:** SLEV intervention

such as lack of recognition of SLEV as a different variety; attitudes still adhering, in some quarters, to Kwéyòl as to its status and usefulness in education; and a strong determination to establish English as the dominant language have all led to much tentativeness regarding language-education policy and instructional approaches in classrooms. The teaching of "English as mother tongue" to speakers of Kwéyòl and SLEV has been the norm, and this has not led to positive educational outcomes for many learners.

While some studies have promoted the use of same-lexicon CIVs to teach the standard, others have cautioned that in cases where the CIV is close to the standard it is sometimes difficult for students and some teachers to detect differences between the two varieties. Studies done in the St Lucian context have shown that when Kwéyòl speakers shift from what Isaac (1986) termed a "basilectal form of St Lucian English" towards the acquisition of forms that approximate more closely the standard, the shift towards full acquisition of the standard seems to become slower and more difficult (Simmons-McDonald 1994, 1999). Studies done in other contexts have reported that the use of CIV varieties to teach the standard may be useful. Siegel (1997) found this to be so in the case of the experimental use of Tok Pisin in education in Papua New Guinea.

Some reports on CIV speakers in other contexts have noted that these speakers are often placed in remedial classes because of their dialect and that the type of instruction provided is not the most beneficial. Winer (1993, 195), writing about English Creole speakers in Canada, recommended that teaching approaches for these children include "knowledge about and acceptance of the language and its culture". She also recommended the use of a contrastive approach to the children's first language in relation to "English language and culture varieties". Nero (2000, 503) made a similar recommendation in her report on a case study of three CIV speakers in New York. She suggested that effective instructional practices for CIV speakers would require teachers to become familiar with the "linguistic, cultural, and educational background" of the students.

Reports on and suggestions for the incorporation of CIVs in education have been varied. Carrington (1976, 36) proposed a set of principles for the use of English-lexicon varieties in instruction. The first principle states that in situations in which a language is "related to the official language, conditions are linguistically unfavourable for its use as a medium of instruction". Simmons-McDonald (1996) suggested that the use of the vernacular as a language of instruction might be unnecessary, since the acquisition data in the case of her subjects in St Lucia had shown that speakers of Kwéyòl had little difficulty in acquiring vernacular structures and most of them seemed unable to shift to SLSE for school purposes. However, the findings of some of the studies referred to earlier in this chapter (Rickford and Rickford 1995; Rickford 1999; Siegel 1997; and selected papers in Tabouret-Keller et al. 1997) indicate that a CIV could be useful in the learning of the L2. Siegel's (1999) review of three programmes that incorporated the vernacular in instruction found in all three cases that the vernacular was helpful. The difference between the three types of programmes Siegel reported on is the use made of the CIV. In the case of instrumental programmes, the CIV is used as a medium of instruction initially to develop literacy, while in accommodation programmes the use of the CIV is accepted in the classroom. In awareness programmes the CIV is actually studied and discussed. Siegel reported that of the three types, the awareness programmes seemed to be most beneficial.

The variability in findings indicates the need for a more careful examination of situations such as the St Lucian case where the question of distinctive differences between SLEV and SLSE will also be a factor that is likely to influence learnability. It may well be the case that where differences between the varieties are transparent to learners, they can use the CIV[8] as a stepping stone towards the acquisition of the second language or dialect. Craig (1971) used the term "area of interaction" to describe situations in which differences between the CIV and the standard may not be easily detected. In such cases, the differences can be said to be "opaque" and therefore less clearly discernible by learners. It seems logical to assume that in cases where the distinctions are opaque, the case for use of a CIV as a language of instruction is weak. However, in such situations, its use for judicious contrast between the varieties in question would be useful.

Certainly in the case of St Lucia, in which experiments in this area have not been conducted, the task of delineating the conditions under which the CIV is likely to be most helpful to learners has to be carefully researched. The model presented in this chapter provides a context in which such research can be undertaken. The intervention for SLEV speakers proposes the incorporation of a rich literature base in English with the use of judicious contrasts between SLEV and SLSE, where appropriate, to raise the awareness of students about the difference between the two varieties. A study by Wilson et al. (2001) reported significant gains in the improvement of literacy skills for creole speakers in Jamaica when a literature-based programme in the language arts was used. Figure 7.3 presents the treatment for SLSE speakers.

| SLSE Instruction (3 hours 15 mins.) | Kwéyòl Instruction (1½ hours) |
|---|---|
| Allows SLSE speakers to:<br><br>• develop early literacy in SLSE<br>• develop academic-language proficiency in SLSE<br>• use SLSE for creative purposes | Allows SLSE speakers to:<br><br>• learn Kwéyòl as a subject and acquire oral proficiency in it<br>• determine contexts in which use of Kwéyòl is appropriate<br>• learn Kwéyòl as a second language and use it for creative purposes |

OUTCOMES
- Early literacy in SLSE
- Academic-language proficiency in SLSE
- Communicative competence and oral proficiency in Kwéyòl
- Literacy in Kwéyòl

**Figure 7.3:** SLSE intervention

The model for SLSE speakers allows for one and a half hours of instruction in Kwéyòl. The intention here is that Kwéyòl will be introduced as a subject for the purpose of developing communicative competency (and oral fluency) in it. If the approach advocated in this chapter is effective, students will also acquire literacy in Kwéyòl and will have the option of using it in contexts that are appropriate. The model recommends the teaching of Kwéyòl for all three groups for several reasons. The first is a second language acquisition/bilingual argument which posits that learners derive cognitive benefits when they acquire two languages in early childhood. The subsequent acquisition of a third language for learners who have "sufficient proficiency in L1 and L2" is said to be much easier than for monolinguals. The benefits, reported in a series of studies (for example, Baker 1993; Bialystok 1991; Cummins and Swain 1986; Diaz 1983; Hakuta 1986, 1990; Hamers and Blanc 1989; Homel, Palij and Aaronson 1987), were summarized by Ovando and Collier (1998, 256). These include cognitive advantages over monolinguals on measures of cognitive flexibility, linguistic and metalinguistic abilities, and concept formation.

The second reason is that in the case of St Lucia, the early introduction of a language for which there is local support – that is, learners can hear the language spoken around them and they have opportunities to use it in the community – instead of one which students must learn as a foreign language, and for which there is no support in the community, such as French or Spanish, makes good sense at the primary level. Further, if the instructional programmes (based on the model) are effective and lead to the learning of the second language, the learning of a third language later on in school or at the secondary level should be easier.

A third reason for instruction in Kwéyòl relates to national character: it would favour the preservation of the unique identity of St Lucia as a bilingual community with strong traditions in Kwéyòl. The existence of Kwéyòl is used as advertisement to attract tourists, but if the language is used by fewer individuals in successive generations, it will eventually disappear as its last speakers die. The situation in Grenada is instructive in this regard. The minimization and eventual loss of Kwéyòl will likely have implications for the cultural preservation that is currently emphasized as a drawing card for tourism.

## Some Implications for the Introduction of the Model

In its initial conceptualization, several factors were identified as possible hindrances to the implementation of the model in the St Lucian setting. These included attitudes to Kwéyòl; the search for approval to include Kwéyòl in the school curriculum, and specifically the role of research in this regard; the availability of materials in Kwéyòl for instructional purposes; and the training of teachers and management of classrooms to accommodate the teaching of Kwéyòl. Some progress has been made in all of these areas, and there are some positive indications of willingness to explore the possibilities of Kwéyòl and CIV in education and assess their benefits to speakers of these language varieties.

### A. Attitudes to Kwéyòl

There are indications that attitudes to Kwéyòl have changed over the years, and the strong negative responses to this variety that once prevailed have become somewhat more muted in some quarters. Some studies have reported that St Lucians have an ambivalent attitude towards Kwéyòl and English. Early studies on the language situation in St Lucia made comparisons between the two languages. For the most part, the views expressed about Kwéyòl were negative, with English being valued as superior. The range of comments in the following examples, taken from publications over the last century, illustrates the changing attitudes.

1. "The negro language is a jargon formed from the French and composed of words or rather sounds adapted to the organs of speech in the black population. . . . It is, in short, the French language, stripped of its manly and dignified ornaments and travestied for the accommodation of children and toothless old women." (Breen 1844, 184)

2. "Patois (Kwéyòl) is inferior to English; it is not a language; it has no grammar; it is only broken French." (Vérin 1958, 164, writing about the language used in the school system and commenting on the "postulates . . . pumped into the scholar's head")

3. "Patois is making [St Lucians] backwards; it is nothing but palawala and it is merely a ploy to keep us back." (Yarde 1989, 1990)

4. Alleyne (1961, 5) found while doing his survey in St Lucia that teachers were ignorant of creole; "they rejected it as unintelligible gibberish and associated it with backwardness".

5. Liebermann (1974, 112) reported that St Lucians expressed "a positive attitude towards Patois" in their daily conversations.

6. Carrington (1984, 6) found, based on his 1966 study, that teachers expressed willingness to use Kwéyòl for explanatory purposes and "a small but increasing number of persons [feel] that Creole represents the soul of the St Lucian people and should be preserved as carefully as possible".

7. Liebermann's 1975 study found that St Lucians seemed to have a higher regard for Kwéyòl than for English; they showed reluctance to admit occasions when they used Kwéyòl but they readily admitted instances when they used English; they rated Kwéyòl versions of a story in a matched-guise test "more confident" and "more wise" than the English versions (p. 487).

8. Simmons-McDonald (1988, 30) reported that attitudes towards Kwéyòl in the teaching profession had changed for the better; 81 per cent of principals reported that they allowed teachers to use Kwéyòl to speak to children in class when necessary and 92 per cent of primary-school teachers reported that they used Kwéyòl with children for a range of purposes.

The first three comments in the set, (1) to (3), expressed by Breen, Vérin and Yarde, respectively, appear to be based on the personal views of these authors about Kwéyòl, as they compared it with English. The other comments, (4) to (8), are representative of varying views that might have been expressed by members of the population and which were derived from information gathered in surveys and reported in papers based on empirical studies.

More recent studies have commented on the increased use and acceptance of SLEV, and recently this variety has been the subject of more detailed linguistic study and analysis (for example, Garret 2004). Although there are some who still espouse negative views towards Kwéyòl, of the type that were expressed by Vérin, Breen and (more recently) Yarde, most St Lucians accept Kwéyòl as a language that expresses the essence of St Lucian culture and identity. In fact, there are concerted efforts by agencies such as the Folk Research Centre and An Tjè Nou ('In Our Hearts'), a publisher of Kwéyòl materials, to promote the study of Kwéyòl and French Creole culture. Greater acceptance of this variety is evident in the more frequent television and radio programmes delivered in Kwéyòl. Further, more prominence is given to events such as the Lawoz ('The Rose') and La Magwite ('The Marguerite') flower festivals and the annual celebration of Jounen Kwéyòl, a day when every St Lucian is encouraged to speak only Kwéyòl. These events have promoted a greater valuation of Kwéyòl and heightened the awareness of younger generations about Kwéyòl and French Creole culture, even though fewer among the younger generations of St Lucians speak the language.

The situation remains one that is essentially paradoxical. There are tensions between the thrust to preserve Kwéyòl on the one hand, and the natural dynamics of change on the other. Preservation efforts are manifested through the promotion of cultural events, such as those mentioned in the foregoing paragraph, as well as through the institutionalization of the use of Kwéyòl and the broadening of its functions, as in the previously discussed acceptance of its use during the proceedings of parliament. Shifts away from Kwéyòl are accelerated by increased exposure to English via the media, increased communication with peoples of neighbouring anglophone islands and validation of English through the education system and its various examinations. The latter has resulted in increased use of English, the emergence and widespread use of SLEV, fewer monolingual speakers of Kwéyòl and fewer speakers of Kwéyòl in general (see Carrington 1984; Simmons-McDonald 1996). These trends have affected attitudes towards the language varieties spoken in St Lucia in recent times.

In a study on such attitudes which tested a sample of teachers using a variety of instruments, Simmons-McDonald (2006a, 67–68) reported the following:

> All the items probing the use of Kwéyòl in education yielded positive responses and favourable attitudes towards its introduction in that domain. This was an encouraging finding since hitherto, resistance to the use of Kwéyòl in education came primarily from teachers. These results indicated a distinctive shift from the first half of the twentieth century when reports were made of students being prohibited from speaking Kwéyòl on the school compound and even being punished for doing so. Responses to the one item . . . that probed attitudes towards the use of SLEV in education were almost balanced: 40 percent agreed that children should not be allowed to speak that language in schools while 43 percent disagreed and 17 percent were uncertain. There was more certitude regarding the use of Kwéyòl in the domain of education than the use of SLEV and this probably was because there was less familiarity with SLEV than with Kwéyòl. Closer inspection of individual items in the four categories provided some further insight into the scores on the attitudinal scale which showed overall positive attitudes towards Kwéyòl. They further indicated that while the attitudes towards Kwéyòl were positive, respondents still valued SLSE, even as they were also accepting of Kwéyòl.

The study also reported a more positive correlation between SLSE and Kwéyòl (0.93) than between Kwéyòl and SLEV (0.54) or between SLSE and SLEV (0.20). A main finding was that SLEV was less highly valued than either Kwéyòl or SLSE, and the valuation of SLSE and Kwéyòl on the traits examined in the study were similar (Simmons-McDonald 2006a, 73).

This report indicates the shift in attitude towards acceptance of Kwéyòl as a positive development in the St Lucian context, one which in turn created a more suitable context for research on the use of Kwéyòl instruction in the school.

## B. Inclusion of Kwéyòl in the School Curriculum: The Role of Research

Since the early 1800s when St Lucia was ceded to the British, English has been the only language of instruction and the one that has been officially promoted for communication in the school setting. Some scholars, cited earlier in this chapter, have suggested that this policy resulted in the emergence of SLEV. Increased tolerance by officials towards Kwéyòl has become evident in their granting of permission for carefully controlled experiments to be done at the primary level. In one such instance, An Tjè Nou, the publishers of a series of folk tales in Kwéyòl, was permitted to introduce these texts in a selected primary school and to teach the students to read them. In another instance, this author was given permission to conduct an experiment in developing literacy in Kwéyòl. The results of that experiment, briefly explained here, have paved the way for additional work to be undertaken with Kwéyòl in education.

A modified version of the model proposed in this chapter was used for the experiment because of time limitations and the fact that permission had been granted to perform the preliminary pilot study with only a small group of learners in grades 5 and 6. A single-subject research design was used (Neuman and McCormick 1995), and the school chosen was in a rural community in the northeast of the island. The sample was drawn from a group of sixty-nine children who had been identified by teachers as having severe reading problems. The initial survey revealed that approximately 60 per cent of the children were reading between two and four grade levels below their actual reading age levels. The pilot study was conducted with three of the older children in the group who all spoke Kwéyòl as their first language. Performance levels were established for each of the children: Ado was reading at a beginning grade 1 level with considerable difficulty and neither Uka nor Dovi could read. A typical teaching day began with the Kwéyòl session, which lasted for forty-five minutes to an hour, followed by an English session which lasted sixty to seventy-five minutes. Afternoon sessions were devoted to individual instruction in areas of difficulty and to providing opportunities for additional guided practice for reading in Kwéyòl and in English. The researcher drew from a rich selection of literature in both languages, appropriate to the students' reading abilities. Reading records of individual performance were taken to determine individual gains over the six-week period of the experiment. Reporting on the development of both languages, Simmons-McDonald (2006b) noted the following for two of the students.

> *Ado*: The trends in Ado's case show a close correspondence in accuracy in reading in both languages. Accuracy percentages for Kwéyòl are higher at the start of the study, but at the end performance in both languages is on par. Overall, Ado's results show a comparable performance in L1 and L2 which strongly suggests balanced development in reading in English and Kwéyòl. (p. 140)

> *Uka*: Trends for Uka show that at the start of the study her accuracy was higher for Kwéyòl than for English. . . . The low accuracy percentages in Kwéyòl at Sessions

4 and 5 reflected her attempts to read more challenging and unfamiliar texts. . . .
During those sessions she maintained a high level of accuracy in English and was
able to read the English texts on her own and with fluency. . . . The data show that
by the end of the study Uka's accuracy percentage in both languages was similar,
in the 90 percent to 94 percent range, which represents an ability to read with
fluency. (pp. 140–41)

The positive results of this pilot study, in which the teaching time recommended
by the model was drastically reduced, are encouraging for bilingual development and literacy in Kwéyòl and English in the St Lucian context if the full
model and teaching approaches are implemented.

## C. Availability of Materials in Kwéyòl for Instructional Purposes

In the past, the issue of availability of materials would have presented a major
challenge in any consideration of introducing Kwéyòl as a language of instruction
in education. However, since the publication of *A Handbook for Writing Creole*
(Louisy and Turmel-John 1983), An Tjè Nou has produced several wonderfully
illustrated books in Kwéyòl for young readers, using the orthography recommended in that handbook. The An Tjè Nou collection forms a good starting core
of supplementary texts for the enjoyment of students and for the development
of fluency skills. Simmons-McDonald (2010, 203) reported the development of
other materials in Kwéyòl for use in an extended implementation of the project.
The texts listed are:

1. *Pwèmyé Liv Kwéyòl Pou Piti Zanfan* ('Introductory French Creole Book
   for Beginners')
2. *Mwen Sa Li: An Liv Kwéyòl Pou Piti Zanfan* ('I Can Read: A Kwéyòl Reader
   for Beginners')
3. *Mwen Sa Konté: An Liv Kwéyòl Pou Piti Zanfan* ('I Can Count: A Kwéyòl
   Reader and Book of Numbers for Beginners')
4. *Apwann Li: Dézyenm Liv Kwéyòl Pou Piti Zanfan* ('Learn to Read: Kwéyòl
   Book 2 for Beginners', a grade 1 text)

She describes the texts further:

The introductory book presents an approach that emphasises the development
of phonological awareness, and the supplementary texts in the series present

materials for reading practice, discussion and comprehension. . . . the text for use at grade 1 presents an integrated approach to the language, and it draws on topics from across content areas of the curriculum to expose students to concepts in other subjects in Kwéyòl. (p. 204)

## D. Training of Teachers and Management of Classrooms

Teacher proficiency in the languages in question is likely to be a factor that will determine teacher willingness to experiment with the model. This issue can be addressed in consultation with the school administration so that teachers who are proficient in both Kwéyòl and English will be assigned to classrooms. Screening for language proficiency is one of the built-in protocols for the study. Training can be conducted in workshops and in on-site training sessions.

Another important consideration relates to the willingness of the school to modify procedures to facilitate implementation of the model. The introduction of the model and related instructional procedures will require several inputs from principals and staff. These include adjustments to the timetable, moving away from discrete slots in which subjects are compartmentalized towards a schedule which allows for blocks of time to give learners freedom to work on projects, read, write, speak, listen, explore concepts, construct meaning from the content to which they are exposed and learn in a holistic way; in short, it means shifting to an integrated approach. Because the classrooms in the selected schools comprise students with heterogeneous language backgrounds, implementation of the three components of the model (in effect, two components, because the SLEV and SLSE components use the same instructional approach) can be effected seamlessly with specified blocks of time for instruction in Kwéyòl and English.

## Conclusion

Despite the challenges outlined in this chapter, the possibility of bilingualism and bi-literacy that the model offers is sufficiently compelling to warrant experimentation. Several benefits are likely to accrue to St Lucian learners if the model and programmes can be used effectively. These include but are not limited to (1) the development of literacy for non-native speakers of St Lucian Standard English; (2) the development of proficiency in Kwéyòl, which can lead to the creation of literary materials by Kwéyòl speakers; (3) increased awareness about the language varieties spoken in St Lucia by the speakers of these varieties; and (4) increased awareness of St Lucian cultural heritage.

If the objectives for the model are realized, the beneficiaries of the innovation will be (1) speakers of St Lucian French Creole, for whom literacy was before now a remote possibility, with advancement through education limited; (2) speakers of SLSE, who will have the opportunity to become proficient in the languages spoken in their country; (3) all learners, who are likely to gain greater cognitive flexibility through bilingual development; (4) the education system, which will have at last begun to tackle in a concrete way the problems which have plagued educational development over the last four decades (and continue to do so); and (5) last, but by no means least, St Lucia itself, which will benefit from the development of its human resources and the contribution of all sectors of the population through their ability to participate actively in the affairs of the nation.

## Notes

1. The term *interlanguage systems* is used here to refer to the language produced by learners in their attempts to use the second or target language that they are learning.
2. SLEV is also referred to as St Lucian Creole English (SLCE; Simmons-McDonald 1996); Vernacular English of St Lucia (VESL; Garrett 2003); and, elsewhere, Creole English.
3. The term *St Lucian Standard English* is used specifically to distinguish it from other standard varieties in the Caribbean. While there is a Caribbean Standard English that is mutually intelligible with other Standard English varieties around the world, the varieties spoken in Caribbean countries vary in some respects in lexicon, so that there are some expressions that may be used by Jamaicans that may not be understood by Barbadians or St Lucians. This results from the different historical backgrounds of each island.
4. Correct use of English is not always consistently stressed in subject areas other than the English lesson, and assessment of subjects other than English does not always take into account correctness of expression in English.
5. See Hazel Simmons-McDonald's research report on teacher–student interaction in primary schools (Department of Linguistics, University of the West Indies, Cave Hill).
6. Several literature texts in Kwéyòl have been published that are appropriate for use in schools.
7. SLEV is now spoken in some rural communities that were once exclusively Kwéyòl domains.
8. This is relevant in cases where the CIV and the standard share the same lexicon.

# References

Alleyne, Mervyn. 1961. Language and Society in St Lucia. *Caribbean Studies* 1 (1): 1–10.

Baker, C. 1993. *Foundations of Bilingual Education and Bilingualism*. Clevedon, UK: Multilingual Matters.

Baratz, Joan C., and Roger W. Shuy, eds. 1969. *Teaching Black Children to Read*. Washington, DC: Center for Applied Linguistics.

Bernstein, B. 1961. Social Class and Linguistic Development: A Theory of Social Learning. In *Economy, Education and Society*, edited by A.H. Halsey, J. Floud and C. Arnold Anderson, 288–314. New York: Free Press.

Bialystok, Ellen, ed. 1991. *Language Processing in Bilingual Children*. Cambridge: Cambridge University Press.

Bollée, Annegret. 1993. Language Policy in the Seychelles and Its Consequences. *International Journal of the Sociology of Language* 102: 85–99.

Breen, Henry H. 1844. *St Lucia: Historical, Statistical, and Descriptive*. London: Longman, Brown, Green and Longmans.

Calfee, R., and S. Freedman. 1980. Understanding and Comprehending. Paper presented at Center for Study of Reading. Urbana, Illinois.

Carrington, Lawrence D. 1976. Determining Language Education Policy in Caribbean Sociolinguistic Complexes. *International Journal of the Society of Language* 8: 27–44.

———. 1984. *St Lucian Creole: A Descriptive Analysis of Its Phonology and Morpho-Syntax*. Hamburg: Helmut Buske.

———. 1988. *Creole Discourse and Social Development*. Manuscript Report 212e. Ottawa: International Development Research Centre.

Craig, Dennis R. 1971. Education and Creole English in the West Indies: Some Sociolinguistic Factors. In *Pidginization and Creolization of Languages*, edited by D. Hymes, 371–92. Cambridge: Cambridge University Press.

———. 1977. Creole Languages and Primary Education. In *Pidgin and Creole Linguistics*, edited by A. Valdman, 313–32. Bloomington: Indiana University Press.

———. 1999. *Teaching Language and Literacy: Policies and Procedures for Vernacular Situations*. Guyana: Education and Development Services.

Christie, Pauline. 1983. In Search of the Boundaries of Caribbean Creoles. In *Studies in Caribbean Language*, edited by L.D. Carrington, D.R. Craig, and R. Todd-Dandaré, 13–22. St. Augustine: Society for Caribbean Linguistics.

Cloud, Nancy. 1994. Special Education Needs of Second Language Students. In *Educating Second Language Children: The Whole Child, the Whole Curriculum, the Whole Community*, edited by F. Genesee, 243–77. Cambridge: Cambridge University Press.

Cummins, Jim. 1979. Cognitive /Academic Language Proficiency, Linguistic Interdependence, the Optimum Age Question and Some other Matters. *Working Papers on Bilingualism* 19: 121–29.

Cummins, Jim. 1984. *Bilingualism and Special Education: Issues in Assessment and Pedagogy.* San Diego: College-Hill.

———. 1994. Knowledge, Power and Identity in Teaching English as a Second Language. In *Educating Second Language Children*, edited by F. Genesee, 33–58. Cambridge: Cambridge University Press.

Cummins, Jim, and Merrill Swain. 1986. *Bilingualism in Education: Aspects of Theory, Research and Practice.* London: Longman.

Diaz, R.M. 1983. Thought and Two Languages: The Impact of Bilingualism on Cognitive Development. In *Review of Research in Education*, vol. 10, editd by E.W. Gordon, 23–54. Washington, DC: American Educational Research Association.

Duffy, Gerald G., and Laura R. Roehler. 1987. Improving Reading Instruction through the Use of Responsive Elaboration. *The Reading Teacher* 40: 514–20.

Frank, David B. 1993. Political, Religious and Economic Factors Affecting Language Choice in St Lucia. *International Journal of the Sociology of Language* 102: 39–56.

Garrett, Paul. 2003. An "English Creole" That Isn't: On the Sociohistorical Origins and Linguistic Classification of the Vernacular English of St Lucia. In *Contact Englishes of the Eastern Caribbean*, edited by M. Aceto and J.P. Williams, 155–210. Amsterdam: John Benjamins.

Hakuta, K. 1986. *Mirror of Language: The Debate on Bilingualism.* New York: Basic Books.

———. 1990. *Language and Cognition in Bilingual Children.* In *Bilingual Education: Issues and Strategies*, ed. A.M. Padilla, H.H. Fairchild and C.M. Valdez, 47–59. Newbury Park, CA: Sage.

Hamers, J.F., and M.H.A. Blanc. 1989. *Bilinguality and Bilingualism.* Cambridge: Cambridge University Press.

Hargis, Charles H. 1982. *Teaching Reading to Handicapped Children.* Denver: Love Publications.

Homel, P., M. Palij and D. Aaronson, eds. 1987. *Childhood Bilingualism: Aspects of Linguistic, Cognitive, and Social Development.* Hillsdale, NJ: Lawrence Erlbaum.

Isaac, Martha F. 1986. French Creole Interference in the Written English of St Lucian Secondary School Students. MPhil thesis, University of the West Indies, Cave Hill.

Jensen, Arthur R. 1968. How Much Can We Boost IQ and Scholastic Achievement? *Harvard Educational Review* 39 (1): 1–123.

Le Page, R.B., and Andrée Tabouret-Keller. 1985. *Acts of Identity: Creole-Based Approaches to Language and Ethnicity.* Cambridge: Cambridge University Press.

Liebermann, Dena. 1974. Bilingual Behavior in a St Lucian Community. PhD diss., University of Wisconsin.

———. 1975. Language Attitudes in St Lucia. *Journal of Cross-Cultural Psychology* 6: 471–81.

Louisy, Pearlette, and Paule Turmel-John. 1983. *A Handbook for Writing Creole.* Castries: Research St Lucia.

McLaughlin, Barry. 1981. Differences and Similarities between First- and Second-Language Learning. In *Native Language and Foreign Language Acquisition*, edited by H. Winitz, 23–32. New York: Academy of Sciences.

Neuman, Susan B., and Sandra McCormick, eds. 1995. *Single-Subject Experimental Research: Applications for Literacy*. Newark, DE: International Reading Association.

Ovando, Carlos J., and Virginia P. Collier. 1998. *Bilingual and ESL Classrooms: Teaching in Multicultural Contexts*. Boston: McGraw-Hill.

Rickford, Angela. 1999. *I Can Fly: Teaching Narratives and Reading Comprehension to African American and other Ethnic Minority Students*. Lanham, MD: University Press of America.

Rickford, John R., and Angela E. Rickford. 1995. Dialect Readers Revisited. *Linguistics and Education* 7 (2): 107–28.

Siegel, Jeff. 1997. Using a Pidgin Language in Formal Education: Help or Hindrance? *Applied Linguistics* 18 (1): 86–100.

———. 1999a. Stigmatized and Standardized Varieties in the Classroom: Interference or Separation? *TESOL Quarterly* 33 (4): 701–28.

———. 1999b. Creoles and Minority Dialects in Education: An Overview. *Journal of Multilingual and Multicultural Development* 20 (6): 508–31.

Simmons-McDonald, Hazel. 1988. The Learning of English Negatives by Speakers of St Lucian French Creole. PhD diss., Stanford University.

———. 1994. Comparative Patterns in the Acquisition of English Negation by Native Speakers of French Creole and Creole English. *Language Learning* 44 (1): 29–72.

———. 1996. Language Education Policy: The Case for Creole in Formal Education in St Lucia. In *Caribbean Language Issues, Old and New*, edited by P. Christie, 120–42. Kingston: University of the West Indies Press.

———. 1999. Developmental Patterns in the Acquisition of English Negation by Speakers of St Lucian French Creole. In *Studies in Caribbean Language II*, edited by P. Christie, Barbara Lalla, Velma Pollard and Lawrence Carrington, 75–99. St Augustine: Society for Caribbean Linguistics.

———. 2001. Vernacular Literacy: Influencing Policy through Pedagogical Experimentation. Paper presented at the annual conference of the American Association for Applied Linguistics, St Louis, MO. February.

———. 2006a. Attitudes of Teachers to St Lucian Language Varieties. *Caribbean Journal of Education* 28 (1): 51–84.

———. 2006b. Vernacular Instruction and Bi-literacy Development in French Creole speakers. In *Exploring the Boundaries of Caribbean Creole Languages*, edited by H. Simmons-McDonald and Ian Robertson, 118–46. Kingston: University of the West Indies Press.

———. 2010. Introducing French Creole as a Language of Instruction in Education in St Lucia. In *Creoles in Education: An Appraisal of Current Programs and Projects*, edited by B. Migge, Isabelle Léglise and Angela Bartens, 184–209. Amsterdam: John Benjamins.

Swain, Merrill. 1981. Time and Timing in Bilingual Education. *Language Learning* 31: 1–15.

Swain, Merrill, and Sharon Lapkin. 1991. Heritage Language Children in an English-French Bilingual Program. *Canadian Modern Language Review* 47 (4): 635–41.

Tabouret-Keller, Andrée, Robert B. Le Page, Penelope Gardner-Chloros and Gabrielle Varro. 1997. *Vernacular Literacy: A Re-evaluation*. Oxford: Clarendon Press.

Tharp, Roland G., and Ronald Gallimore. 1991. *The Instructional Conversation: Teaching and Learning in Social Activity*. Santa Cruz: National Center for Research on Cultural Diversity and Second Language Learning.

Vérin, Pierre M. 1958. The Rivalry of French Creole and English in the British West Indies. *De West Indische Gids* 38: 163–67.

Vygotsky, Lev. 1962. *Thought and Language*. Cambridge, MA: Harvard University Press.

Winch, Christopher, and John Gingell. 1994. Dialect Interference and Difficulties with Writing: An Investigation in St Lucian Primary Schools. *Language and Education* 8 (3): 157–82.

Wells, G. 1986. *The Meaning Makers*. Portsmouth, NH: Heinemann.

Winer, Lise. 1993. Teaching Speakers of Caribbean English Creoles in North American Classrooms. In *Language Variation in North American English: Research and Teaching*, edited by A.W. Glowka and D.M. Lance, 191–98. New York: MLA.

Yarde, Clive. 1989. Patois Making Us Backward. *Voice*, 26 August.

———. 1990. Patois Emphasis: A Ploy to Keep Us Back. *Voice*, 10 February.

# 8

# The Role of Grammar in English-Language Teaching in the Anglophone Caribbean

IAN ROBERTSON
*University of the West Indies, St Augustine*

M ajor changes in approaches to and methodology in language learning and teaching in the twentieth century have been premised essentially on theoretical issues. Little attention has been paid to actual research or practical considerations and developments. An examination of the major paradigm shifts in approaches to language teaching reveals that the direct-method, audio-lingual, notional functional, reading and communicative methods may all be traced directly to shifts in theoretical perspectives on the nature of language itself and on evolving theories of language learning and language acquisition. Richards (1985, 43) claims that "such approaches and techniques are promoted and justified through reference to intuitively appealing assertions and theories, which, when repeated by those in positions of authority, assume the status of dogma".

In recent times, the communicative approach has probably been the one with the greatest appeal to teachers of language. This appeal stems, in part, from the fact that it has the potential to resolve the long-standing debate among language teachers on what constitutes real knowledge of a language. It is this knowledge, it is argued, which should be used to determine the target skills and abilities for language learning and teaching.

## Knowledge of Language

Positions on what constitutes "knowledge of language" have evolved with the development of linguistics. Chomsky's (1957, 1965) answer to this question is based on the assumption that every language is dynamic and infinite, though the rules by which any specific language may operate are finite and form part of a set or subset of universal features of human language. This theoretical position represented a radical shift from the behaviourist position, which assumed that though any language might be very large, each was finite. Under these conditions, it was therefore theoretically possible to know the entire language. More than that, it was assumed that language was merely another form of behaviour (Skinner 1957) and that the way to acquire language was principally through mimicry and memorization. The evidence adduced by Chomsky from studies of first language acquisition challenged the prevailing perceptions of what was acquired.

In particular, Chomsky introduced the notion of native-speaker competence to account for what really constituted knowledge of language. The notion is in part similar to the notion of *langue* developed by Saussure in 1922 and is used to refer to the system of rules that the native speakers of a language have to master in order to facilitate production, interpretation and the development of grammaticality judgements.

It is this underlying competence which provides both the target and the model for approaches to language learning and teaching. For many approaches to language learning and teaching, it is the ability to internalize the rules of a language and to operate them in a manner similar to that described for the native speaker that is the hallmark of a good language learner. In this context, the role of grammar in language learning and teaching has come under close scrutiny, especially since attempts have been made to determine just how native speakers acquire language and to use these principles underlying first language acquisition to inform language learning and teaching.

## Explicit Grammar and Language Learning

One important issue which arises out of this is the role of explicit grammar teaching in the language-learning process. Since attempts to develop approaches and methodologies for language teaching and learning have assumed as axiomatic the need to follow as closely as possible natural acquisition behaviours, it became necessary to consider the role of explicit grammar teaching in native language acquisition.

Writers like Krashen may be read to imply that explicit grammar teaching plays little or no part in normal language-acquisition behaviours and that it should therefore have only a minimal role in language learning and teaching. Krashen (1981, 1) distinguishes between conscious language learning and subconscious acquisition and argues that "subconscious language acquisition appears to be more important". He claims that language acquisition

> requires meaningful interaction in the target language – natural communication – in which speakers are concerned, not with the form of the utterances, but with the messages they are conveying or understanding. Error correction and explicit teaching of rules are not relevant to language acquisition . . . but caretakers and native speakers can modify their utterances addressed to acquirers to help them understand, and these modifications are thought to help the acquisition process.

This view has attracted some followers.

Though the proposition may be attractive, it is fundamentally flawed. There is clear evidence from some of the early research in child language acquisition (such as Brown 1973), as well as from the most casual observation, that such teaching practices as modelling, expansion, repetition, direct correction, positive and negative reinforcement, and even instruction ("Don't say this, say these") are part of the natural acquisition process. While it is true that there is no classroom situation and no programme in normal acquisition contexts, it is clear that there is significant focus on explicit attention to grammar.

A much more significant and important consideration for the role of grammar in language teaching comes from a second perspective on what constitutes knowledge of language. Hymes (1971) presented the alternative notion of communicative competence, which challenges the restriction of competence to grammar only. According to Crystal (1990), this notion focuses on "the native-speakers' ability to produce and understand sentences which are appropriate to the contexts in which they occur". In this context, grammar becomes merely one of the essential components of competence. The others are sociolinguistic competence, pragmatic competence and discourse competence. These various components of communicative competence and the need to achieve them challenge the position that grammar should be the focus of language teaching. At its most extreme, this alternative has resulted in a debate as to whether fluency or grammatical accuracy should take precedence (Brumfit 1984). The debate itself challenges the focus on grammatical accuracy as against communicative effectiveness. Celce-Murcia and Hilles (1988, 1) point out that "in the past sev-eral years many ESL professionals have come to assume that second-language (L-2) learning is very much like first-language (L-1) acquisition. Their argument is that providing 'comprehensible input' (language addressed to the learner that he or she can understand) is really all that a foreign- or second-language teacher can or should do to facilitate acquisition."

Celce-Murcia and Hilles (1988, 2) concede that the communicative approach to language teaching is attractive, but they add, "There is equally appealing and convincing evidence that a communicative approach can lead to the develop-ment of a broken, ungrammatical, pidginized form of language beyond which students can never really progress. Such students are said to have 'fossilized' in their acquisition of the language."

These two positions together provide adequate reason to re-examine the validity of the issues involved in the evolution of language-teaching approaches and methods. It is also important to challenge the unquestioning acceptance of some of the basic assumptions that underpin language teaching and learning.

The focus of this chapter is the role of grammar teaching in language educa-tion in the anglophone Caribbean. The issues are addressed from a theoretical perspective.

## Grammar

Among language teachers, there is a general lack of consensus about the nature of grammar itself. A considerable part of the debate could be avoided if there were some clarity as to what constitutes grammar and how concepts of gram-mar may be distinguished from the teaching of it. The distinction is important if approaches to and methodologies for the teaching and learning of language are to be kept separate and distinct from the grammar itself and from its relevance to the language teaching and learning process.

The grammar of any language, written or unwritten, is simply the set of rules by which acceptable utterances in that language may be constructed or inter-preted. At its simplest, the study of grammar is the study of the ways in which words and their component parts combine to express meaning in any particular language. The study of grammar helps learners to develop an informed aware-ness of any language and of how it works. It also provides a point of reference for those who need a clear position or principle on which to base an operational activity, what Krashen would refer to as a *monitor*.

Grammars may be prepared for a range of purposes. A *reference grammar* is a comprehensive description of the structural principles on which a language operates. Such a grammar attempts authoritative and comprehensive coverage of the system of rules on which a particular language operates. A *descriptive grammar* is a systematic description of language as found in a sample of speech. Such grammars analyse the rules that might be derived from the study of samples of actual speech. A *theoretical grammar* goes beyond description to provide insights into the principles underlying the workings of the subsystems and systems of that grammar. A *pedagogical grammar* is usually a simplified or restricted description of the grammar of any language written to facilitate teaching and learning of that language. A good pedagogical grammar selects those aspects of the grammar which are necessary to service the specific purposes of the learning exercise. The principles for such selection should always be clear.

Another important distinction which should be drawn is that between *formal grammar* and *traditional grammar*. Formal grammar, in its strictest application, refers to the study of linguistic forms, their structures and their distribution. It is often mistakenly linked to traditional grammar by the fact that both terms are used to describe what takes place in the classroom. Specific lessons that focus on teaching and learning grammar are often referred to as "formal grammar lessons" or "teaching grammar formally". The type of grammar most frequently used for teaching is traditional grammar, with its prescriptive rules and regulations. As a consequence, the two types of grammar, formal and traditional, have become closely associated and the terms are conflated to the point where "teaching formal grammar" has come to mean making formal arrangements for the teaching of grammar. Traditional grammar, as noted earlier, is not always based on strict linguistic analysis but on perceptions which particular grammarians might have about how the language works or, more often, ought to work. In many instances, traditional grammars are linguistically inaccurate, especially in those cases where they seek to impose the rule system of one language (especially Latin, which is often seen as the model for all languages) on other languages. This is especially so when languages such as English are erroneously assumed to have been derived from the language being used as a model.

Decisions about the teaching of grammar are often based on conflicting perceptions and misconceptions. This is especially true for formal grammar. Wherever it is linked with traditional grammar, the tendency has been to reject it because of the many inherent inaccuracies of the latter. Traditional grammar, which has come under scrutiny and criticism by linguists, is usually the type of grammar that is rejected because of its manifest inaccuracies brought about by the reliance on prescription rather than description.

## Knowing Grammar

Sandra McKay (1990) claims, "At the heart of this controversy [about whether grammar should be taught at all] is the question of what it means to teach grammar." Of equal significance is the question of what "knowing the grammar" means. For some language teachers, this knowledge is the ability to verbalize aspects of the rule system by which a given language operates – the ability, for instance, to provide definitions of word classes such as nouns and verbs, and grammatical functions such as subject and object. This type of grammatical knowledge is sometimes referred to as "knowledge about the language". The usefulness of such an exercise, especially when what is verbalized is inaccurate in the manner indicated for traditional grammar, has often been questioned. Indeed, such verbalizing or externalizing of grammatical information is generally seen as being of questionable value in language learning and teaching. There is a need, however, to bear in mind the various possible issues related to differing learning styles. Some persons do learn better through the conscious application of rules. The understanding about just how far knowledge about language facilitates operation of linguistic systems is as yet unclear. This is particularly important in the case of adult second language learners, since these learners often rely on their ability to rationalize. They consciously use overt understandings of grammar as a handle to facilitate their learning of a second language. But the distinction between "subconscious language acquisition and conscious language learning" (Krashen 1981, 1) is not neat since many processes of conscious language learning, such as error correction and provision of models, are part of normal language acquisition.

Other teachers view "knowledge" as the ability to operate the systems of the language effectively. They place a premium on the ability to use the language rather than to verbalize understandings of how it works. There can be little doubt that where the focus is on communication, the ability to operate the principles is of greater significance. Again, it must be emphasized that there is no clear understanding of the facilitating role which knowledge about language might play in such communication. Adult learners, for instance, and perhaps adolescents as well, are known to perform better if they can identify specific rules by which to take linguistic decisions. Their knowledge about grammar serves as a convenient reference point for editing their linguistic production. In a sufficient number of cases this function is performed with such automaticity that little or no difference in the fluency may be detected between these speakers and those who could be said to have "acquired" the language. There is therefore no conclusive proof that the explicit teaching of grammar and the attention to knowledge about grammar should be rejected entirely in deference to the development of the ability to use grammar. Indeed, explicit focus on grammar might well enhance the process of learning.

Celce-Murcia (1985) suggests that decisions on the teaching of grammar must be made on an informed and rational basis, and she lists as some of these considerations the age of the learners, their cognitive styles, the levels of proficiency desired, the linguistic background of the learners and their purposes for learning the language. Dulay et al. (1982, 94) support this through their claim that "age and personality are individual characteristics of individual learners which have been shown to have a marked effect on second language development".

The following guiding principles might be added to these arguments.

- Although knowledge of grammar, especially explicit knowledge, does not guarantee knowledge of the language and the ability to use it, it is clear that the person who does not know the grammar does not know the language. In other words, to know a language one must have control of the grammar, though one need not have the ability to verbalize that knowledge (Ellis 1994, 230–32).
- For some learners, and in some learning situations, the ability to verbalize grammar knowledge might well enhance the ability to operate the language effectively.
- Grammar is never an end in language learning, but it is a means to an end. The ultimate aim is to use language effectively, accurately and elegantly. This cannot be based solely on the grammar.
- The ability to use the language should never be judged solely on the control of grammar that the user displays. There is the more important need for appropriateness and sensitivity to register.
- Grammar is best acquired through use rather than by rote memorization and explication.
- Acquiring grammar in a relatively restricted context such as a classroom requires sufficient exposure to adequate models. It is this exposure which facilitates the use of linguistic intuitions and acquisition of the underlying grammar principles of the target language.

- Effective language learning and teaching require maximum opportunities to practice. This fact clearly implies that the lecture on grammar is as ineffective a teaching tool as is rote learning of rules, since neither is directly linked to usage. Often students can verbalize rules that they seldom operate.
- Finally, it is important that teachers and learners alike be aware that the grammar of the language impacts on the entire range of interpretation, expression and aesthetics of language. Often, discussions of grammar in relation to language learning and teaching tend to be restricted to considerations of mechanical form and of basic classroom exercises. However, control of grammar, as demonstrated in (a) to (d) below, is critical to all areas of language use.

In examples (a) and (b) below, the speaker exploits the control of grammar to affect the message.

a. He gave the book to his friend. (*not to his sibling*)
b. She gave her friend the book. (*not the pen*)

In (c) and (d), the article is critical to the positive or negative interpretation of the utterance.

c. He has few good ideas. (*negative*)
d. She has a few good ideas. (*positive*)

At the more sophisticated literary levels, the exploitation of grammatical possibilities to achieve a range of different cognitive and affective effects on perspective and other elements clearly indicates that the simple, mechanistic view of the role grammar plays in language is, at best, naive. It is the use of the grammatical possibilities of inversion that lifts the following lines from prose into poetry.

> Earth hath not anything to show *more fair*
> *Dull* would he be of soul who could pass by
> A sight so touching in its majesty.
> (William Wordsworth, "Westminster Bridge")

There therefore appear to be good reasons to pay conscious attention to grammar. First, grammar is the *sine qua non* of language knowledge. The person who does not know the grammar simply does not know the language. This does not necessarily imply that the person who knows the grammar knows the language, since grammar is not the end but the means to the end. The end is efficient, effective communication in all contexts, allowing users to access a wide range of information and to participate meaningfully in many types of interactions.

Grammar also provides a useful principle for organization and sequencing of experiences to facilitate learning and acquisition. Indeed, one of the criticisms made of some other approaches was that they did not display the same level of facility for organizing the learning experience. However, the question of whether such rigid organization is an asset or not is raised by approaches which advocate total immersion. It has even been argued, quite correctly, that the sequencing used in the organization of grammar-based syllabuses is often different from the sequence in which features emerge in the natural setting. This is the logical outcome of attempts to provide a sequence which facilitates pedagogy and learning rather than acquisition.

Ellis (2006, 167) frames the debate in this way:

> Two major questions need to be considered with regard to grammar teaching in second language (L2) pedagogy:
> 1. Should we teach grammar at all?
> 2. If we should teach grammar, how should we teach it?

He notes further that, unlike Krashen and those who hold similar positions on the role of grammar, "others . . . have argued that grammar teaching does aid L2 acquisition". He focuses in particular on grammar as consciousness-raising.

It may be argued further that history and experience are also on the side of grammar-based approaches, since these are known to have worked with a significant enough proportion of language learners to indicate that the approaches do have some level of effectiveness. In addition, although the competing approaches are often superior in their communication focus, none can boast of a production rate as consistently excellent as those grammar-based approaches that are sensitive to the real issues.

## The Caribbean

Two assumptions are basic to current language learning and teaching practice in the Caribbean territories under consideration here. The first of these is the conviction that studies of first language acquisition provide the most appropriate basis for language learning and teaching. The second is that the territories under study here fit neatly into one or another of the language-learning paradigms of first, second or foreign language or second dialect learning. It is the latter with which this chapter takes issue.

There is good reason to regard the language situation in the countries under consideration as unique. While the Caribbean learning environments have some similarity to second and foreign language situations, and even more similarity to what are popularly described as second dialect situations, there is sufficient reason to treat these environments simply as language learning in creolophone contexts. They have a number of features that differentiate them from any of the language-learning contexts identified above. Consequently, any approach that is based on partial similarities is likely to be restricted in its effectiveness.

As Craig (2006, 61) notes, unlike the case of Spanish speakers learning English, "A group of vernacular speakers would find it difficult, unless they have been deliberately trained in language awareness, to recognize the difference between their vernacular and English." It is therefore useful to consider these and those in similar situations as a special sub-group of language learners.

In the Caribbean contexts under consideration here, the first language of the majority of the population is a creole with a lexicon drawn primarily from English or, in the cases of St Lucia and Dominica, from French. The creoles are the languages of widest currency in these societies, even though the language of officialdom, power, upward social mobility and, in certain social circumstances, prestige, is a local or regional standard version of English. There is sufficient lexical, syntactic and even semantic overlap between the popularly used creoles and the target standard to give the impression of a simple dialectal relationship. These similarities often mask fundamental differences and serve to give the creole speaker a false sense of control of the target.

For the Jamaican student, for instance, the following structure might have at least two interpretations.

1. From a girl I learnt to cook.
    a.  A girl taught me to cook. (I learnt to cook *from* a girl.)
    b.  I learnt to cook *since I was a girl*.

The parallel is true of the following structure in Guyana.

2. The boy went running.
    a.  The boy went running. (*ran away*)
    b.  The boy *was* running.

In both of the above examples, the first interpretation is easily compatible with the target language and the second is really a creole sentence masquerading as standard. The real problem is that this kind of correspondence often leads to a false sense of control on the part of the creole speaker.

The distinctions extend to word class membership, as well as to semantics. In a text published by the Guyana Ministry of Education, the following sentence appears below a picture in which a boy and a girl are about to enter a shop.

John and Mary *go in* the shop.

Given the picture stimulus, it is reasonable to assume that the focus is on physical movement. In the creole of that territory, *to go in the shop* does not focus on movement into the shop, but rather on the act of shopping or the purpose for going to the shop. It would be perfectly normal to ask a child to go in the shop for someone. That child would focus on the purpose rather than on physical movement. Similar situations may no doubt be found in several language-learning situations and contexts. However, the range and complexity of such occurrences in creole situations in the Caribbean are beyond those encountered in other situations.

The motivation to learn the official language is affected negatively by the false sense of security and control of standard English. In addition, while it is normal for comprehension of language to exceed production, the gap is much wider in the case of the creole speaker. Because of the partial overlap, creole speakers seem to understand considerably more of the target than they can produce (though the extent of true understanding might be very suspect). It is therefore important to develop approaches that help to disabuse learners of the many false assumptions which characterize creolophone situations.

The problem is not restricted to the learners only. Often the primary stakeholders – parents, planners, trainers of teachers, policy makers – are themselves as misinformed as the language learners themselves.

Apart from low levels of motivation, the limited number of language-learning contexts restricts the degree of exposure to English, thereby reducing the opportunities for modelling and practice and impacting negatively on the learning process. In most instances, there are few opportunities beyond the classroom for further interaction with standard English. Even in the classroom, the model presented may be suspect. The situation is often further compromised by the fact that many classroom teachers are not themselves aware of the issues, and they often perpetuate practices that run counter to their own objectives. According to Craig (2006, 62), "The teachers themselves of vernacular speakers often get carried away by the cognitive or meaning-focused aspects of the English tasks and neglect the focused aspects. . . . but the point is that if both form and meaning are included in the teaching objective, then one portion of the objective should not be attended to while the other position is ignored."

It is not uncommon for teachers, in particular those who are not responsible for the teaching of English, to use the first language of the students as the norm, rather than as a socio-psychological facilitator. These very teachers complain about the inability of students to access information that is presented to them in texts written in English.

The issue is not a simple one, as it involves and sometimes clashes with issues of national self-awareness and a positive linguistic self-concept. In many instances, students are not willing to identify with the persons who use the standard and may therefore serve as models for their own development. For many, speaking standard English is culturally uncomfortable or even unacceptable, representing as it does a way of life that is part of the upper or even foreign social levels and tastes. This position is often reinforced by the existence of sufficient significant models of success among creole speakers who do not appear to have been hampered by their lack of control of English. Such persons might attain the level of folk heroes, and some may even owe their success to their proficiency in Creole rather than English. The considerable international reputations of such icons as Robert Lester Marley (Bob Marley) and Louise Bennett, for instance, rest upon their sophisticated exploitation of the vernacular.

The range of variation between the target and the home language/vernacular is at its widest in the Caribbean classroom. For a few students, the standard might be their home language. For many, the remote creole forms the basis of their daily interactions. For yet others, there is an area of interaction between the two extremes. In any one classroom, therefore, there may be first and second language and second dialect students alongside creole speakers, all taught by the same teacher, who may also have the ability to slide from one variety to the other with some (sometimes unconscious) facility. For each subset of students, there is an equally complex set of beliefs and understandings about what they speak and about its relation to the target.

In such a complex situation, it is imperative that the language teaching issues be as uncluttered as possible if there is to be any significant level of success. Appropriate linguistic development must assert the bona fides of the creole languages. At the same time, realistic ways must be found to ensure competence in the official language.

Finally, in the creole-language contexts under scrutiny, there is little accessible codification of either the creole language or the local standard version of English that is supposed to serve as the target. There is even less clarity about the domains of use. Indeed, in many of these societies, persons with minimal competence in the official language have managed to rise to positions of prominence in a range of areas.

This combination of factors is perhaps unique to the Caribbean. It should therefore be seen as definitive of the Caribbean language-learning context. These factors, more than anything else, justify any attempt to re-examine the role of grammar in the teaching of the official language. The significance of the linguistic background of these learners needs to be given adequate consideration. There is an absolute need to disabuse Caribbean language learners of their false sense of linguistic competence if the right attitudes to acquiring the standard are to be encouraged. The most secure way to do so is through the use of conscious focus on grammar.

For the Caribbean student trying to develop competence in standard English, an overt focus on grammar is necessary if the desired levels of accuracy, fluency and elegance are to be attained. The knowledge of grammar will help the learner to recognize the fundamental differences between the creole with which he or she has great facility and the target. This explicit knowledge will provide a convenient reference point for motivating those who could easily be misled about their levels of control of English by improving the levels of conscious awareness of the difference between the two.

## Issues of Application

It is not the aim of this chapter to deal with classroom solutions in any detail, but it is important to give some indication of possible courses of action. Appropriate action should not be left to chance. The following issues are therefore raised for consideration.

Teachers of standard English must be properly informed on the total language situation in their particular territories and on the implications of the special relationship between the local creole and the target language. In addition, they should themselves be good models of the standard, since in all likelihood they will represent the only consistent model to which students are guaranteed exposure. What this indicates is the necessity for teachers of English in creole situations to have a high level of linguistic training to facilitate their classroom practice at all levels.

As far as grammar teaching is concerned, teachers may be guided by a few principles. On the question of the selection of grammar, choices could be guided by the notion of necessity and usefulness. The grammar points selected ought to reflect an awareness of those forms which students do not control or which have considerable potential for misinterpretation and misuse as a result of the close parallels between the two systems. The intention here is to ensure that all instances of misinterpretation and misunderstanding are resolved through the promotion of fluent, accurate English usage.

In order to ensure this, the information presented to students should be clear and accurate. A good example is the rule for pluralization in English. Since creoles do not pluralize in the same ways in which English does, and especially since the more widely used form in English is determined by sound, it is important that the correct English rules be understood. One popular traditional grammar book says it in this unfortunate way: "Add 's' or 'es' if you find you cannot *say* 's'" (my emphasis). The rule is inaccurate and misleading.

In the first place, the rule for English is more comprehensively captured by recognizing that voicing and the presence of sibilants in the final position of the root combine to determine which of the several suffixes is used: /s/ after voiceless nonsibilants, as in *cat/s/*; /z/ after vowels and voiced nonsibilants, as in *bag/z/*; and /iz/ after sibilants, as in *church/iz/* and *bridg/iz/*.

Second, adding *-s* or *-es*, which are written symbols, if you cannot *say* "s" seems to conflate speech with writing. At any rate, it is easy enough to say "s" after the vowels, but the pronunciation is a voiced sound.

The creole speaker has special problems here. In creole, there is a tendency to simplify consonantal clusters. Pluralization in English produces a number of the precise clusters that creoles tend to avoid. Awareness of this fact could facilitate the control of both localization and concord, problems that are so highly stigmatized in creole speakers' attempts to use English.

In order to ensure that learners fully grasp the usefulness of the exercises, all grammar teaching should focus on the meaningfulness of the element being taught. This implies that no grammar teaching should focus exclusively on formal accuracy but should extend to the coverage of meaning and the significance of the particular form. A useful consideration here would be to ensure that grammar points are always introduced and used in a meaningful context. This should be further strengthened by ensuring that the student is provided with sufficient opportunity to practise the use of any aspect of grammar in realistic communication settings, rather than as empty form.

## Summary

The essential argument of this chapter is that the teaching of English in creole contexts in the Caribbean requires some explicit attention to the teaching of grammar. However, there is a need for a clear understanding of the nature of grammar and of what it means to teach grammar. It is also argued that the Caribbean contexts are sufficiently different from other types of language learning situations to warrant specific attention to grammar. These considerations are seen to have far-reaching implications for teachers of English in the region with regard to their preparation and their practice.

## References

Brown, Roger. 1973. *A First Language: The Early Stages*. Cambridge, MA: Harvard University Press.

Brumfit, Christopher. 1984. *Communicative Methodology in Language Teaching: The Roles of Fluency and Accuracy*. Cambridge: Cambridge University Press.

Celce-Murcia, Marianne. 1985. Making Informed Decisions about the Role of Grammar in Language Teaching. *TESOL Newsletter* 19 (1).

Celce-Murcia, Marianne, and Sharon Hilles. 1988. *Techniques and Resources in Teaching Grammar*. New York: Oxford University Press.

Chomsky, Noam. 1957. *Syntactic Structures*. Gravenhage: Mouton.

———. 1965. *Aspects of a Theory of Syntax*. Cambridge, MA: MIT Press.

Craig, Dennis R. 2006. *Teaching Language and Literacy to Caribbean Students: From Vernacular to Standard English*. Kingston: Ian Randle.

Crystal, David. 1990. *The Cambridge Encyclopedia of Language*. Cambridge: Cambridge University Press.

Dulay, Heidi, Marina Burt, and Stephen Krashen. 1982. *Language Two*. New York: Oxford University Press.

Ellis, Rod. 1985. *Understanding Second Language Education*. Oxford: Oxford University Press.

———. 2002. Grammar Teaching-Practice or Consciousness Raising. In *Methodology in Language Teaching*, edited by Jack Richards and Willy A. Renandya, 167–74. Cambridge: Cambridge University Press.

Hymes, Dell. 1971. *On Communicative Competence*. Philadelphia: University of Pennsylvania Press.

Krashen, Stephen D. 1981. *Second Language Acquisition and Second Language Learning*. Oxford: Pergamon.

McKay, Sandra. 1990. Language Minority Education in Great Britain: A Challenge to Current US Policy. TESOL *Quarterly* 24 (3): 385–405.

Richards, Jack C. 1985. *The Context of Language Teaching*. Cambridge: Cambridge University Press.

# 9 | The Landing Point: The Bilingual Education Project and the Grade 4 (2008) Results

HUBERT DEVONISH AND KAREN CARPENTER
*University of the West Indies, Mona*

## The Stakes

The stakes were high. The 1953 UNESCO report on the use of the mother tongue in education (UNESCO 1953) raised the question of the role of Caribbean creole languages in this domain. At that time, the focus was Haiti. By the time of the Conference on Creole Language Studies that was held in Jamaica in 1959, the discussion had spread to the Commonwealth Caribbean. The matter was hotly debated at an open forum held during that conference and documented by Le Page (1961). This became the platform from which a large body of research would issue (e.g., Carrington 1978; Craig 1999). This research had as its central focus children who were native speakers of a creole language lexically related to English. The primary question was how conditions could be created which would allow such children to acquire effective and consistent control of English, the official language of education.

The need for a new model was the result of the overall failure of the "English as a mother tongue" approach. This had not produced large enough numbers of school leavers with the requisite levels of competence in English. The researchers viewed themselves as seeking language-education solutions for the education systems of the emerging independent Commonwealth Caribbean of the 1960s to 1980s. They generally viewed these systems as in crisis in relation to English-language teaching and learning.

This body of work made certain assumptions to begin with. One was that the public would not accept the formal use of a creole language in school as a language of instruction, a subject of instruction and a medium for acquiring and using literacy. The other was that creole languages did not have sufficient autonomy in relation to English, because of the supposed existence of a continuum relationship between creole and English. This, according to the received wisdom, would prevent English-lexicon creoles from being formally used in education in those countries where English was the official state language and language of education. This was often linked to the absence of a widely accepted standard writing system for these creole languages.

Some important consequences came out of these initial assumptions. Nearly all of this pioneering research work was directed at how Craig's (1999) monoliterate transitional bilingual (MTB) approach could be implemented. This was an approach which allowed for the oral use of the children's native language, creole, in the formal education system, but not for its use in writing. The greatest and most visible impact of this research on policy was the Ministry of Education, Youth and Culture (MOEYC) of Jamaica's language education policy (2001). This policy document was eventually tabled in parliament as the official policy on language education.

The language education policy (MOEYC 2001) both reviewed and benefited from the mass of preceding research on the subject. It proposed, as the preceding research had, that an MTB approach was the only viable option. The policy did accept that full bilingualism or biliterate transitional bilingualism were ideal for the Jamaican situation. These options, however, were impractical. Like the research on which it was based, the policy document made the assumption that Jamaican society would not accept formal use of Jamaican in writing. There was, in any case, according to the document, no standard writing system for Jamaican (Creole).

One response to the language education policy was a proposal for the 2004 Bilingual Education Project (BEP), spearheaded by the Jamaican Language Unit. The proposal sought to implement, with the endorsement of the MOEYC, a trial of the fully bilingual approach with a view to demonstrating that it could and should be implemented at the primary school level. The BEP proposal was sceptical of the received wisdom that the public would resist the implementation of a programme using Jamaican alongside English as a formal medium of instruction, as a subject and as a medium of acquiring and exercising literacy skills in schools. This scepticism was subsequently supported by the results of the 2005 National Language Attitude Survey of Jamaica (Jamaican Language

Unit, 2005). The BEP proposal also challenged the assumptions that there was no standard writing system for Jamaican and that the language did not have the resources to be used in technical, educated discourse.

The proposal put forward the details of a fully bilingual education project for three primary schools in Jamaica. The point of the project would be to establish that options such as full bilingualism and transitional biliterate bilingualism, identified as ideal but impractical by the language education policy, could in fact be implemented. The justification for the project was to demonstrate that a fully bilingual programme could be implemented in an effective and sustainable manner. Once this could be established, official language-education policy would be free to implement the approaches which it considered ideal. The ideal would have been made practical.

## The Theoretical Background

There was a central argument for implementing the project in the form of a fully bilingual programme, which was that it developed among children a competence in both Jamaican and English, the two languages widely used in Jamaica. This justification was supplemented by reference to the numerous claims in the literature about the cognitive benefits of bilingual education (Craig 1999; Cummins 1979; Scribner and Cole 1981). The proposal used some of the best-documented pieces of research in that area, those based on the seven hundred thousand records of minority students in the United States researched by Thomas and Collier (1997, 2002; Collier and Thomas 2004). Thomas and Collier (1997, 53–55) were able to show that fully bilingual education predicts high academic performance, not only in the languages themselves, but across all subjects. Programmes in which both languages were maintained throughout the entire education process, and were given equal roles and functions, were shown to produce the best academic outcomes. They showed superior results to those produced by programmes that adopted either transitionally bilingual or English as a second language methodologies. This influenced the design of the BEP in Jamaica. It was designed to be fully bilingual, studiously avoiding those features characteristic of transitional programmes.

The bilingual nature of Jamaica and regions with similar language environments had been seen by linguists, including Craig (1971, 1999), and by educators as a "problem" which had to be overcome by research and improved teaching methodology. The position taken against the background of Thomas and Collier's (1997) research was that the existence of two widely used languages within Jamaica was an advantage which the education system should benefit from. The language situation provided children in the society with the opportunity to enjoy the cognitive advantages which come from fully bilingual, as opposed to transitional bilingual, education.

It is worth noting that the model of full bilingual education adopted for the BEP, involving the equal and continuing use of both languages, has come to be called "dual language education" (Torres-Guzmán 2002). We shall, however, for the purposes of this chapter, retain the term "full bilingual education", in keeping with the terminology used in the original proposal.

## The Project Design

In 2004, the Jamaican Language Unit at the University of the West Indies, Mona, approached the MOEYC about a project that would implement full bilingual education in a small group of schools. It was designed to address the primary concerns expressed in the MOEYC's 2001 language education policy about the formal use of Jamaican, namely:

1. the lack of a standard writing system for the teaching of Jamaican (otherwise referred to by the ministry as the "home language");
2. the absence of written teaching material in Jamaican; and
3. the perceived lack of public support for children being educated in Jamaican.

There was an implied additional concern: Do the demonstrated advantages of fully bilingual education in countries outside of the Caribbean transfer to the peculiar language situation of Jamaica? Even though this question was not raised in the language education policy as a concern (MOEYC 2001), the reluctance to contemplate bilingual education can be assumed to be partly due to such reservations.

Ideally, the BEP should have covered six years of education. Some of the best research on the subject had indicated that pupils had to have been in fully bilingual education for between five and seven years before the positive impact of bilingual education could begin to be measured (Thomas and Collier 1997). However, based on the advice and wishes of the MOEYC, there had to be a modification in the original concept. The BEP would be implemented over grades 1 to 4, and the project would last four years.

The real judgement of the project would be in the answer to the question of the actual success of full bilingual education in Jamaica. Therefore, shortening the time span ran the risk of there being, at the end of the project, results which showed no benefit to the project's pupils. In fact, there was a strong chance that they would still be showing a deficit relative to those pupils outside the BEP. Such a result would have been pounced on by those hostile to the approach as proof that the method was ineffective.

The Jamaican Language Unit was faced with the chance of missing the opportunity to implement the BEP while waiting on perfect conditions. We had no choice but to gamble.


## Official Approval

In early 2004, the Jamaican Language Unit made a formal proposal for implementation of the BEP in three primary schools, to involve full bilingual education for four years in the two main languages of the society, Jamaican and English. This required the sanction of the MOEYC, and the latter granted permission for a BEP pilot project to go ahead in the three primary schools. The (then) minister of education, youth and culture herself, Maxine Henry-Wilson, expressed support for the project in person and gave it her blessing. The official letter from the ministry stated that it was "very pleased to be associated with the work undertaken by the Jamaican Language Unit. We fully endorse your proposal to conduct a pilot project in Bilingual education for primary school children enrolled in grades 1–4 in three institutions" (MOEYC 2004).

The following year, Henry-Wilson was interviewed by a newspaper reporter who was in the process of collecting information for an article which turned out to be quite sympathetic to the project:

> But Henry-Wilson, though acknowledging that while the new education policy speaks to some of the issues discussed by the researchers, was noncommittal on implementing bilingual instruction on a formal scale after Devonish's project wraps up in 2008. . . . "They are doing some fieldwork through the formal education system and we would like to see whether in fact the views expressed are true, that is, whether they will prove that the students would be more productive," said the education minister. . . . "But we must be mindful that English is a global language; Patois isn't," she added. . . . "India has their local dialect, but the country recognises the importance of speaking English. . . . One of the assets we need to optimise is that we do have English as a formal language, it's universal,

and we need to ensure that our children are able to mine that advantage." (Arlene Martin-Wilkins, "The Patwa Experience . . . Mek wi trai di patwa", *Sunday Observer*, 20 November 2005)

The honourable minister's commitment, or lack thereof, to implementing bilingual instruction more generally was, as she stated in the article, dependent on "whether they prove that the students would be more productive". Her definition of what constituted "more productive" was clear: it was the children's ability to function in English. She had, after all, expounded on the glorious advantages afforded globally to speakers of English. The BEP proposal had stressed the potential advantages of the project for the children's cognitive development and had addressed the prospect of improved mastery of content subjects. However, given the role which competence in English plays in the social hierarchy of Jamaica, the effect of the BEP in that area was critical. It was this which would determine support for or opposition to a more general implementation of the bilingual approach.

## Project Promises

The BEP was a pilot project in full bilingual education for primary-school pupils. It would track, over a period of four years, cohorts of children who were taught in a full bilingual programme from the time of their entry into grade 1 until the end of grade 4. The project was aimed at determining the most effective means of encouraging full bilingualism for the primary level in Jamaican (Jamaican Creole) and standard Jamaican English (SJE). The promises it made which are relevant to the present chapter were as follows:

- The BEP would, at a minimum, do no harm, notably to pupils' competence in English.
- The BEP would produce an increase in language arts skill levels in English among pupils within the project relative to those in traditional modes of instruction.
- The BEP would produce an increase in absolute literacy levels of pupils in the project, as manifested in their literacy in their native language, Jamaican, as compared with the literacy levels of non-project pupils for whom English was the only language of literacy.

The BEP was planned to run for four years. It began in May 2004 with the training of teachers, and bilingual instruction in the schools commenced the following September. All participation was on a voluntary basis on the part of schools, specific teachers and parents of pupils. Parents were also briefed on the nature of the project and individual written consent was sought for the inclusion of the children in the four-year process. The BEP was initially quite ambitious, and by its second year it included four schools and some six streams. By the third year, in spite of expressed agreement to the contrary, school internal reorganization and streaming had taken place, which compromised the internal composition of the groups of children who were originally part of the project. This made it difficult to identify groups of children who were in continuous receipt of bilingual instruction. For purposes of ensuring the validity in the findings, research for the project had to focus on what by the beginning of the fourth year was the only group of students who had had four consecutive years of bilingual instruction. These children had begun with the BEP in grade 1 of their primary education and had continued in the project through grade 4.

Each year of the project was divided into four separate phases: (1) translation of teaching materials; (2) teacher training in bilingual delivery; (3) implementation within the schools; and (4) project evaluation.

## Measuring the Results: The Grade 4 Literacy Tests

### Time Is of the Essence

The issue of time was critical given the short duration of the project: four years rather than the preferred six. The BEP fitted the description of what Collier and Thomas (2004) call a "one-way enrichment dual language programme" – that is, a programme which is fully bilingual in L1 and L2, and in which all of the children have the same L1. This fact was significant and of concern to the project designers since, with reference to the enormous body of data collected on such programmes in the United States, Collier and Thomas (2004, 5) noted, "In every study conducted, we have consistently found that it takes six to eight years for ELLs [English-language learners] to reach grade level in L2, and only one-way or two-way enrichment dual language programs have closed the gap in this length of time. No other program has closed the gap in this length of time." These findings were similar to those made in Thomas and Collier (1997, 36, 53).

Collier and Thomas (2004, 5) further stressed the limitations of all programmes that were not "dual language". None of these had been able to close, in the long term, more than half of the achievement gap with native English speakers. Native speakers of English continued to improve their language competence in their L1, even while English-language learners tried to catch up with them. L1 speakers of English presented a constantly moving target. English-language L2 learners, therefore, could only close the gap by making more than one year's worth of progress in their L2 with every year of schooling. It was this which the children in the dual language enhancement programmes studied by Collier and Thomas (2004) had achieved. This fact made such programmes stand out relative to all other programme types, such as transitional bilingualism and English as a second language.

The moving-target issue did not present the same problem for the dual language BEP that it would have elsewhere. The hoped-for positive results for the four-year course of the BEP lay in the nature of the comparison group in the Jamaican context. It was not L1 speakers of English who were being taught monolingually in their L1. Rather, it was the non-project children of the same grade within the same primary school. These, like the BEP group, were not native speakers of English and had Jamaican as their L1. This latter group was being taught using a hybrid of approaches, including that of English as a Mother Tongue. They as a target were not, therefore, moving as quickly as they would have had they been native speakers of English. This made the four-year target date marginally more achievable than otherwise might have been the case.

## The Test Instruments

The Grade 4 Literacy Test is part of the normal annual evaluation activities of the MOEYC. It is administered toward the end of the school year, in the May–June period. It is nationally administered and used as a guide to the literacy competence of children at grade 4. In cases where children fail the test, a ministry-mandated intervention takes place to get the children to a point where they pass the test and can move on to grade 5. The BEP administrators were interested in the results of tests administered in the May–June 2008 period, the time at which the BEP pupils and their non-BEP counterparts would have completed grade 4.

In the case of the BEP children, there were areas of literacy competence not measured by the national tests: namely, their literacy competence in Jamaican.

The BEP pupils were, in the period of May–June 2008, given a Grade 4 Language Arts and Literacy Test in Jamaican. It was designed to conform as closely as possible in form and difficulty level to the equivalent national Grade 4 (English-language) Literacy Test being administered to the BEP children in that year.

The test was in two parts. The first, which we will call Test 1, consisted of word recognition and reading comprehension components. Test 2 involved two writing tasks.

The word recognition section had forty questions. Twenty of these required pupils to match the picture with the correct word, involving a choice from a list of four words. For the other twenty questions, students were expected to match the word with the correct picture, selecting one of four pictures.

The reading comprehension component had seven passages and thirty questions in total. Students were required to read the passages carefully before choosing their answers from the possible A, B, C or D.

In Test 2, there were two writing tasks. In task 1, pupils were asked to complete a registration form to join their local library. Task 2 was a letter writing activity. Students who used Standard Jamaican English in the writing task were penalized as the test was in Jamaican Creole and all questions and answers were to be given in that language.

The marking scheme for Test 2 was based on the MOEYC's training package for writing tasks, which gave relevant guidelines on the marking of writing tasks for the official English-language version of the test. Based on the guidelines and the quality of their work, the pupils were then assigned levels of mastery, from one to four, for each task, in a manner similar to that done for the equivalent official English-language test.

## Results and Analysis: The Grade 4 Literacy Test

Let us examine first the pattern of highest scores across the tests for the two groups.

**Table 9.1:** Mean Scores on Grade 4 Language Arts Test 1 (Jamaican and English)

|  | BEP Jamaican | BEP English | Non-BEP English |
| --- | --- | --- | --- |
| **Word Recognition (/40)** | 36.6 (91.50%) | 36.94 (92.35%) | 37.46 (93.65%) |
| **Reading Comprehension (/30)** | 15.77 (52.56%) | 18.06 (60.2%) | 17.635 (58.78%) |

**Table 9.2:** Mean Scores on Grade 4 Language Arts Test 2 (Jamaican and English)

|  | BEP Jamaican | BEP English | Non-BEP English |
|---|---|---|---|
| **Writing 1 (/4)** | 3.17 (79.17%) | 3.176 (79.4%) | 3.216 (80.04%) |
| **Writing 2 (/4)** | 2.67 (66.67%) | 2.5 (62.5%) | 2.635 (65.88%) |

In word recognition, the non-BEP English group received the highest mean score of the three. In the case of reading comprehension, on the other hand, it was the BEP English mean score that came out the highest, over those for non-BEP English and, surprisingly, BEP Jamaican. In writing task 1, the highest score went to non-BEP English, while in task 2, the highest score went to BEP Jamaican.

One can also analyse the data from the perspective of absolute literacy skills achieved. We see that in Test 1, the word recognition score for non-BEP English is 1.3 per cent ahead of the next highest, that for BEP English. In the case of reading comprehension, by contrast, the score for BEP English is ahead of the next highest score, that for non-BEP English, by 1.42 per cent. In Test 2, writing task 1, the non-BEP English performance is very marginally ahead of that for BEP English, by 0.64 per cent. By contrast, in the case of writing task 2, the BEP Jamaican performance is ahead of the next highest, that for non-BEP English, by 0.79 per cent. This suggests that in absolute terms, the BEP group and the non-BEP group have about equal levels of performance, but these levels are distributed differently: the BEP group is strongest in English reading comprehension and Jamaican writing task 2, and the non-BEP group leads in English word recognition and English writing task 1. Viewed differently, however, the BEP group as a whole is showing literacy in two languages, while the non-BEP group demonstrates literacy in only one.

The other perspective from which to view the data is that of which group has demonstrated the highest levels of literacy in English. In this case, the non-BEP group has the lead in three of the four areas, with a maximum lead of 3.38 per cent. The BEP group leads in the fourth area by 1.42 per cent. In order to get a better picture, we could find the mean of the four percentage scores for each component of the test for each group. If we treat the four test parts as having the same weighting, we would end up with non-BEP in the lead with 74.59 per cent, BEP English with 73.61 per cent and BEP Jamaican with 72.48 per cent. The non-BEP group is marginally in the lead, ahead of BEP English by less than 1 per cent, with BEP Jamaican coming up 1.1 per cent behind BEP English.

Looking at these figures, the question arises as to the effect of the BEP intervention. It is clear that the performance of the BEP group in English was about normal for the particular school, by comparison with the non-BEP group. This occurred in spite of the fact that the actual exposure to English of the BEP group would, at least in principle, have been less than that of the non-BEP group. Exposure to English in the BEP classroom would have been shared significantly with Jamaican, by comparison with the non-BEP classes, where English would have been the dominant if not sole language of instruction. The BEP group, by this stage, does not show any deficit relative to the non-BEP group.

Certain conclusions are clear. The period that it has taken for the L2 scores of the BEP group to catch up with the non-BEP group, four years, is shorter than might have been expected from the literature. The time ranges predicted, as identified by Thomas and Collier over time, were, respectively, five to seven years (1997), four to seven years (2002) and six to eight years (Collier and Thomas 2004). The BEP results for Jamaica provide circumstantial evidence supporting the view of Craig (1999) that situations such as those involving a traditionally low-status creole language and a lexically related high-status European language are special. They create peculiar handicaps for the learning of English, as compared to other language learning situations. The fact that the BEP group was on par with the non-BEP group at least as early as year four suggests that the non-BEP approach was particularly ineffective. This amplifies the positive effect of the fully bilingual approach.

The similarity of the BEP pupils' mean score in English to that of the non-BEP group is of importance if we accept the model of progression in bilingual education presented by Thomas and Collier (2002) and Collier and Thomas (2004).

## A Note on Gender Effects

The issue of gender has been invoked as one which has significant effects on learning outcomes in the formal education system in Jamaica. There might be some insight to be gained, therefore, in examining the results according to gender. The statistics are presented below in tables 9.3 to 9.6.

When we analyse the results according to gender, non-BEP females performed the best of all groups on word recognition and writing tasks 1 and 2. BEP males, however, performed the best on reading comprehension.

The group that did not lead the pack on any of the sections of the test was non-BEP males. They, in fact, had the lowest performance of all four groups in

**Table 9.3:** Mean Scores by Gender on Grade 4 Literacy Test 1 (Jamaican and English), Females

|  | BEP Jamaican | BEP English | Non-BEP English |
|---|---|---|---|
| Word Recognition (/40) | 36.65 (91.62%) | 37.12 (92.79%) | 38.89 (97.23%) |
| Reading Comprehension (/30) | 16.76 (55.88%) | 17.71 (59.02%) | 17.79 (59.29%) |

**Table 9.4:** Mean Scores by Gender on Grade 4 Literacy Test 1 (Jamaican and English), Males

|  | BEP Jamaican | BEP English | Non-BEP English |
|---|---|---|---|
| Word Recognition (/40) | 36.54 (91.54%) | 36.76 (91.91%) | 36.59 (91.47%) |
| Reading Comprehension (/30) | 14.46 (48.21%) | 18.41 (61.37%) | 17.09 (56.96%) |

**Table 9.5:** Mean Scores by Gender on Grade 4 Literacy Test 2 (Jamaican and English), Females

|  | BEP Jamaican | BEP English | Non-BEP English |
|---|---|---|---|
| Writing 1 (/4) | 3.29 (82.35%) | 3.29 (82.35%) | 3.46 (86.61%) |
| Writing 2 (/4) | 2.71 (67.65%) | 2.59 (64.71%) | 2.82 (70.54%) |

**Table 9.6:** Mean Scores by Gender on Grade 4 Literacy Test 2 (Jamaican and English), Males

|  | BEP Jamaican | BEP English | Non-BEP English |
|---|---|---|---|
| Writing 1 (/4) | 3.00 (75.00%) | 3.06 (76.47%) | 3.07 (76.63%) |
| Writing 2 (/4) | 2.62 (65.38%) | 2.41 (60.29%) | 2.52 (63.04%) |

three of the four sections. In the fourth, writing task 2, they did manage to out-perform the BEP English males by a tiny margin. However, for that component, it was the BEP Jamaican males who submitted the highest scores, with a lead of 2.34 per cent over non-BEP English.

The above points to a trend also observed in relation to other data, most notably the performances on the Grade 3 Language Arts Diagnostic Test, the results of which are discussed by Devonish and Carpenter (forthcoming). In the grade 4 test, again, we find the following pattern: non-BEP females perform the best, followed by BEP females, then BEP males and then, bringing up the rear, non-BEP males.

Judging by such data, the BEP intervention seems to have had the most positive effect on males. These results raise the tantalizing prospect of gender-specific language-education policies within the Jamaican education system. Do we have here an indication that, while benefiting boys, the BEP does little or nothing for girls' language development? Given the association of Jamaican with non-conformity and English with conformity, is formal use of Jamaican the means of addressing male alienation from the education system? And if so, and given that such alienation does not seem to be as significant a problem for females, does it mean that dual language/bilingual programmes of the BEP type might have to be implemented on a gender-specific basis? These are interesting questions requiring further research.

## Conclusion

The BEP did achieve the first of its promises, that of doing no harm. This could be measured by the fact that the BEP pupils' performance on the Grade 4 Literacy Test was on par with that of their non-BEP grade cohort in the project school. This achievement, made within four years, has to be appreciated in the context of the five-to-seven-year time range that past bilingual/dual language programmes have required to demonstrate their positive effects. The results of the BEP also have to be evaluated against the background that students schooled solely in English initially make dramatic gains in the early grades, whatever type of programme they are in, and this misleads teachers and administrators into assuming that the students are going to continue to do extremely well (Thomas and Collier 1997, 34).

The results of the Grade 4 Literacy Test in English show that the ambition of achieving the same gains as those promised by a six-year programme were not realized in the four-year BEP project. The English-language competence of the BEP pupils was not greater than that of the non-BEP group by the end of four years.

In all this, the major achievement of the BEP was to demonstrate that a fully bilingual programme involving the use of an English-lexicon creole and English could be implemented in a Caribbean setting. Its main goal, which was to document the steps that need to be taken to do this, has also been achieved. The debate around the actual implementation of such a programme on a national scale has just begun.

## References

Carrington, Lawrence D. 1978. Language Problems in Schools of Today. *Trinidad and Tobago Review* (January).

Collier, Virginia P., and Wayne P. Thomas. 2004. The Astounding Effectiveness of Dual Language Education for All. *NABE Journal of Research and Practice* 2 (1): 1–20.

Craig, Dennis R. 1971. Education and Creole English in the West Indies: Some Sociolinguistic Factors. In *Pidginization and Creolization of Languages*, edited by D. Hymes, 371–91. Cambridge: Cambridge University Press.

———. 1999. *Teaching Language and Literacy: Policies and Procedures for Vernacular Situations*. Georgetown, Guyana: Education and Development Services.

Cummins, James. 1979. Linguistic Interdependence and the Educational Development of Bilingual Children. In *Review of Educational Research* 49 (2): 222–51.

Jamaican Language Unit. 2005. *The National Language Attitude Survey of Jamaica*. Kingston: University of the West Indies. http://www.mona.uwi.edu/dllp/jlu/project.

Le Page, Robert, ed. 1961. *Creole Language Studies II: Proceedings of the Conference on Creole Language Studies* (University of the West Indies, Mona, 1959). London: Macmillan.

MOEYC (Ministry of Education, Youth and Culture). 2001. Draft language education policy. Typescript.

———. 2004. Letter from the permanent secretary. 6 May.

Scribner, Sylvia, and Michael Cole. 1981. *The Psychology of Literacy*. Cambridge, MA: Harvard University Press.

Thomas, Wayne P., and Virginia P. Collier. 1997. School Effectiveness for Language Minority Students. Washington, DC: National Clearinghouse for Bilingual Education.

———. 2002. A National Study of School Effectiveness for Language Minority Students' Long-Term Academic Achievement. Berkeley: Center for Research on Education, Diversity and Excellence, eScholarship Repository, University of California. http://repositories.cdlib.org/crede/finalrpts/1_1_final.

Torres-Guzmán, María E. 2002. Dual Language Programs: Key Features and Results. *Directions in Language Education* 14 (Spring): 1–16.

# 10 | The Varilingual Language Use of Trinidadian Secondary-School Teachers

VALERIE YOUSSEF
*University of the West Indies, St Augustine*

There is much debate concerning the status of and relationship among different language varieties throughout the Caribbean. All territories share the co-existence of standard and creole varieties of language, but the ways in which these varieties interact vary tremendously, sometimes cutting across lexifier languages, as in a territory like St Lucia where a French Creole coexists with standard English (SE) and an anglophone mesolect, and, more frequently, embracing the interaction between one or two creole varieties and a co-lexifier standard, as in Jamaica. In addition, the range of language competence across the contact languages and the levels of code-mixing are both highly variable.

In these situations, children have been found to have difficulty upon entering school if they are taught exclusively in a standard variety that is not the native language variety of the majority; considerable time has been spent by language education experts, including most particularly the late scholar, linguist and educator Professor Dennis Craig (e.g., 1971, 1976, 1999, 2006), to devise education systems that will allow students to most effectively acquire two and sometimes three varieties, including the local standard. The role of teachers and their language in these situations is clearly crucial; they are often held responsible for their students' so-called language failure by those outside of the school system. A poor work ethic is often cited, as is language incompetence; it is argued by laypeople in these societies that the teachers themselves do not know standard language, much less how to teach it. Older persons hark back to "the good old days" when standard language use was enforced by the use of "bamboo" and children, at least those who survived in the system, "really learned Standard". All of this is highly speculative, both with regard to language use in schools and also with regard to the specific competence of teachers; while there have been two major studies of language attitudes of teachers in Trinidad and Tobago, namely by Winford (1976) and Mühleisen (2001), teacher language has not been investigated systematically until very recently (cf. Deuber and Youssef 2007; Mohammed 2008).

My concern in this chapter is to describe the language varieties used by Trinidadian secondary-school teachers in their classrooms. In the community at large, contexts for production of standard English are minimal, and classroom interaction provides the most consistent space for potential development of this variety. A study conducted by students of the University of the West Indies' Special Project in Linguistics class during the academic year 2006–7, however, indicated that for the most part, teachers *do* use standard English, although their speech includes some switching to mesolectal Trinidadian Creole (TC), usually as appropriate to very specific contexts of interaction with their students. They exhibit what I have elsewhere described as varilingual competence (e.g., Youssef 1996), such that their inter-varietal language production is a manifestation of a coherent whole, applicable to their roles as educators in a twenty-first-century Caribbean sociolinguistic complex. The concurrent study completed by Mohammed corroborates the findings of this study in a remarkable way.

## The Caribbean Linguistic Milieu

Linguists even outside the Caribbean are familiar with the notion of a post-creole continuum, which has been used to describe language situations in which a creole language interfaces with a standard. This notion was explicated by DeCamp (1971) at a conference held in 1970 at the Mona campus of the University of the West Indies, which resulted in a seminal text out of the papers presented there, entitled *Pidginization and Creolization of Languages* (Hymes 1971). Within that text, DeCamp described the continuum construct as embracing the interface between an acrolect (standard variety), a mesolect (midway between creole and standard) and a basilect (a deep creole variety, usually mutually unintelligible with the standard). Jamaica and Guyana were the particular societies most readily described by this model, which argued for unidirectional and ongoing change towards the standard in the course of time; it was also argued that a continuum could only exist in circumstances within which the lexifier code was consistent across the different language varieties.

Since that time, the construct has been modified both through theoretical reinterpretation and through observation and description of actual language situations. Derek Bickerton (1975) devised a method of measuring the linguistic progress of persons across the continuum space using an implicational scale model which he applied specifically to the Guyanese context, but others, like Carrington (1980), argued that the continuum model could not mirror reality, which was necessarily multidimensional, allowing for variation at any point on the continuum as well as along it.

Time has indicated the capacity for relative stabilization of Caribbean language situations in circumstances in which the varieties each have strong functional value. The creole has proven to have tremendous functional value as the code of solidarity, emotion and nationalistic awareness and representation. It is not moving into extinction but is vibrant and increasingly used, at least at the mesolectal level. A study conducted by Youssef (2001) in Tobago indicated that older educated persons used more standard than young people, who appeared to have latched on to the mesolect as their preferred variety. Furthermore, a continuum has been shown to develop cross-linguistically in territories like St Lucia, with an English-lexifier mesolect developing between the French Creole basilect and the standard English acrolect (Simmons-McDonald 2008).

For countries like Trinidad and Barbados, it has been argued that the continuum spans the interaction of two varieties: a mesolect and an acrolect. Winford's (1972) major study of language use in Trinidad used Labov's classic sociolinguistic method to investigate, define and delineate the varieties used in Trinidad. He studied two communities, one rural and one urban, and found predictable patterns of style-shifting across four socio-economic levels; he made a significant argument for the creole having a separate system of predication from English (Winford 1988), a major break with Labovian theory (Labov 1972), which had thus far posited a common underlying system in the contact varieties investigated. In so doing, Winford brought discussion of what really constitutes a speech community into reconsideration in the Caribbean context, arguing that it was a shared set of linguistic norms which defined such a situation rather than the capacity to produce the norms, which is extremely variable among speakers. An individual attending a funeral or going for a job interview, for example, would know exactly what varieties he or she should appropriate even without necessarily being able to actually produce them.

The realistic description of language competence was posited as varilingual by Youssef (1990) in assessing the emerging language competence of small children differentially exposed to the creole and the standard in Trinidad. She found that the acquisition of language went hand in hand with the capacity to mix language varieties effectively according to the language situation in which each child found him- or herself. While each child's balance of production was different, since it depended explicitly on his or her previous language exposure, there was no delay at all in the development of the capacity to vary language with acute stylistic sensitivity. Subsequently, the model was extended and applied to adult speakers' language competence and production in both Trinidad and Tobago (Youssef 1996). Its defining characteristics include full or partial competence in two or three codes, and the capacity to code-switch among them. However, the model acknowledges that it is possible for competence in one code to be only partial, although full or partial competence in all is not excluded. Youssef noted that the linguistic situation is so intensely mixed, and between varieties that historically have been increasingly closely related, that it is not always possible to posit a matrix language as Myers-Scotton's (1996) did for code-switching societies like Kenya, where intense switching entails dissimilar languages in contact. In Trinidad and Tobago, a standard verb form may co-occur with a creole pronominal and a creole word ordering, as in "Allyuh asked him to stay?", making any pronouncement on the sentence as ultimately creole or standard nigh impossible. Additionally, present-tense forms, save for the third-person singular, are identical in their unmarkedness in both varieties.

Further, though an individual may use a preponderance of creole or standard features in a particular context, the appropriate blend of varieties is what is critical to his or her language performance and competence. To assess the language performance of such an individual as standard but displaying creole features, and to go further to surmise that the mix is owing to a lack of full competence in the standard, would be to miss the mark entirely. The creole is most often used at contextually strategic points to maximize communicative efficiency.

## The Language Education Situation

It was Dennis Craig (1971) who first drew attention to the fact that the language-learning situation for young creole speakers in school in the anglophone Caribbean is somewhere between a first language and a second language situation, since the lexicon is largely shared between the two varieties they are likely to be using; they know some standard structures well, and others passively, while remaining ignorant altogether of the workings of some others. Craig showed us (1971, 1999, 2006) that the way forward was to design teaching and learning in such a way that the structures to be taught are treated differently according to the level of familiarity with which they are known. If we do less, we will find that students will withdraw because of boredom, since their perception is that they know English already, albeit badly, and that perception will be reinforced by an approach which takes either the native or foreign language teaching approach exclusively. Although the latter two volumes cited above provide very precise instruction for how to develop our students' language, this language-learning tool which Craig produced has hardly been seriously utilized, at least in Trinidad and Tobago, and some students emerge from secondary school with stronger competence in creole than in standard.

Although the creole was recognized as a language in its own right by the Ministry of Education of Trinidad and Tobago in 1975 (Carrington and Borely 1978), the precise mechanisms for its appropriate validation have remained ill-defined. In former times, the standard variety had been pursued as the route to educational success and its literature was valued as part of a culture of postcolonial learnedness, but since independence in 1963, Trinbagonians have become more conscious of their own culture and more ready to accept the language resource of the creole. Kamau Brathwaite has defined the creole as a "nation" language for the Caribbean and as a form of "revolution": "English it may be in terms of some of its lexical features. But in its contours, its rhythm and timber, its sound explosions, it is not English, even though the words, as you hear them, might be English to a greater or lesser degree" (1984, 13).

Teachers in Trinidad and Tobago, like most of the educated population, alternate between a mesolectal creole and a local standard in their own informal speech, and since each code has value for its speakers there is no reason for them to exclude the creole entirely, even from the classroom context. While standard English is recognized as the language of education and considered discussion, the creole has a very real value as the language of solidarity and of local identity. For youth, discovering themselves and their identity in a twenty-first-century world, to eschew the language of their former colonizers in favour of varieties which represent their lived experience as independent Caribbean citizens is clearly desirable, especially for intra-group talk. This opposition of functions for the different language varieties has allowed for both to be readily exploited in a range of settings, which today includes parliament, the university and church. Controversy still surrounds the notion of there being a local standard, but that variety, clearly defined by both phonological and grammatical features, is part of our everyday usage and needs to be distinguished from any other international variety on those grounds (Youssef and James 2004; Youssef 2004).

Today, we find several agencies being blamed for the failure of our students to learn English: teachers, parents, students themselves, the educational system, linguists in the university – the list goes on, and with the blame go many misconceptions, both about language attitudes and about language capacities. The real need is for motivation towards the standard as the language of international communication and advancement, but this has been differentially promoted. It has been shown that teachers do have ambivalent attitudes to the creole (Winford 1976), but that they are becoming more positive in the course of time (Mühleisen 2001). Recent work by Selvon-Ramkissoon (2008) indicates, however, that even our curriculum planners feel they lack the necessary expertise to design a language curriculum for appropriate inculcation of standard English among their students. Teachers themselves often tell us in the university, where we meet them as students, that they feel ill-equipped to deal with the language situation in the classroom. Winford's early study indicated that teachers perceived the creole as "bad" English, but Mühleisen (2001) found a shift in this regard, with the stigma attached to the variety gradually disappearing. When questioned in detail, teachers seemed cognizant of code-mixing in both studies, however. In this later study (Mühleisen 2001, 68), they responded as follows to a question on the circumstances in which they would use Trinidadian Creole in the classroom:

| | | |
|---|---|---|
| a. | to break classroom tension | 76.7% |
| b. | to facilitate student comprehension | 74.4% |
| c. | to increase student interest and response | 60.0% |
| d. | to prevent students from getting bored | 48.9% |
| e. | for personal conversation with students | 43.3% |
| f. | for reprimanding and scolding | 21.1% |
| g. | to keep discipline and control | 18.9% |
| h. | other purposes | 06.7% |

How teachers actually negotiate the intensely mixed language situation in the classroom and what variety or varieties they produce had hardly been investigated in Trinidad before this study, save for one early dissertation (Baptiste 1978), which argued that a separate teacher code existed. The way in which teachers today carry out their classroom interactions is of critical interest since it is necessarily a significant model for students in a territory where parental speech and the language of the wider community exhibit a preponderance of creole features. In the context of the current study, some teachers commented on their own language production in the classroom, indicating that they deliberately switched "to make a point", but that they "normally" spoke standard English.

It is important to note for the present time that there is a work by Mohammed (2008), an Indo-Trinidadian working at the University of Texas at Austin, which reports very similar findings to our own even though it focused on the primary school in Trinidad, where it might have been expected to find more creole. Her study was based on the in-class talk of thirteen Trinidadian teachers at the Standard 5 level, and she also collected data from focus-group interviews on teacher attitudes to classroom talk. She also compared the classroom talk to the language required of the students in their school-based assessments. She found a low production of TC by teachers, with a mean rate of one "Trini" item per one hundred words, with the categories of major usage found to be unmarked forms in present and past, and then *in(g)* forms without the auxiliary *be* for present continuous usage. Some conflation of the latter form type into that of the former categories seems to have inflated the unmarked tally, however. Mohammed recognized strategic usage of the creole by teachers, which caused her to comment:

> Counter to potential beliefs that poor performance on standardized tests are the result of "poor" language choices made by teachers, this study provided no evidence that students are instructed in the vernacular, nor that their performance on the test has a direct relationship with their teachers' use of "Trini" features. In fact, the linguistic patterns found here could be interpreted to mean that students are provided with good models of code-mixing, which is an essential tool in a varilingual context.... Should this finding be replicated ... in varied settings ... it could be used as evidence that varilingualism itself is being taught in classrooms and that teachers should not be overly concerned with their use of Trini in the classroom. (pp. 140–41)

For too long it seems that commentators have talked about "talking creole" or "talking standard" without sufficient recognition that it is the judicious mixing of both varieties that has become the norm for appropriateness in a large range of contexts. Deuber (2009) is also working with the data set to be described below, and she has commented on the level of creole usage among the teachers in relation to their students. She notes that the student level is considerably higher than that of the teachers, but she fails to describe standard usage in the same detail as that of specific creole features; this might make it appear as if they are speaking more creole than they actually are. She too concludes, however, that "Standard English retains an important role as a medium of instruction", while at the same time noting the current tolerance of the wide use of the creole by students and the use of creole as a complementary medium for the teachers. She argues for more functional teaching of the standard, as others have done (Craig 1999; Youssef 2004).

## Methodology

A new corpus of teacher language which has been compiled at the University of the West Indies in St Augustine as part of a larger corpus of English in Trinidad and Tobago will provide the basis for investigation of the actual classroom language use of these speakers. As mentioned in the introduction to this chapter, this was collected as part of a research project undertaken in its initial stages by students in a final-year undergraduate linguistics research course who were learning how to collect data and analyse it in a corpus linguistics frame. Subsequently, much more data has been added, since Dagmar Deuber and I embarked on collection of a subset of the International Corpus of English (ICE) Caribbean component for Trinidad. Deuber spent the 2006–7 academic year, in which the initial data was gathered, at the University of the West Indies, St Augustine, and made a significant input to the class in question.

In order to sample teacher speech at the secondary-school level, the research students in the exercise were advised to divide Trinidad geographically and to identify for sampling rural and urban schools in northern, southern and central parts of the island. Because these young investigators were engaged full time in their studies or in their work as teachers, they were not able to sample Tobago. Access to schools was also a problem as without contacts of some kind, students found that they were often denied entry. Nevertheless, we achieved a fairly broad sampling, managing to sample in northern, southern and central Trinidad. Since we knew that we might find different levels of standard according to differences in school type as well as age, race and gender of teachers, we took these factors into account as far as possible; however, access issues impinged on our overall coverage in these areas and the numbers of teachers sampled according to age, ethnicity and gender did not allow for anything more than suggestions for future investigation. In the final analysis, the data were drawn from fifteen different secondary schools. The classes recorded varied from literature through mathematics, sociology and science; approximately half were fifth- and sixth-form classes in the context of which students are prepared for the CXC examinations and the Caribbean Advanced Proficiency Examinations (CAPE). These examinations have international recognition and are acceptable for university entry worldwide.

Student investigators worked as far as possible in groups of four at each school, and they would aim to record two class lessons as well as two conversation sessions among a group of teachers, controlled to a fairly formal topic, such as language use in the schools. Each student was made responsible for the recording and transcribing of one session of at least two thousand words. With fifty students, this gave us a sample of one hundred thousand words, which were transcribed according to the requirements of the *ICE Markup Manual* (Nelson 1996, 2002) and computerized as a substantial corpus for analysis. The subset of data to be analysed here is drawn from fifteen texts in the category "class lessons".

For purposes of this chapter, I have focused most specifically, but not exclusively, on the form of the verb phrase as produced by the informants in question. It is arguably the most central feature of the language system and allows for disambiguation between standard and creole more consistently than any other feature. The major analysis for the study identified all finite verb forms as either standard or creole and at the same time considered carefully the precise contexts in which the creole, which was used as a minority variety among the teachers, was produced. The verb forms were quantified for each speaker as creole or standard but there was a significant qualitative element to this investigation as each context of usage of the different forms was carefully scrutinized. There were, of course, other creole features in sentences with creole verb forms, so that these features do come to attention in the streams of discourse represented. Finally, consideration was given to forms which might arguably have been considered Trinidad Standard as distinct from International Standard, since they represent calques, evidencing creole functions in standard forms. The varietal neutrality of many of the contact forms is also described.

# The Findings

## *Majority Usage of Standard*

The clearest finding from our investigation was that all teachers used standard English primarily, and that only one of the fifteen recorded seemed marginally non-fluent in its use, as adduced from errors in production. These non-fluencies occurred in the speaker with the highest creole production at 32 per cent, and may have been accounted for by his concern at being observed in class, for he also made a spelling mistake on the blackboard which he subsequently corrected. Far from being limited, the teachers were fluent in SE, with minimal errors of production in the entire corpus. Equally clear, however, was that they did not consider it appropriate to use standard English exclusively. While they used it for the overall impartation of information to their students, a majority used TC on occasions to question their students directly. Tables 10.1 and 10.2 give a detailed breakdown of percentage of SE use by teachers and specify contexts for usage of creole. Teachers are identified by numbers, according to age and gender, for reasons of confidentiality, and, in the same vein, schools are only identified by locality.

## *Language Production According to Age*

## Over 45 and Under 25

Interesting distinctions appeared according to age, with the two female teachers and one of two male teachers over 45 years making minimal usage of creole, as well as one young man under 25. The first older female, speaker 2a, used SE exclusively, and the other, speaker 2b, almost exclusively (99 per cent). It is notable for speaker 2b that she is from Tobago, where I have elsewhere noted high production of standard English among older and professional persons (Youssef 2001). The male who used standard 97 per cent, speaker 4b, used creole on four isolated occasions, three of which were utterances in which he modelled creole speech in the wider community to his students with the opener "What do we say?" An example is given below:

1. Right and because of that constant bombardment from the TV or the radio, OK, you internalize it and that is their hope. . . . You internalize it right, and a lot of us do not think before we vote, because what do we say: "Me father was PNM" or "Me, I born UNC."

**Table 10.1:** Language Use by Teachers in Trinidad, Females

| Code | Age Range | School Locality | Subject | Class Level | Qualifications | Ethnicity | Language Use | Standard Percentage |
|---|---|---|---|---|---|---|---|---|
| 1a | 26–45 | South | Accounts | Form 6 | BSc, DipEd | Afro | Creole relational and direct questions | 79/99 (80%) |
| 1b | 26–45 | South | Integrated Science | Form 2 | MSc | Indo | Creole relational, direct orders and questions | 190/226 (84%) |
| 1c | 26–45 | South | Maths | Form 2 | Secondary | Afro | Less apparent pattern, but some creole in direct questions | 117/133 (88%) |
| 1d | 26–45 | South | Literature | Form 2 | University | Mixed | Low-level creole but present in direct interface with students | 190/205 (93%) |
| 1e | 26–45 | Central | Sociology | Form 6 | University | Mixed | Low-level TC, not contextually motivated; structurally specific | 170/182 (93%) |
| 1f | 26–45 | Central | Spanish | Form 1 | University | Mixed | Creole for direct interface with students; reprimanding | 27/35 (77%) |
| 1g | 26–45 | North | Business | Form 4 | MBA | Mixed | Low-level TC; first form in series; 2 lexical items account for 7/10 forms | 105/115 (91%) |
| 1h | 26–45 | North | Accounts | Form 4 | BA, BSc | Afro | Relatively high creole level; used to express empathy with students | 95/129 (74%) |
| 2a | 46–65 | North | Literature | Form 5 | University | Indo | All SE | 100% |
| 2b | 45–65 | North | History | Form 6 | University | Afro (from Tobago) | Almost exclusively SE | 206/208 (99%) |

**Table 10.2:** Language Use by Teachers in Trinidad, Males

| Code | Age Range | School Locality | Subject | Class Level | Qualifications | Ethnicity | Language Use | Standard Percentage |
|---|---|---|---|---|---|---|---|---|
| 3a | 26–45 | North | Metalwork | Form 2 | University | Afro | Creole relational, direct questions to students | 157/172 (91%) |
| 3b | 26–45 | North (rural) | Agri-cultural Science | Form 5 | BSc | Indo | Highest level of TC | 97/143 (68%) |
| 3c | 26–45 | Central (rural) | Spanish | Form 1 | University | Indo | Creole relational, setting up Spanish scenarios | 137/162 (85%) |
| 4a | 46–65 | South (prestige school) | Chemistry | Form 6 | University | Indo | Largely monologue, no questions; often starts utterance with TC, e.g., "We goin'" | 156/180 (87%) |
| 4b | 46–65 | North | Social Studies | Form 5 | BA | Indo | High level of SE; TC stylistically conditioned to "What do we say . . ." sequences | 128/132 (97%) |
| 5a | Under 25 | South (prestige) | Sociology | Form 6 | MPhil | Indo | Only one creole form; has lived abroad for 4 years; decreased varilingual competence? | 144/145 (99%) |

It is only in his giving a typical utterance type from what we might call the supposed "man in the street" that this older male teacher goes into the creole.

The other older male, 4a, with 87 per cent, is not marked out by his level of standard versus creole, but by the fact that he did not use the creole to relate to students but would begin his monologues with a creole form and then switch to standard; he was also unique among the teachers in consistently operating without any interactivity with his students.

The age of these teachers reflects very clearly their own time of schooling and the prevailing language and language teaching ideologies of that time. They would most likely have been educated in the 1970s around the time of the Ministry of Education's statement on the validity of the creole in 1975, when language attitudes towards the creole were only just beginning to change and when the school domain was still very much the preserve of standard English. For this reason, they may have been less motivated to produce the creole.

The other atypical result was found in the single teacher recorded in the under-twenty-five age range, speaker 5a, who maintained standard at a 99 per cent level also. What rendered him additionally atypical – and which in his case might be construed as more influential on his language habits than his age was – was that he had just spent four years abroad in a standard English–speaking environment.

Of particular concern, apart from the eschewing of the creole by the above group, is their lack of stylistic variation in using it. While its production was clearly stylistically constrained for the majority of teachers in the 26–45 age group, there were no constraints of the same type among this group. The creole was not used for specific direct questions to students, to make very specific points to them or for the sake of establishing some kind of empathy or identity. In fact, there was an apparent failure to be cognizant of the capacity for exploitation of mixed usage in the classroom for maximal effectiveness, other than in the single case of the teacher who directly imitated creole speech.

## The 26 to 45 Age Group

Usage among the 26 to 45 age group is very different, at least for females, among whom 60 per cent (6/10) teachers use creole but most specifically in direct interaction with their students. 33.3 per cent (2/6) of the male teachers followed this patterning also, but this can less readily be commented upon since the number of male teachers was lower, rendering it difficult to claim typicality in the sample. For the rest, it is a very important finding, since it demonstrates clearly that, far from interspersing creole with standard at random, teachers use their two varieties strategically for maximal stylistic effectiveness. Since the creole is the language of solidarity, it is natural that they would use it when specifically relating to their students, and its use demonstrates their varilingual competence to use each variety appropriately in balance with the other to fit their given situations. Some examples follow to demonstrate the various sub-types of usage. Creole features are in italics.

## Relevant Examples, Direct Questions

First of all, we have speaker 1a teaching a sixth-form accounts class in South Trinidad. From the table, it can be noted that she had a relatively high creole level, at 20 per cent overall. Specific typical tokens are listed below with glosses in parentheses, explicating the TC features. Each grammatical feature is explicated only once.

2. If it's the wrong size, the wrong shape it *eh good* . . . that's an allowance for those reasons. For those reasons, you will get discount on what you have purchased. You buy *plenty plenty plenty* you will get a particular discount on the amount you're buying – some terms at the bottom of the purchase invoice that will tell you when you have to pay *eh right* . . . (Using a real example to make a point to student group)
(*Eh* is a negative marker in the TC predicate system. "Plenty plenty plenty" is an example of reduplication within it.)

3. When we buy in credit what's the name of the account *we usin*? (Asking a direct question)
(*-In[g]* stands for continuous/habitual marking without an auxiliary verb.)

4. Remember when we bought the goods on credit we had credited accounts payable. If we now *payin* for it then remember we go back to our what? Our rule for liabilities credit to increase so if we *reducin* it, it will be debit to decrease, all right? (Example and question)

5. What are our credit entries? We *payin* cash, remember. Cash is an asset. To increase *we* debit we reduce *we* credit. So we *payin* cash. Well, how is this cash coming out? We are not paying fully three thousand five hundred, we are paying cash of three thousand four hundred and thirty. Remember we *work* that out? How we *get* that? (Real example and direct questions)

(*We* is the first-person plural possessive adjective in the TC system; the unmarked verb form signifies completive marking and is often loosely equated with the past.)

There is considerable contrast here with streams of speech which are more purely informative and less relational and where we find no creole usage:

6. "Shipping point" means that the goods are placed on board the carrier by the seller and the buyer pays the freight cost. "Destination" means that the goods are placed free on board to the buyer's place of business. All right. So for the buyer and the seller the information will be different. If it's "FOB shipping point" – this is on page 188 – it means that the seller is not paying and the buyer has to pay the freight cost. That will be like your carriage inwards that you would have learnt in form four and form five, because the seller now has to include in the cost of good that he has purchased the freight cost.

In the above example, the teacher is interfacing with the text and providing theoretical background relative to the examples presented in the earlier extracts.

Another teacher, Speaker 1b, is teaching an integrated science class at form 2 level. As we might expect, her class is more interactive throughout than 1a's, perhaps because it is at a much lower class level. However, the level of creole use is actually lower, at 16 per cent, though it is also used most specifically for questions and directives to students. A point that should be made is that there is very little percentage predictability according to relative interaction or class level, since each teacher's baseline for moving between creole and standard is different, dependent on his or her own language background and experience. We might note that this speaker does have education up until the master's level, contrasting with the bachelor's degree plus Diploma of Education of the first speaker; it is hard to say whether this would bring about a difference in standard production, and we would need a much more detailed bio-profile on each individual to be sure. The point to be made, however, is that stylistic variation is occurring, and not random mixing.

Here are some examples from this lesson:

7. And at the beginning of that chapter we see the heading "Solution and Suspension". Everybody *seein* that? (Direct question)

8. Right, so we *goin an* write some notes before you all forget. (Directive to students)
   ("Goin an" is a marker of immediate future in the TC system.)

9. Write it down next to it. Sugar. Now we *goin to* write down what is a solvent.
   (Directive)
   ("Goin to" is another future marker in the system, used without an auxiliary verb.)

10. Yes. I want a sketch of it, so don't colour it and put the same amount of circles
    *you all seein* there. (Directive to students)
    ("You all" is an associative plural marker.)

This contrasts with a stream of discourse like the following:

11. Figure three, point two. We're seeing that. And what happened there? Some
    solute is put into the solvent and all the solute doesn't dissolve, so therefore we
    can't consider it a solution. But then when the solute starts breaking up it starts
    distributing itself throughout the solution and as a result it becomes a solution
    then, oh sorry, it distributes itself in the liquid which is water and when it has
    come to that point where it's evenly distributed which is the third diagram we
    see it has formed a solution.

Once again, above, we see that the informative and explanatory material is
delivered in consistent standard English.

## Reprimanding, Exhorting, Motivating

An interesting variation on the range of creole usage is found in speaker 1h,
as she delivers a form 4 accounts lesson in Tunapuna in North Trinidad. As a
student complains bitterly that she is not coping with the work in contrast to all
the other students, the teacher replies thus:

12. Because you're not trying hard enough. Because you *concentratin* on play more
    than anything else and *hangin* out with boys. And those boys will leave you behind.
    And that is why I spoke highly of Yadap yesterday, because he not *hangin* out *an*
    *playin* around. I haven't seen him. *You not seein* him in the office in trouble. And
    that's excellent. And there is nothing wrong with you. And if you continue telling
    yourself there is something wrong there will be something wrong. You could learn
    it and you could do it. Didn't you just call out the answer for one there for me.
    (*Not* is a negative marker, an alternative to *eh*, slightly closer to standard.)

Superficially this may appear like a case of "reprimanding and scolding", and
perhaps it is to some extent, but it can also be seen as encouraging, motivating,

making the point to exhort the student to do better with the proviso that she does have the capacity and must not undermine herself. I would call this kind of talk also relational, encouraging and motivating. There is a solidarity element in it, since it is female-to-female speech and confronts inter-gender performance as a necessary motivator.

A more straightforward case of reprimanding is found in the case of the form 1, female Spanish teacher, who uses the creole when checking on the stage her students have reached when doing some written work:

13. *You all* still *workin*? Why you *takin* so long?

14. Why you all *peltin* [unintelligible word]?

## Setting the Scene

A final sub-type of stylistic variation occurs in a foreign language lesson, a Spanish class at the form 1 level, where two teachers from Central Trinidad, a male and a female, share a class. The male takes the majority of the class and sets the scenes for his students which are subsequently going to be rendered by them in Spanish. He starts off in SE but shifts to TC in the process of setting up the scene, using the kind of example which his students can relate to in terms of topic and geographical reference point:

15. Now, let's suppose Ahmed is talking to this girl on the phone for a few weeks and he wants to organize. He wants to go on a date, so he wants to meet her by Sauce Doubles in Curepe . . . and then he went on the date. He *eat* a doubles and a juice, *get* diarrhoea from the pepper sauce and as soon as he *reach* home, Devanand *call* and *say*, "Boy, what this girl like?"

This kind of patterning occurs on three separate occasions in his forty-minute lesson. He clearly aims to bring realism to the scenarios through his use of personal examples rendered in the students' own vernacular variety.

## Forms in a Series

A different kind of patterning, not stylistically motivated in the same way, is recorded for male teacher 3b, who has the highest level of TC usage in the group as a whole, at 32 per cent, and whose speech production is less fluent in standard than the rest of the teachers. He maintains sequential use of the same lexical item, as in the examples below:

16. We *talkin* about plants eh.

17. What we talking about is, we talking about when reproduction of new plants so we *dealin* with corn, if we *dealin* with peppers.

18. One of the main sections when we *dealin* with propagation, we *talkin* about where we use everything except seeds.

It should be added that he does also have the kind of stylistic variation recorded for the majority of speakers, using TC forms to question or to relate directly to students.

Like speaker 3b, female speaker 1g, at 91 per cent, uses TC forms to the very limited extent that she does so, in a series, as in the following:

19. But when they *producin* for the London Carnival . . . and they *producin* those exclusively for export, so that will be surplus production. So when Poison *producin* for Barbados Crop-Over that production . . . domestic production will be zero.

Patterning appears to be according to lexical item for her rather than being motivated by the situation, encouraged by the repetition of the lexical item, and perhaps paralleling the production of formulaic expressions without deep-level processing.

## Calquing

Two other features of the teachers' speech are worthy of mention. First, they do show evidence of using standard forms with creole meanings, or calquing, by imposition of a standard-looking item on a creole function. The verb forms which are seen being used in this way are *had* and *would* or *will*. Some examples of each are given below. The first, again from 1g, is a two-sentence sequence which mixes creole forms, standard and calquing, where *will* is used for the standard *would*, but on the creole irrealis pattern where there is no distinction between future and conditional marking.

20. All right, so one does use buds and one does use grafts because we know we could take a mango and put it in the ground and it *will grow*. We know we could take a orange seed and put it in the ground and it *will grow*.

The next is an example of *had* usage in a simple past or relative past context. A regular TC feature is the use of *did*, which in basilectal creoles is usually rendered by *bin*, to mark events which are finished with in the past, almost removed from relevance, reversing the perfect meaning associated with the unmarked form in many cases. Across the board in Trinidad, educated speakers are now using *had* in this same function rather than as a standard pluperfect rendering. Speaker 1e, with a 93 per cent level of SE production, teaching a sixth-form sociology class in Central Trinidad, uses this form several times:

21. So I *had also asked* for people to . . . yes, I *had also asked* for people to bring their handouts.

22. Now what we *had started* last day as well, we started looking at the handout.

Speaker 1a, teaching her accounts class at sixth-form level, also uses this form:

23. We *had originally done* what? Credit the account merchandise inventory thirty-five hundred. So now we have to do what?

Finally, the use of *would* and *could* is to be noted where *will* and *can* would most usually be used in SE. These forms are common in the speech of the form 2 male metalwork teacher, 3b:

24. We *would* not be able to scribe a circle but we can find the centre of a circle.

25. OK. What is a scriber? You *could* show me?

All of these forms occur as part of the idiolect of specific teachers. While they are relatively commonly heard in the broader Trinidadian context, they do represent a particular type of learning common among educated speakers, who are conversant with both languages in contact but also embrace such interlingual feature between the two. As such forms are heard frequently by students, it is likely that they will become more entrenched and arguments will arise over whether and to what extent they can be taken as part of standard Trinidadian

English, a variety which is hotly contested among intellectuals and on which papers like this intend to shed more light.

## Neutral Forms

Earlier in the chapter I mentioned that it is not always possible to discern a matrix or dominant language variety in the code-mixing recorded in the country. This is because unmarked forms in the present tense, as well as some modals, are neutral in that they can occur in both creole and standard and cannot be definitely ascribed to either variety. I give some examples of this not as illustrative of particular speakers or of style-shifting but simply of this phenomenon:

27. *Don't* let your eye *fall out* over there. You want to hear him, right?

28. Apparently you all *like* him, right?

29. *Look at* your list so that when I *ask* you, you *don't have to keep* us waiting.

30. Anybody in these two rows *go ahead.*

Superficially, we might assess the above verb forms as SE. However, in doing so, we would do well to recognize that, given the heavy stigmatization of the pre-verbal marker *does* in semi-formal contexts, the creole itself utilizes an unmarked form in present contexts, with only the third-person singular distinguishing between them by reason of the addition of *-s* – for example, "he *likes*".

The imperative is also unmarked in both varieties. Given the creole question form, uninverted in (27) and (28) with the TC tag *right*, we need to mark utterances like the above as neutral rather than as TC or SE.

## Overall Findings

First, teachers are using both standard and creole varieties in a judicious and appropriate manner, given the language background of their students and the present-day norms for language use in Trinidad and Tobago. They are displaying varilingual competence, balancing the use of the two varieties according to a norm for classroom usage which rests, for this group, at a mean level of 85 per cent for females and 86 per cent for males, in both categories under forty-five.

Given the exceedingly low level of males sampled, however, we cannot make an overall comment on usage according to gender.

In contrast to the above, three out of four teachers over the age of forty-five produce standard English at an average rate of 99 per cent and do not code-switch, but again we must bear in mind that we are looking at a very small sample. Two of these teachers are also addressing sixth-form classes, where more standard usage might be expected. Age, then, would not be worth mentioning if it were not for the fact that this differential might be expected on a larger scale given the shift in language attitudes since this group were in school themselves, and because it also concurs with Mohammed's findings (2008, 144).

There is little apparent differential according to school subject or level. Only two vocational subjects are represented and while one, agricultural science, has the highest rate of creole use (32 per cent), the other, metalwork, has a low rate (9 per cent). The high rate of creole use might reflect the background of the teacher himself as well as the rural location of the school in which he is teaching. While sixth-form classes look impressively standard, with a mean of 8 per cent creole production, three of the older teachers are teaching these levels, as a result of which age is conflated with class level and more investigation is necessary. Deuber (2009) speaks of a level of code-mixing which appears to relate to subject, but we certainly need more data to verify this.

Of more importance for this study are the precise contexts in which the teachers use creole and the consensus among them in this arena. Creole is used by almost all teachers for direct questions or comments to the students, and to a lesser extent to establish realistic local context effectively, to establish relationship and for exhortation and motivational efficiency. The light which is shed on motivated functional mixing indicates that, far from slipping into creole because of a lapsing level of standard English competence, teachers are shifting to improve the quality of their communication with their students, and are, in fact, creating their own standards for language usage given a lack of specific instruction from the Ministry of Education, which, like the entire country, seems to think still in terms of bare alternatives with respect to use of the contact varieties.

It is worth mentioning also that the verb features which teachers use are generally those which Winford (1972) identified as being less stigmatized and more common across the range of formal and informal settings, namely the use of -in(g) without the auxiliary for continuous marking, and Ø marking for past/perfective usage, the former category being more prevalent than the latter. In contrast, the pre-verbal marker *done* does not occur and the habitual *does* occurs only seven times in the entire data set under scrutiny. That there is some calquing going on, as well as some overlap among the contact systems, is also clear, but perhaps this is inevitable given the level of fusion which the contact codes have reached.

## Conclusions

As teacher language in Trinidad gets more attention, we are obliged to recognize that teachers have their own "language education policy", and that the society should acknowledge an astute competence that they exhibit in relating to their students, a competence which appears to have changed in time towards a judicious blending of the creole with majority standard usage. It has now been nearly forty years since the Ministry of Education officially recognized the creole as a language in its own right, and change has come during the intervening period. What we learn demonstrates the ignorance of commentators in the wider society who speak derisively of teacher use of creole without recognizing that their use of it is stylistically appropriate in their more informal interactions with students. The data are useful to us for demonstrating the kind of language use that we have long been loosely aware of in the wider society but have not begun to describe or quantify before now.

It is clear that we need to go further in defining a local standard, but it is likely that linguists will never quite agree on the exact status of calqued forms or the mixing of functions associated with modal verbs which describe irrealis categories. More important, it seems we are coming into a time where language description needs to change, to remove its blinkers and to recognize that speakers normatively do not necessarily use a single variety; what is standard and what is creole is ultimately less important than how we blend them, and the need to get this right supersedes the need to be total masters of both in the context of the individual speech community. If we are to teach effectively according to functional variation, our teaching has to encompass an admission that mono-varietal language competence is not an option in a varilingual context.

## References

Brathwaite, Edward Kamau. 1984. *History of the Voice: The Development of Nation Language in Anglophone Caribbean Poetry.* London: New Beacon Books.

Bickerton, Derek. 1975. *Dynamics of a Creole System*. Cambridge: Cambridge University Press.

Carrington, Lawrence D. 1980. Images of Creole Space. *Journal of Pidgin and Creole Languages* 7 (1): 93–99.

Carrington, Lawrence D., and Clive Borely. 1978. *The Language Arts Syllabus 1975: Comment and Counter-Comment*. St Augustine: University of the West Indies, School of Education.

Craig, Dennis R. 1971. Education and Creole English in the West Indies. In *Pidginization and Creolization of Languages*, edited by D. Hymes, 371–91. Cambridge: Cambridge University Press.

———. 1976. Bidialectal Education: Creole and Standard in the West Indies. *International Journal of the Sociology of Language* 8: 93–134.

———. 1999. *Teaching Language and Literacy: Policies and Procedures for Vernacular Situations*. Georgetown, Guyana: Education and Development Services.

———. 2006. *Teaching Language and Literacy to Caribbean Students: From Vernacular to Standard English*. Kingston: Ian Randle.

DeCamp, David. 1971. Towards a Generative Analysis of a Post-Creole Speech Continuum. In Hymes, *Pidginization and Creolization of Languages*, 349–70.

Deuber, Dagmar. 2009. Standard English in the Secondary School in Trinidad: Problems, Properties, Prospects. In *World Englishes: Problems, Properties, Prospects*, edited by L. Siebers and T. Hoffmann, 83–104. Amsterdam: John Benjamins.

Deuber, Dagmar, and Valerie Youssef. 2007. Teacher Language in Trinidad: A Pilot Corpus Study of Direct and Indirect Creolisms in the Verb Phrase. Proceedings of the Corpus Linguistics Conference, University of Birmingham, 27–30 July.

Hymes, Dell, ed. 1971. *Pidginization and Creolization of Languages*. Cambridge: Cambridge University Press.

Labov, William. 1972. *Language in the Inner City: Studies in the Black English Vernacular*. Philadelphia: University of Pennsylvania.

Mohammed, Sarojani S. 2008. Trini Talk or the Queen's English? Navigating Language Varieties in the Post-Colonial, High Stakes Climate of "Standard Five" Classrooms in Trinidad. PhD diss., University of Texas at Austin.

Mühleisen, Susanne. 2001. Is "Bad English" Dying Out? A Diachronic Comparative Study of Attitudes towards Creole versus Standard English in Trinidad. *Philologie im Netz* 15: 43–78. http://web.fu-berlin.de/phin/phin15/p15t3.htm.

Myers-Scotton, Carol. 1996. *Social Motivations for Code-Switching*. Cambridge: Cambridge University Press.

Nelson, Gerald. 1996. The Design of the Corpus. In *Comparing English Worldwide: The International Corpus of English*, edited by S. Greenbaum, 27–35. Oxford: Clarendon.

———. 2002. Markup Manual for Spoken Texts. http://www.ucl.ac.uk/english-usage/ice/manuals.htm.

Selvon-Ramkissoon, Nicha. 2008. The SEMP Language Arts Curriculum (Levels 1–3): An Overview from Conceptualization to Enactment. Cross-Campus Linguistics Research Day, University of the West Indies, Cave Hill, 22 April.

Simmons-McDonald, Hazel. 2008. Comparative Patterns in the Acquisition of English Negation by Native Speakers of French Creole and Creole English. *Language Learning* 44 (1): 29–74.

Winford, Donald. 1972. A Sociolinguistic Description of Two Communities in Trinidad. DPhil diss., University of York.

———. 1976. Teacher Attitudes towards Language Variation in a Creole Community. *International Journal of the Sociology of Langu*age 8: 45–75.

———. 1988. The creole continuum and the notion of the speech community as the locus of language. *International Journal of the Sociology of Language* 71: 91–105.

Youssef, Valerie. 1990. The Development of Linguistic Skills in Young Trinidadian Children: An Integrative Approach to Verb Phrase Development. PhD diss., University of the West Indies, St Augustine.

———. 1996. Varilingualism: The Competence behind Code-Mixing in Trinidad and Tobago. *Journal of Pidgin and Creole Languages* 11 (1): 1–22.

———. 2001. Age-Grading in the Anglophone Creole of Tobago. *World Englishes* 20 (1): 29–46.

———. 2004. "Is English We Speaking": Trinbagonian in the Twenty-first Century. *English Today* 20 (4 October): 42–49.

Youssef, Valerie, and Winford James. 2004. The Creoles of Trinidad and Tobago: Morphology and syntax. In *The Handbook of Varieties of English*, vol. 2: *The Americas and the Caribbean*, 320–38. The Hague: Mouton de Gruyter.

# PART 4

## ISSUES OF CONTEXT

# 11 | Coexisting Discourses and the Teaching of English in the Creole-Speaking Environment of Jamaica

KATHRYN SHIELDS BRODBER
*University of the West Indies, Mona*

Teachers of the English language at the high-school level in those Caribbean territories designated as "anglophone" have usually shared an agreement on the linguistic features of that target language which they need to include in their programme. Guided by texts designed for the purpose, and armed with knowledge about what has traditionally proved difficult for learners of English in a creole-speaking environment, they have focused on the direct teaching of aspects of grammar that need constant reinforcement, such as tense, concord and the like, as well as variation in sentence structure, the elimination of fragments, the meaning of various transitional words and phrases, paragraphing and style. Passages from both Caribbean and non-Caribbean writers are usually chosen as models from which students are led to infer and then implement the "best practices" which are their aim, while peer reviewing provides opportunities for them to critique each other's work as they improve their editing techniques.

Since the success of such programmes is measured by examinations of the Caribbean Examinations Council (CXC), sat at the end of grade 10 or 11 of the secondary system, students of the English language in creole-speaking territories have generally been expected to develop skills and competencies in using grammatical English clearly and precisely for informative, expressive and persuasive purposes, and to demonstrate an understanding of meaning derived from a variety of texts written for such purposes. In the syllabus reproduced by Craig (2006b, 261–66), it is instructive that there is no direct reference to essay writing, although instructions, explanations, statements of evidence, circulars, notices and announcements, summaries and reports, cables, telegrams, advertisements, formal letters and minutes are all included.

Following on from his 1966 publication on teaching English to creole speakers, Craig (1999, 2006b) has consistently made a case that successful delivery of programmes in what he calls Teaching English to Speakers of Related Vernaculars (TESORV) must be bolstered by teachers' and students' development of language awareness – not only of the target language, but also of their vernacular language. Recognizing the cognitive benefits L2 learners derive from the parallel development of their L1 and L2, as well as the obvious differentials in learners' L2 awareness and their recognition of the L2 being far in advance of their production, he emphasizes that "vernacular-speaking learners of English need a strong conscious awareness of the formal linguistic characteristics of both their own language and the English they are attempting to learn". He continues, "The linguistic content of English teaching has to focus heavily on [those] aspects of English . . . which are in contrast with vernacular features" (2006b, 7).

Craig (2006a, 111–12) also reiterates the need not only for teachers to have developed language awareness concerning such contrasts, but also for students' continuing language awareness about their creole first language and culture to be central, for the following purposes:

- exploration and expression of the child's own perceptions, ideas and thought processes;
- through the latter, a maintenance of continuity and the achievement of adequate maturation of the child's cognitive development (Cummins 1979a, 1979b; Long 1990); and
- creation of an adequately rich background of ideas and understanding that can serve as the content of second language (SE) learning.

One of the aims of language awareness about the creole-influenced vernacular (CIV) L1 is to pinpoint and develop strategies to deal with associated practices that could be potentially problematic for learners of the L2. Craig (2006b) provides detailed resources to guide teachers on morphological and syntactic contrasts between the two languages: "some forms of English words and sentence structures that can be selected for direct teaching to CIV speakers" (p. 237); "a programme for maintaining the home language and culture, and strengthening the language awareness of pupils" (p. 242); "some activities in the direct teaching and learning of language structure" (p. 246); and "some purposes for the creative utilisation of language structures" (p. 267). However, although he identifies code-shifting (p. 41) as a problematic practice which he asserts learners must be taught to resist, especially in contexts where English is the target, he does not address, through discussion or resources, the discourse context or any other related practices of CIV teachers and learners which would have to be incorporated within a comprehensive TESORV programme.

The practices of code-shifting and code-mixing constitute one of the more obvious features of linguistic discourse, marking changes in the contemporary sociolinguistic environment of the Caribbean, and potentially contributing to the derailing of learners' efforts to develop communicative competence (Hymes 1972) in their European target language. While change is occurring at varying rates throughout the different territories, the upsurge of local identity issues, combined with a focus on post-independence local norms of behaviour and value systems, has meant that some degree of change has been inevitable.

The territory with perhaps the most marked and vibrant sociolinguistic change reported is Jamaica. Christie (1998, 21) provides evidence of the genesis of this change, described in a revised version of her 1992 paper, as "a few obvious trends in relatively formal Jamaican English". Using examples from material collected between 1977 and 1982, from a wide range of oral and written sources, she points to the deliberate use of Jamaican Creole in formal writing and speech by those who would have detached themselves from such a practice in the past; however, she emphasizes that at that time, 1982, "the trends . . . [were] far from general even in the usage of the persons quoted" (p. 34).

Shields Brodber (1992) points to the rapid progress and vibrancy of this change, which she claims is a consequence of the proliferation, in the late seventies and early eighties, of talk radio programmes which had their advent in the late sixties. She attributes to this source the gradual elevation of Jamaican Creole to public-formal status, providing the primary means for ordinary citizens to express their opinion in the language(s) of their choice. The role of educated Jamaican hosts in facilitating the change – not only by accommodating to the usage of their callers, but sometimes also by selecting creole for their commentary and analysis – is also discussed. The pervasiveness of the change leads Shields Brodber (1997) to pronounce a requiem for English in Jamaica.

In such a context, there is increasingly less tension between the characteristics conventionally associated with the linguistic behaviour of the privileged, educated members of society and those viewed as belonging to that of the general population. For obvious reasons, higher value has traditionally been attached to the practices of the former category, which have gained acceptance as marking public interaction. Accompanying the spread of the creole language to public-formal domains, however, has been the gradual collapse of some of the distinctions between private and public interaction, leading to an increasing prominence of locally evolving creole discourse practices. These relate to, for example, appropriateness in language choice and use, contexts of formality, norms of politeness, the structure of conversation, the conduct of argument and the negotiation of conflict.

The above has obvious implications for teachers of the target language, who must be ever cognizant of the decreasing number of target-language models at the disposal of their students and who are required to supplement and reinforce classroom goals. These should address not just the levels of morpho-syntax and lexico-semantics, but also the discourse practices required for mastery of the target language, and integration within that community. On the assumption that the development of learners' communicative competence in the target language is their primary goal, and that the route to be taken begins at the place where students exist, teachers have no option but to develop an awareness and a thorough working knowledge of the discourse environment and norms which characterize the communicative competence of students in their native creole language. This must constitute the starting point of their effort.

## Encoding Formality in a Culture of Informality

A major casualty of the blurring of the norms distinguishing public from private communication is attention to established codes of formality. These are not just procedures to be observed for their own sake; they assume social meaning, shared by those who subscribe to them. Teaching of the target language becomes a major source of exploring this meaning, especially when there are no obvious parallels in the discourse of learners' creole language; therefore, it provides learners not only with models of target-language conventions, but also with practice in the ways in which they are observed.

In this section, the focus of the discussion is on some examples of politeness conventions related to formal target-language discourse, which teachers of creole-speaking learners would need to address. A primary concern of politeness strategies is the non-invasion of the personal space and time of another, categorized as "negative politeness" (Brown and Levinson 1987). This is marked, for example, by a speaker's use of an apology before requesting the time, or signifying respect by the use of titles to those of higher status. Showing appreciation and admiration for others, or indicating connection and solidarity with them through the use of familiar terms of address, on the other hand, is described as "positive politeness".

Creole discourse, at least in Jamaica, seems to focus on positive politeness activity, such as giving a "big op" (encouragement, compliment); greeting others using terms of endearment and familiarity, even when paying respect ("momi" to an unknown female older than the greeter); and issuing personal, sometimes overtly sexual compliments to passers-by ("ku di bompa" as a comment of appreciation of a female's ample derrière). Such strategies, deemed as constituting an invasion of the personal space of another, are not acceptable in formal English discourse, concentrating as it does on maintaining a polite distance between interlocutors, especially if they are strangers. Further, sociocultural differences in interpretation may also lead to their being considered offensive.

In order to heighten students' awareness of the importance of observing formal, and especially negative, politeness codes in the appropriate circumstances, a classroom teacher would need to design activities for them to identify such distinctions: in their daily interaction at home, at school with peers and school officials, at interviews and at church. The teacher could also have them analyse the dynamics of the language of varying relationships in literary texts, movies and plays of different cultures and levels of formality. Recasting in formal, standard English telephone text messages from friends, as well as those conveyed through social media, should also provide excellent material and opportunities for students to recognize and analyse informal elements which they replace in the formal register.

## Observing Protocol

For formal events such as banquets and awards ceremonies, for instance, there are conventional prescriptions related to the rules of protocol to be followed in the mode of dress deemed suitable, the organization of the formal proceedings, the welcoming of dignitaries and other guests, and the language considered suitable for the delivery of speeches. Individual guests may introduce informality in a number of ways – for example, by wearing casual dress or code-switching in conversation; however, the organizers, invited speakers and other main participants in the event are normally expected to observe formal conventions. School officials, in particular, are often assumed to constitute models in this regard. Thus, deviation from established norms, such as the absence of a structured, scripted programme, or the shelving of protocol in its delivery, becomes a point to be noted in a cycle of change, especially if the person breaching the convention is one expected to uphold it.

An example from the fiftieth-anniversary banquet of a Jamaican high school, held in the ballroom of a hotel at seven in the evening, illustrates this point. As the principal rises and moves to the podium to extend a greeting and welcome on behalf of the school, the audience has certain expectations. These include her reading from a list, arranged in order of status, the names and designations of the dignitaries, who include the chairman and members of the Board of Governors, special guests including bishops of the church with which the school is associated, members of the administration, student leaders, parents and alumni. When, in the absence of a list or any other visible written text, the principal's greeting is simply, "All protocol observed", it promotes discomfort in many of the guests, who, after the function, exchange their negative evaluations of this greeting.

Social meaning, embodied in cultural practice, is transmitted through codes of discourse. The expectations of invitees to a formal banquet, about which they have been informed through a formal, printed invitation, include their hosts having fully prepared themselves to perform the roles assigned to them, and exhibiting some comfort with the associated codes. The initial complaint of the guests is about what they consider the inappropriateness of the greeting, in a context about which the intended formality is not in doubt. Following on from this, and certainly of greater consequence, is their primary concern about how this breach of protocol will be interpreted, encoding, as it seems, inadequate recognition of the dignitaries, and indicating less than the required respect for their status. Thus, the principal's non-observance of the conventions of formality – perhaps a result of her under-preparation – becomes a means through which she has delivered what her guests consider to be an insult, and a threat to their negative face needs.

Not only does such a principal expose her own discomfort with the formal procedures of the discourse of the target language; she also loses a significant opportunity to provide a model for those students attending the function, who often do not appreciate what a formal welcome entails, particularly in a situation in which this is not addressed by target-language teaching within the context of the classroom.

The aware classroom teacher would have students role-play formal functions such as prize-giving ceremonies, graduation exercises or a school-leaving banquet, and take them through the processes, expectations and appropriate discourse associated with welcoming guests, delivering the valedictorian's speech, giving the vote of thanks and so on. Such an approach would promote the comfort of both teachers and students with such protocols.

## Formal Terms of Address

As has been noted above, negative politeness can be marked by the use of titles and formal terms of address to strangers or to acknowledge social distance between interlocutors, whether created by anonymity, inequality of status resulting from differentials in age, class or roles, or even the expression of displeasure or disagreement between them. In a growing culture of informality, the distance between interlocutors is reduced, as the more relaxed communication of private spaces is transposed to that of the public domain. It is not uncommon to overhear, in Jamaica, telephone receptionists at government and professional offices employing the informal "love" and "man" as substitutes for the conventional "sir" and "ma'am" used to address anonymous callers.

Changing norms in this regard are continually illustrated in talk radio, in which hosts alternate the more formal "sir" and "madam" with a range of choices, including terms of endearment, in response to callers whom the ensuing conversation indicates they do not know. The result is a lessening of the initial distance between them, and the creation of a relaxed atmosphere. Examples from the public media feed naturally into public discourse at a general level, with the effect of making what purports to be formal interaction less formal than it has been in the past.

Examples 1 to 3 below, from radio talk shows in Jamaica, illustrate this point. In example 1, the host's use of "sir" maintains the traditions associated with addressing an anonymous male caller.

## *Example 1*

> Host: Hello?
> Caller: Missa P?
> Host: Yes, *sir.*
> Caller: Good morning, *sa.*
> Host: Good morning to you, *sir.*

> (*Perkins on Line*, 25 October 2004)

In example 2, the caller repeats "hello" as if he is not certain whether he is currently on air. The host's repetition of the greeting and formal title alerts him to the fact that it is his turn. Once this has been established by his acknowledgement of her by name and title, she responds with a term of endearment to encourage conversation.

## Example 2

H: Good afternoon. THIS is *Disclosure*. Let's go to the phones.
C: Hello? Hello?
H: Hello, sir, you are on the air.
C: Hello?
H: Yes, sir.
C: Good afternoon, Ms H.
H: Good afternoon, darling.
C: Yes, I have two point here.

(*Disclosure*, 6 October 2004)

There is sometimes a mismatch between the tone of the host and that of the caller, as is illustrated in the informal alternatives, one of which is creole, chosen by the host in example 3, in response to callers' formal greetings. In section (a), the host's response indicates the relaxed atmosphere in which he conducts all his conversations. "Howdi", an informal local reduction of "How d'you do?", is used in conjunction with the male sibling referent, "brother". In (b), the correction to the time of day is made in creole, pre-empting any possible threat to the caller's face.

## Example 3

(a) H: *Laing and Company*. Good afternoon.
    C: Good afternoon, Mr L.
    H: *Howdi, my brother.*

(*Laing and Company*, 8 November 2004)

(b) H: This is TL.
    C: Good afternoon, sir.
    H: Maanin *mi pikni.*

(*Laing and Company*, 14 November 2004)

Classroom exercises designed to facilitate students' awareness of the functions, in context, of these alternative styles of greeting could focus on students' collection and discussion, in class, of a range of openings and closings of conversations noted from electronic and social media. Teachers could also have students compose dialogues and conversational routines in various formal settings, and involving strangers and superiors. Through role play which is critiqued by other class members applying the Hymes (1972) SPEAKING conventions, students gain practice in performing these routines in styles appropriate to the context, and in recognizing those which are inappropriate.

## Email Communication with Teachers

In the area of writing, Internet communication and text messaging have also contributed to the de-formalizing of communication. Formal written communication between, for example, students and their university lecturers, has given way to missives using the on-line vehicle. In such exchanges, the relaxed orthography, conversational tone and increasing informality in the style adopted all limit the viability of a formal approach. Some students have reported such ease with computer-mediated communication (CMC) via social media, that they have to make a conscious effort to reformulate messages to maintain an appropriate distance from those receiving them, and to do careful editing with respect to their academic presentations.

## Expressing Disagreement with Others' Points of View

Another important way in which the discourse of the native language is carried over to that of the target language is in contexts of public disagreement. Talk radio in Jamaica, one situation in which public disagreement is continually conducted, is replete with interactions in which disagreement is expressed, not in terms of evaluating opposing views and opinions, but of personal attacks on their proponents. This may be vaguely disguised, as in the case of a seemingly innocuous comment repeatedly made by a certain host, on what he regards as misrepresentations of his stated opinions: "Sir, I cannot be held responsible for the limitations of your understanding." It may also be delivered as a direct insult.

In the exchange recorded in example 4, the host, a minister of religion and psychologist who hosts both a religious programme and a talk show, insists on keeping the content of the programmes separate. He is upbraided by a frequent caller, who repeats his criticism of the discussions related to sexual matters aired on the talk show. This host's response is personal and face-threatening – an obvious indication of his exasperation, perhaps because he has so often repeated his rationale in the past. Also interesting is his manipulation of varieties: a Jamaican Creole-English code-mixed insult; informal English (incorporating a non-inverted question) for the advice given; and formal English for his editorial comment. In this comment, he addresses his radio audience, making reference to the caller in the third person, as if he is not present – perhaps because the producer has, by then, disconnected him.

## Example 4

C: Why you won' pray fo' people?
H: Iz bikaaz you kyaan du ANYTHING. Why you don' wan' me to talk about sex! If you can't have sex, why you don' go to the doctor? He thinks sex is nasty. He jus' has a nasty mind.

*(Dear Pastor, 20 March 2009)*

Televised parliamentary exchanges in which personal attacks are employed are another rich source of models of disagreement. A newspaper account of an exchange in one such debate is presented below.

## Example 5

But it was the classifying of the concerns by Senator AJ Nicholson, Leader of Opposition Business in the Senate, over the length of incarceration as "foolish and nonsensical" by Leader of Government Business in the Senate, Attorney General and Justice Minister, Senator Dorothy Lightbourne, that electrified the atmosphere in the chamber.

"Oftentimes we make these suggestions, they are not taken on board and there are consequences. If someone is going to regard this as nonsense, I think that's an idiotic approach," Knight said, provoking sounds of protest from Government senators. (*Jamaica Observer*, 12 July 2009)

Where such public disagreements are conducted in English, it is realistic to assume that target-language learners could be confused into considering their style and focus a model of formal English discourse. They therefore have to be given practice in recognizing and separating the in-your-face personalizing of contentious issues and those who promote them, from the impersonal, dispassionate responses to and analysis of opposing views. Newspapers, television news clips, public conversations and interviews are potentially good sources of data and analysis in this regard.

## Transferring the Oral to the Written

One obvious characteristic of a primarily oral communicative space is the intricate development of the oral milieu, with speech acts derived from oral speech events achieving primacy over those associated with any other mode. These constitute language learners' schematic knowledge – their background and sociocultural knowledge (content schemata) on the one hand, and their understanding of how discourse is organized in an appropriate response to contextual constraints (formal schemata) on the other (Carrell and Eisterhold 1983). It can be no surprise, then, that oral and informal elements are often evident, not only in the spoken presentations students make in class, but also in the submissions which they author and present as formal essays.

Examples 6 to 11, excerpts from problematic essays of applicants to the University of the West Indies, Mona, in the English Language Proficiency Test[1] of March 2007, have been included to illustrate this point. Several of them exhibit general weakness in written English;[2] however, I have left them as in the original, since it is the transfer of oral to written components of style which is of concern here.

The instructions on this test were, in part, as follows:

> Write a FORMAL ESSAY of about 300 words on the following set question. . . . Discuss with reference to your society and/or other societies TWO or THREE of the major issues arising from any ONE of the following [a, b or c].

In none of the examples discussed below, however, did it seem that the candidates, if indeed they had read the instructions, had mastered the style required. The following two examples are responses to the topic of skin bleaching. The author of example 7 uses informal phrases, such as "white folks", as well as the local phrases "pretty hair" and "picky picky head", which, to her credit, she puts in inverted commas.

## Example 6

> From the days of slavery until now people still believe that being white is better
> than being black. Back in slavery days, most white folks were masters and had a
> lot of black persons as slaves. Even now that we are emancipated, we seem to still
> not be free from slavery. But how can we be free, when mothers are seeking fathers
> with light complexion and we would call "pretty hair". When the child is born and
> attending school, the parent is ensuring that the child does not mix with the black
> "picky picky" head child.

In example 7, the author addresses several issues related to skin bleaching:
the legacy of slavery, self-rejection, peer pressure and health risks. The style,
however, is not that of a formal essay. From the first paragraph, the tone is didactic, with a first-person speaker addressing an audience as "we black people" – a
collective – in a manner characteristic of female single-sex conversation (Coates
1996). By paragraph 3, the author assumes an oral preaching style, rather than
that of a dispassionate discussant, addressing an audience directly in the second
person, as "[you] people". Colloquialisms such as "I guess" and "trust me" contribute to the informal, oral nature of the text.

## Example 7

> I strongly believe that we should love our skin, therefore I don't think anyone,
> whatsoever should destroy it. I believe that we black people should respect our
> colours bearing our ancestors in mind, and also our heroes and heroine that
> fought for us in time of slavery so that we can be free now.
>
> People our skin is too sensitive and beautiful for us to be destroying it. After
> all none of us made ourselves, none of us choose to be black. I guess none of us
> knows what God is doing, but trust me he does. . . .
>
> What little I know about relationship is that it should not be about the colour
> of a person's skin it should be about love, trust and communication. So people
> someone is persuading you to do it leave them instantly they don't want you.

In example 8, the topic is the use of cellular telephones. An essay which
begins, from a stylistic point of view, as exposition, moves seamlessly by paragraph 3 into a narrative, annotated by one examiner as a "rambling story" and
exhibiting very little adherence to English grammar, before ending with an
informal exhortation: "keep it positive".

## Example 8

In todays society, cellular telephone plays an important role. Cellular telephone is the device that is used to do most of our communication in all parts of the world, hence manufacturers are making them in different shapes, size and different features, to do other things than to communicate in your leisure. . . .

There are lots of human beings out there that all they can think about is violence stealing and killing. Those are the one's who use cellular telephone to do bad things. For example Tom who lives in the "ghetto" have a gun and he knows Jim from up town, Tom use his cellular telephone to inform Jim that he is coming uptown to rob one of his rich friends. Jim now use his cellular telephone, call one of his rich friends to meet him at x point. At this time Jim already call Tom and inform him of the location where he will meet Jim and his rich friend. When they all reach there destination Jim introduce Tom to his rich friend, they sat and they eat peacefully.

A few minutes later Tom pulled a shot gun from his waste and told Harry which is Jim friend to give him all the money he got. Harry replied. I don't have any money. Tom eventually shot Harry in his chest chest and ran. Later in the night the news report that three men were sitting at x point eating when one pulled gun hitting the other in the chest was taken to the UHWI where he was pronounced dead. I strongly agree that cellular phone is use full and important, so i urge anyone with a cellular phone to use it wisely and keep it positive.

Didactic, conversational and promotional voices characterized many of the essays presented in this English Language Proficiency Test. Example 9, on the staging of the 2007 ICC Cricket World Cup which took place in the West Indies, is generally informative, although the author assumes a didactic voice in the "We as people need to understand" of the second sentence.

## Example 9

Another concerns of many are, the fact that persons will not be able to enter the stadium with food items, radios, weapons and etc. We as people need to understand that previous cricket games here are not like the ICC Cricket World Cup. Hence certain traditions will not be accepted at a international competition such as this.

Example 10, however, captures the excitement and anticipation of a promotional piece encouraging the participation of fans.

## Example 10

> The World Cup Cricket lovers have been rushing to get their tickets. What a great event taking place in our back yard? This competition is one of the greatest of all times; therefore all eyes will be glued to the television set.
>
> Firstly the it is gateway to Tourism. The Caribbean will now welcome the entire world. Aren't you happy that Jamaica is apart of it? We will share with the world our food and different culture with some of the greatest competitors and visitors. What an exposure?

Example 11, from an essay on a recent outbreak of malaria in Jamaica, reads as if it were a government information service advisory, especially in the instructions offered at the end of the paragraph. In this case, abbreviations such as "e.g." and "etc." and phrases such as "or evenings", included as an afterthought to the old-fashioned "when night is drawing near", also add informality to the text.

## Example 11

> If a person is contagious or affected with Malaria there are many preventative methods to get treated, otherwise if persons are not affected but is present in areas that the disease is affecting the preventative methods should be taken up in hand and be done right away. For example, close windows and doors when night is drawing near or evenings, discard any item where water can be catched eg. Old tyres, cans etc,

All the excerpts quoted above have in common an incorporation of informal, spoken features within a text presented as a formal essay. There is no reason to believe that the writers have not been taught the mechanics of formal essay writing; rather, it is likely that, under examination pressure, they have resorted to what they know best: the creole discourse of their everyday existence. It is also possible that this has been reinforced in the classroom itself, since teachers at all levels often lead the discussion of essay topics in class, encouraging wide participation and focusing on content, rather than code or style.

Teachers may use problems in student writing, such as those presented above, as a basis for discussion among students, from a variety of perspectives: targeting revision of the creole segments to formal English; the informal, oral components to formal writing; idiomatic creole to idiomatic English and so on.

Focused discussion in class can clarify the reasons for the revisions made. Similar use may be made of everyday conversations in literary texts, which can be reworked to achieve a sense of appropriateness to different audiences, requiring changes of language, voice and register. Class exercises and discussion can clarify the changes generated by student proposals.

## Conclusion

The examples analysed above are problematic because of the transfer of oral, informal discourse to formal expository essays. This chapter has argued that such a problem is likely to arise from limitations in teachers' active awareness of the effects of major differentials in the discourse practices of the creole language and the target language, which constitute potential stumbling blocks in students' (as well as teachers') communicative competence in that target language.

Developing, as it seems, general competencies required for life – although not necessarily academic life – after secondary schooling, the CXC English A examination appears to have been reserving a focus on formal written essays in English for CAPE, which is sat at the end of grade 12 or 13.[3] What this means is that many first-year tertiary-level students, including in- and pre-service teachers, who leave school at the end of grade 11, demonstrate severe weaknesses with regard to their mastery of the formal registers of spoken and written English, and especially of the requirements of formal essay writing. Further, it is clear that even when discourse constraints in writing are addressed, and the discourse of classroom interaction is increasingly being informed by research, a holistic view of the social environment and social spaces of creole-speaking learners, with investigation of the discourse practices which characterize them, does not necessarily inform the practice of TESORV.

One obvious result of the sociolinguistic metamorphosis presented in the introduction as exemplified by Jamaica is the merging of public and private spaces, with a concomitant blurring of the distinctions previously made between public and private communicative behaviour. The expectations and practice of language educators have to be sensitive to the new reality. Without the spoken and written models of the past, and with the erosion of the standards associated with them, learners are at a distinct disadvantage – a challenge which teachers have to address in their target-language teaching. Analysis of these new environmental challenges must be at least a part of their response.

## Acknowledgement

I am grateful to the English Language Proficiency Test Unit, Department of Language, Linguistics and Philosophy, University of the West Indies, Mona, for access to the test scripts quoted above.

## Notes

1. Dyche (1996) discusses some of the results of the 1988 and 1999 tests in relation to the academic performance, in different disciplines, of some of its candidates.
2. The examples presented have not been edited.
3. CAPE also requires presentations of formal English speech.

## References

Brown, Penelope, and Stephen C. Levinson. 1987. *Politeness: Some Universals in Language Usage*. Cambridge: Cambridge University Press.

Carrell, Patricia L., and Joan C. Eisterhold. 1983. Schema Theory and ESL Reading Pedagogy. *TESOL Quarterly* 17 (4): 553–74.

Christie, Pauline. 1998. Trends in Jamaican English. In *History and Status of Creole Languages: Papers by Pauline Christie*, 19–34. Kingston: UWILing Working Papers in Linguistics.

Coates, Jennifer. 1996. *Women Talk*. London: Blackwell.

Craig, Dennis R. 1999. *Teaching Language and Literacy: Policies and Procedures for Vernacular Situations*. Kingston: Educational and Development Services.

———. 2006a. The Use of the Vernacular in West Indian Education. In *Exploring the Boundaries of Caribbean Creole Languages*, edited by H. Simmons-McDonald and I. Robertson, 99–117. Kingston: University of the West Indies Press.

———. 2006b. *Teaching Language and Literacy to Caribbean Students: From Vernacular to Standard English*. Kingston: Ian Randle.

Cummins, James. 1979a. Educational Implications of Mother Tongue Maintenance in Minority-Language Groups. *Canadian Modern Language Review* 34: 395–416.

———. 1979b. Linguistic Interdependence and the Educational Development of Bilingual Children. *Review of Educational Research* 49: 222–51.

Dyche, Caroline. 1996. Writing Proficiency in English and Academic Performance. In *Caribbean Language Issues, Old and New*, edited by P. Christie, 143–59. Kingston: University of the West Indies Press.

Hymes, Dell. 1972. Models of the Interaction of Language and Social Life. In *Directions in Sociolinguistics: The Ethnography of Communication*, edited by J.J. Gumperz and D. Hymes, 35–71. New York: Holt, Rinehart and Winston.

Long, Michael H. 1990. Maturational Constraints on Language Development. *Studies in Second Language Acquisition* 12 (4): 251–85.

Shields Brodber, Kathryn. 1992. Dynamism and Assertiveness in the Public Voice: Turn-Taking and Code-Switching in Radio Talk Shows in Jamaica. *Pragmatics* 2 (4): 487–504.

———. 1997. Requiem for English in an "English-Speaking" Community: The case of Jamaica. In *Englishes Around the World*, edited by E.W. Schneider, 57–68. Amsterdam: John Benjamins.

# 12 | Literature for the Caribbean Classroom

*Retired Senior Lecturer, School of Education*
*University of the West indies, Mona*

## Preamble: Dennis Craig and Literature

There is a painting on the administrative building at the University of Guyana of a child reading a book. On the open page is Dennis Craig's much-anthologized poem "Flowers".

The visitor to the University of Guyana will know immediately not that Dennis Craig had been vice chancellor there, not that he was a famous language educator, but that he was a poet. Creative writing is in fact a little-known aspect of Professor Craig's life. He wrote both prose and poetry, beginning with a prize-winning short story while he was still in school. In 1998, his collection *Near the Seashore* (Craig 1999) won the coveted Guyana Prize for Literature in the Best First Book category. However, I am pretty sure that students who have read and studied the poem "Flowers" in their school poetry books do not recognize its author when they meet him later as Craig in books on language education.

Literature was never far from Dennis Craig's concern, although his work was mainly on language. There is a series of books, well known in the 1970s and 1980s, that is becoming recognized again by the Ministry of Education in Jamaica after the revival by Wilson et al. (1983): it is the Language Materials Workshop Primary Language Arts series (Wilson, Craig and Campbell 1978).

All throughout the texts are stories and poems for children. The *Story Time* volume, which is included at each of the different levels in the series, presents books exclusively of literary selections from local and foreign writers. Craig had a great respect for the literary tradition and an appreciation of its power. Literature was a subterranean stream constantly refreshing his concerns with language. I feel privileged to be allowed to write this chapter and consider it fitting that a collection in his honour should include a section concerned with literature in the Caribbean classroom.

## Introduction

In the introduction to his exposition on the West Indian novel, Glynne Griffith identifies "the tradition of critical practice which differentiates the formal aspects of literature from literature's cultural realm" as a hindrance to the location of literature's sociopolitical intent and argues for "real engagement with the question of cultural concerns" (1996, xvi). Such a comment was reasonable at a time when literature in the anglophone Caribbean meant English literature and the selections offered to students said, in Olive Senior's oft-quoted words, "nothing about us at all" (1985, 26). But that time has long gone. There are people in their forties now who read poems and stories written by Caribbean people in their school and university classes. Yet recent discussions with graduate and undergraduate students in education suggest that students, certainly at the high-school level, are not enthusiastic about literature, not even Caribbean literature, and that teachers themselves are afraid of the subject – especially of poetry. Tyson (2003, 173), reporting on interviews with teachers of upper-level high-school classes, confirms this: "Some teachers also believe that there are teachers who fear and dislike poetry and so transmit their fear to the students." It is a chicken-and-egg situation: teachers are afraid so they avoid it; students get too little and so do not come to enjoy and love it.

It is my contention that there are young people in the schools waiting to enjoy whatever relates to their environment and that teachers can capitalize on that predisposition. The challenge is to select material that is interesting and to present it in an interesting way. This chapter constructs and comments on two units that can be modified for use at secondary or tertiary levels of the school system in any Caribbean territory. The first is a unit around a baptism by water and is for use in a literature course in high school or an introductory course in literature at university or teachers' college. It combines poetry and story with other art forms. The other is constructed around a natural phenomenon common in most Caribbean islands: a hurricane. Content information mixes easily with prose and poetry in that unit, giving literature the functional side that sceptics tend to say it lacks.

The audience of my concern is the large group of young people in Caribbean classrooms; my conduit to them is the teacher who comes to the university to be retrained by following the Bachelor in Education programme in the teaching of English. The units presented here were greeted with some excitement by one such group. They are not meant to be at all prescriptive but are prototypes for unit preparation.

A thematic approach to the construction of teaching units is by no means new. What I propose here is the thematic unit stretched beyond its usual limits. In the first unit, the extension is into creative material not usually considered literature. In the other, there is the same kind of mixing, but the reading includes material that is technical, and the aim of the unit is to make technical information clearer and more relevant and so more easily accessible to the students. In both cases there is multi-sensual stimulation, encouraging an interactive classroom. While both units have been used in a course, Introduction to the Teaching of Literature, the second may be used as well in courses in a number of social-science programmes where literature enhances technical information. This kind of mixing of material is more natural than the segmentation too often practised in the classroom. Edward Baugh (2001, 154), writing on the arts in education, makes a point that supports this thinking: "We must recognize . . . that the line we draw . . . between literature and the other Arts, is not at all precise, to the extent, for example, that plays are also literature, or poetry is also a performance art, and dance is theater, and everything is everything else."

## Unit 1

This unit is centred around a religious ceremony: a baptism by water. Religion is a popular theme in the Caribbean. Many churches use baptism by water as the means of inducting the newly converted into the congregation of the "chosen". Today, that baptism is largely in a sanitized pool inside the church, usually covered, to be uncovered as required. Historically, the ceremony took place in a river. In contrast to that method is the practice in "established" churches of confirmation, the laying on of hands, for the induction. Baptism there is usually reserved for infants, and the water is placed in a font inside the church. Baptism in the river may be considered traditional and is by far the more dramatic method. Visual and audiovisual items related to this practice are easily available. The discussion within the unit runs to questions of economics, class and language in a society where these are never far from the daily experience and about which students have a lot to say when they feel comfortable enough to express their views.

The unit is introduced with "Confirmation Day", a short story by Olive Senior, which may be read aloud to the class by the teacher. It is a short enough story to be read in class, and my experience is that students of all ages like to listen to a story. The eventual focus is on two passages which describe contrasting modes of induction into religious communities. A young girl is being confirmed into the Anglican (Church of England, Episcopalian) community of which her father's family is a part. During that ceremony, she is remembering the contrasting baptism which she had experienced earlier in her mother's church, a Pentecostal community. A point is being made here about social class. The induction into the middle-class, established church is contrasted with the induction into a church usually associated with lower-class communities. The distinction between the communities is less real today than it was perhaps forty years ago when the story is set. Class is not the focus of the unit, but it cannot be ignored in a story such as this, where even the difference in the type of cloth from which the girl's dress is made on the different occasions gets mentioned: cotton as against guipure. What is to be noted and particularly appreciated is the detail with which Senior paints each scene and draws the reader in. The point of view is that of the young girl. Her reverie guides the reader. The following is her present:

> Now we are in another time another church and the smell of incense mingles with the smell of the church and the smell is the smell of the aged. . . .
> And I think as the bishop stands there in robes trimmed with gold chanting words that sound as if he speaks in a foreign language that Confirmation will transform me too, utterly. And the smell of the church will be transformed into the smell of the bats in the nave of the church, into a world of fonts and gravestones. (1986, 82)

This is counterposed to the related experience of her past:

> I in my white shift not guipure but cotton my knees trembling with the early morning cold went down and fought with all my might not to go a second or a third time for in the bottom of the river I had seen the mud and the reeds and

the terrible reality of His existence and knew that if I went down three times I would be obliterated by His greatness. And the day became a day of the brothers and sisters who were not my brothers and sisters singing and praying praying and singing for me and my mother crying crying for me Oh-Oh-Ohhhhhhh!!!! (p. 83)

Discussions about the two events and students' personal experiences of similar or related events may extend the unit in unexpected directions. Other material includes visual and audiovisual representations of baptisms. There is a reproduction, from a calendar, of a piece by a Jamaican artist. It shows a preacher dipping a female convert into the water of a shallow river whose water flows over huge stones. In the river and on its banks are worshippers all dressed in white; the women's heads are tied with white cloth. The preacher is not dressed in white, but the man who helps him hold the woman under is. All are passionately involved in the proceedings. Someone in the class will remember the mud and reeds the young girl in Senior's story saw in the bottom of the river.

A newspaper clipping, a photograph of two bishops performing a real baptism in the Rio Cobre in St Catherine, Jamaica, passed around or projected onto a wall, provides the kind of authenticity which might reassure those students who have never witnessed such a baptism.

There is a recording from the CD *It Was the Singing* by Edward Baugh. The voice is strong and eloquent. A copy of the poem from the collection of the same title is circulated *after* the listening. The relationship between the photograph and the poem will be immediately clear, and between both and the passage from "Confirmation Day". It is a short poem, "Detail from 'Ritual of the River'" (2000, 35), and it runs in part:

> strapping young preacherman dipping
> them, cool morning water, hands sure as faith,
> the faithful rejoicing singing them over

Finally, there is a music video, "Revival Time", by the popular Jamaican singing group Chalice. The chords on the keyboard support the lively initial chorus:

> Aamen Aamen
> Aamen Aamen
> Aamen

The lead singer is a young man dressed like a revival preacher with his white robes and turbaned head. A crowd of similarly robed faithful stand watching and singing on the riverbank. The pastor figure is a young man with a sweet, clear voice which soon takes over with:

> Children children
> come to the river
> you want to born again
> you want to feel brand new . . .

He takes one of the faithful and plunges her backwards into the river water.

The order of presentation of material is not meant to be prescriptive. The teacher can decide on his or her own order. The discussions include detailed comparisons between the different renderings of the same event. Questions of point of view and of artistry loom large. The description of the Anglican confirmation from Senior's story provides an excellent foil for the more dramatic representations.

This unit is a prototype. The chosen theme might be anything that catches the teacher's fancy or that he or she has the materials to support. In this case, it was the picture on the calendar that struck me first. The other pieces came together afterwards. In the actual class, however, the audio aspects (Baugh's voice) and the music video were most highly appreciated. I imagine that teachers taking a unit such as this into the classroom would hardly hear the oft-repeated comment that literature is boring. Students can identify with all the materials presented. The words of the song in the music video validate the fact that poetry is not only words on the page of a textbook but lyrics people in the society sing all the time. As the unit progresses, students might come to write their own poems and to make critical judgements about them. In terms of culture and environment, an added advantage is that the unit introduces for some, for others reinforces, knowledge of an event that is part of the local culture. When I presented this unit, the participants seized the opportunities for discussing aspects of class, religious practice and language use. I am sure the participants in the classes to which they eventually took this or similar units would have responded in the same way.

## Unit 2

This unit is one which may be used to enhance courses in environmental science, agriculture, public health or any other related area. The unit is constructed within a social studies framework. The theme is "Tropical Phenomena". The event is a hurricane, a phenomenon which Caribbean people are constantly required to cope with. The unit responds in part to the request that literature be made to seem useful to other subjects, and while I do not feel that literature needs to be defended in these terms, I do feel that it can bring the classroom close to the environment and help with the enlightenment and the transformation each generation of educators hopes the classroom will perform on students.

The hurricane affects human life and the environment in a frightful way. The more information the population has about it, the more prepared people can be. The unit begins with factual material which is theoretical in the sense that it describes a phenomenon which cannot be immediately experienced. The literary and artistic material described here gives it life. The factual material in the taught unit was taken from a booklet on disaster preparedness. It is material, however, that is available in any geography or environmental science book. In the actual teaching of the unit, as a pre-unit activity, the class might be asked to solicit material from a government division or to use the library or the Internet.

The first literary piece is "The View from the Terrace", a short story by Olive Senior (1989). This story is in fact a complex comment on race, class and social behaviour in Jamaica presented in fine graphic prose. It is a story guaranteed to interest any group. Wind and rain are responsible for how the story ends. A well-to-do crippled retiree watches, from a wheelchair set on his terrace, the construction of a house on a precarious spot on the hillside in his immediate line of vision. His unspoken comment on the inadvisability of building a house at that location is made more believable by the fact that he is a retired civil servant, who on his job was required to select land for building houses. Eight years and many children after he first notices the activity of the single female adult, wind and rain dislodge the house and the squatters:

> Then there was a night when he thought his own roof would go so heavy was the pounding from the rain, the heaviest they said afterwards in seventy years . . .
>
> When the rains cleared, he saw that the house on the hillside had really gone. Bits and pieces of zinc and wood scattered and shored up against the cotton tree were all that remained. (p. 109)

The story ends with an ironic twist, in which the woman and all her children end up in the man's backyard and the details of her story as related by his caregiver unnerve him to such an extent that something bursts in his head "like rain". When the house is put up on the hillside again there is nobody to notice.

The possibilities for reaction and discussion on aspects of the society – class, gender relations, economics – are endless and easily relate literature to life. Of course, there is an appreciation of the quality of the prose and the construction of character.

Following this are two poems by Derek Walcott. One is a short poem, fifteen lines, written early in his career: "The Hurricane (after Hokusai)", from the collection *In a Green Night* (1962). It is a comment on a piece of art by a Japanese artist, on a hurricane at sea. Walcott, an artist himself, paints with words what another artist has put on canvas. It begins:

> Come where on this last shore of broken teeth
> All spume and fury of snorting battle-horses,
> Wild waves and trees are lashing their drenched hair
> Like treacherous women come to grief . . .

Additional life and sound are added to the canvas with the activity of a "mad, old fisherman dancing on his barge" and the unlikely detail of "salt delight of wrinkled eyes" (p. 69).

The other selection is a later description, an excerpt from *Omeros* (1990). The poet here is not limited by what is in a painting. The hurricane is alive, and truly destructive. This one reads like a lived experience. The poet personalizes the behaviours of the different actors in the performance of an extremely energetic hurricane. He finds in Greek mythology a reason for the behaviour of the elements. The poet who elsewhere relates the configuration of the isles of Greece to the Caribbean archipelago links a Caribbean experience to Greek fable. Cyclone/Cyclops is made master of the enterprise. Of course he has accomplices:

> The Cyclone, howling because one of the lances
> of a flinging palm has narrowly grazed his one eye,
> wades knee-deep in troughs. As he blindly advances,
>
> Lightning, his stilt-walking messenger, jiggers the sky
> with his forked stride, or he crackles over the troughs
> like a split electric wishbone. His wife Ma Rain
>
> hurls buckets from the balcony of her upstairs house
> She shakes the sodden mops of the palms and once again
> Changes her furniture, the cloud sofas' grumbling casters
> Not waking the Sun . . .

(pp. 51–52)

The visual and aural aspects of the description are likely to excite anyone who has ever witnessed a hurricane. Comparable descriptions in other material will appear later in the unit. The description further concerns itself with features to which every student can relate. This kind of activity takes place even when hurricanes do not actually hit. They are part of the "preparation" in case:

> there is a brisk business in candles
> in Ma Kilman's shop. Candles, nails, a sudden increase in
> the faithful, and a mark-up on matches and bread
>
> (p. 52)

The features of the hurricane are clear. Fork lightning has two strikingly different manifestations. Deluges are made out to be effects of Ma Rain mopping her house, and the sound of thunder is related to her changing her furniture around. The hurricane is full of pictures and of noises and sounds which seem clearer and louder than the "snorting battle-horses" of the earlier poem. This selection has the added advantage of making Walcott, even later Walcott, accessible. This is important. I have heard this poet's work described by teachers as "difficult". A gentle introduction here humanizes the writing and might well begin an incursion into it for some fascinated student.

The centre of the unit is the music video "Wild Gilbert", in which Jamaican popular performer Lloyd Lovindeer (1989) sings while vivid pictures of wind and rain in action and different people reacting to them slide across the screen. As in the Walcott poem, the descriptions are personified. The metaphors are close to the bone. Walcott's Ma Rain hurls buckets from the sky ("her upstairs house"). They fall on the floor, where the video shows Lovindeer's hurricane survivor sweeping it away endlessly: "Water come eena mi room / Mi sweep out some wid mi broom". Pictures in the video of the coconut trees with their leaves looking like they're trying to escape from the trunk illustrate the activity of the Cyclops in the first two Walcott lines above. But Lovindeer drags the hurricane into the twentieth century by having a householder look for his treasured possession:

> Oonu see mi dish
> Oonu see mi dish
> Anybody oonu si mi satellite dish?

Lovindeer does not go to Greek mythology but instead makes a connection with a children's nursery rhyme in a memorable pun:

the little dog laugh
to see such fun
di dish run away wid di spoon.

The video includes an interview of Lovindeer by a young journalist who wants to find out, *inter alia*, the nature of the creative event. His responses are simple and quite in contrast to the sophistication of the lines he eventually produces. Metaphors close to the Caribbean reality written in high dramatic style are his métier. He tells the journalist how he noticed that several houses had lost their roofs, so he wrote about that. In the actual song it becomes: "The roof migrate without a visa", allowing the hurricane to be a facilitator in illegal migration. This is a topic near to the mind certainly of every Jamaican. It is discussed in the newspapers constantly as relatives and friends are found out and deported chiefly from cities of the United States, where they have managed to stay without the necessary papers. And everyone in all the islands is aware of the long lines of people waiting in all weather to get into the American Embassy to request a visa.

The interview with the journalist offers the teacher (and eventually high-school students) a peek into the mind of the artist: a notion of how the creative imagination works its act of transformation on raw material. If this is a literature class, there is a natural link here with figures of speech and how they can be used effectively. The lyrics of this video are an excellent example of poetry written in the language of the community. The lines in the earlier video about the baptism pointed to poetry in places where it may not have been so labelled. The several verses of Lovindeer's song, with the possibilities for close analysis, take that activity to a higher level.

## Conclusion

The construction of the units above is an exercise in selecting material focusing on a particular topic. Beach and Marshall (1991, 189–90), citing advantages of the topic unit, point to the fact that "students can relate their own information about a topic to the texts in the unit". The term "text" in the units described here is understood in its widest sense, as material selected from any aspect of the arts. As the students relate texts to their lives, they may make suggestions which teachers can add to these open-ended units every time they use them. The suggestions may take the units into areas more familiar to the students than those the teacher selected: drama, dub-poetry, calypso, for example. The Caribbean is an extraordinarily literary environment. As soon as the teacher broadens his or her perspective in terms of what is accessible classroom material, the richness of the culture allows the unit to go along paths not thought of at first. The materials, particularly those which appeal to multiple senses, are interesting and have the ability to hold the attention of students. If we believe that the average human being has an attention span of no more than twelve minutes, then interactive exercises which evolve from the kind of material we are considering here should be encouraged. There is room for comparisons not only between the earlier and later poems by Derek Walcott, but between the non-fiction description of a hurricane and the literary descriptions of it, as well as between both and the filmed representation in the video. There is room for discussion with peers, and most importantly there is room for students' own creative output in story, poetry, art and music around the selected themes.

I mentioned earlier the exposure this kind of unit can provide. In the case of the hurricane, there will be students who are like the "young bud" in the "Wild Gilbert" video who have never experienced one but have been told or have read about the devastating experience. By the end of the multi-sensory presentation, the young person will be close to having had it.

An interactive classroom session is highly valued in educational circles today. With regard to the teaching of literature, Round's comment is to the point: "Teachers of literature will aim to create a rich interactive learning environment in the classroom which encourages a life-long enjoyment of literature" (1997, 295). Even larger claims are made for the teaching of literature, claims which make it urgent that teachers operate in such a way as to engage the students in a lasting fashion. Anne Turvey (2005, 181), in the editorial for a volume of *Changing English*, says: "Literature and literature teaching provide a site for what may be the most profound transformations, as teachers engage with pupils in reading and making connections between 'the world of the book and the world of its readers.'" Units like the above, which draw on material from the environment and material which reflects a response to all the senses, are arrows on the road to the hoped-for transformation.

Lorna Down (2003), writing on the subject of literature as a classroom tool for transformation and sustainability, describes an interesting and successful presentation of Earl Lovelace's novel *The Wine of Astonishment* in a Caribbean classroom. This particular presentation pushes the ideas suggested in the units above even further. The themes are abstract and therefore more difficult to illustrate. The teacher is concerned with alerting students to the "historical context of enslavement, colonialism, of dominant and subordinate power relations". Down describes the imaginative activity in this way:

> Using an integrative approach, [the teacher] created the opportunity for students to present content . . . from their other subject areas, including history, social studies, religious education. Employing graphics and visuals, students produced two "texts" – one they wrote when they described Caribbean society, using only graphics, and the other they helped to write as they collated writings, objects, pictures, into a collage. Students were then encouraged to note the connections between the novel being studied, the extra-textual material, and the text they had created. (p. 94)

Every time a teacher succeeds in firing the imagination of the class in this way, the transformation which optimists hope the classroom can facilitate draws nearer to being realized.

## Acknowledgement

Some sections of this chapter appear in the volume *Teaching Post-Colonialism and Post-Colonial Literatures*, edited by Anne Collett et al. (Aarhus: Aarhus University Press, 1997), as part of the article "From Periphery to Centre: Teaching Caribbean Literature within a Post-Colonial/Commonwealth Context".

## References

Baugh, Edward. 2001. The Arts in Education: The Arts for Life. *Caribbean Journal of Education* 23 (1–2): 153–61.

———. 2000. Detail from "Ritual of the River". In *It Was the Singing*. Kingston: Sandberry Press.

Beach, Richard, and James Marshall. 1991. *Teaching Literature in the Secondary School*. Orlando, FL: Harcourt Brace.

Craig, Dennis R. 1999. *Near the Seashore*. Georgetown, Guyana: Education and Development Services.

Down, Lorna. 2003. Literature: A Classroom Tool for Transformation and Sustainability. *Caribbean Journal of Education* 25 (2): 91–102.

Griffith, Glyne. 1996. *Deconstruction, Imperialism and the West Indian Novel*. Kingston: The Press, University of the West Indies.

Lovindeer, Lloyd. 1989. Gilbert Yu Gone. Kingston: Prolific Productions.

Round, Sue. 1997. Becoming a Teacher of Literature. *Changing English* 4 (2): 295–304.

Senior, Olive. 1985. Colonial Girls School. In *Talking of Trees*. Kingston: Calabash.

———. 1986. Confirmation Day. In *Summer Lightning*. Harlow: Longman.

———. 1989. The View from the Terrace. In *Arrival of the Snake Woman*. Harlow: Longman.

Turvey, Anne. 2005. Who'd Be an English Teacher? *Changing English* 12 (1): 3–18.

Tyson, Esther. 2003. Unchartered Territory: Teachers' Adaptation to the Caribbean Advanced Proficiency Examination (CAPE) Literatures in English Curriculum. *Caribbean Journal of Education* 25 (2): 170–74.

Walcott, Derek. 1962. The Hurricane. In *In a Green Night*. London: Jonathan Cape.

———. 1990. *Omeros*. London: Faber and Faber.

Wilson, Don, Dennis R. Craig and Hyacinth Campbell. 1978. *Language Materials Workshop (LMW): Primary Language Arts Series*. Kingston: Ministry of Education.

Wilson, Don, and Hyacinth Campbell, with Betty Wilson. 1983. *Language Arts for Primary School*. Kingston: Heinemann Educational (Caribbean).

# 13 | Common Problems in Teaching French as a Foreign Language in the English-Official Caribbean

JEANNETTE ALLSOPP

*University of the West Indies, Cave Hill*

The teaching of French in the English-official Caribbean, including Barbados, is undoubtedly the teaching of a foreign language, there being no speech community in our territories to provide any practical, constant backup such as would occur if French were a second language in the society. A quick overview of the history of foreign language teaching in the English-official Caribbean will show that this area of education as a whole only began to assume any serious importance after the emancipation of slaves in 1834. However, it is necessary to provide a brief sketch of the Caribbean language situation as a whole before that period.

## A Brief Overview of the Caribbean Language Situation

During the pre-emancipation era, the language situation in the Caribbean in general developed out of contact between peoples brought about by the settlement history of the region. The indigenous population largely disappeared after the arrival of the Europeans, unable to withstand the strange diseases, strange animals and gunpowder brought by the latter, and as a result European indentured labour was recruited to cultivate tobacco, which was the main crop at the time. When sugar replaced tobacco as the main crop, a much larger workforce was needed, thus sparking the "Sugar Revolution", as it was called – the historical event that gave rise to the triangular Atlantic slave trade, which brought millions of West African slaves to the Caribbean. Their importation into the Caribbean specifically to work on the sugar plantations introduced a new linguistic dimension into the region, as the hundreds of West African languages brought by the slaves merged with the languages of the European masters to form new varieties, or contact vernaculars, which were very limited and rudimentary forms of language used for the specific purpose of sugar cultivation. These ultimately became "creoles" as they gained wider currency of usage in Caribbean societies, including the English-official Caribbean.

The newly formed languages, or creoles, existed side by side with the European languages that had already been brought into the region by the colonial masters: namely, Spanish, English, French and Dutch, the former socially stigmatized because they were spoken by the large mass of slaves and the latter regarded as the elite variety because they were spoken by the socially and politically dominant planter classes. Those creoles or creole-influenced vernaculars that developed, such as Bajan dialect, came to be the L1 or first language of the majority of speakers in the anglophone Caribbean.

This is the language situation which present-day Caribbean societies have inherited and which has influenced significantly the learning and teaching of English and foreign languages in the Caribbean region, particularly the English-speaking Caribbean, with which this chapter is specifically concerned.

## Foreign Language Teaching and Learning in the Post-Emancipation Period

In the post-emancipation Caribbean, foreign languages were learned only for the sake of erudition, since a good education guaranteed social mobility for newly freed slaves. It was only in the early decades of the twentieth century that foreign languages began to be taught as part of the school curriculum of secondary schools in the anglophone Caribbean. As Allsopp (1995) points out, since the best schools in all the territories of the English-speaking Caribbean were grammar schools, patterned after the English grammar schools, their curricula were largely faithful replicas of the English grammar-school curriculum, with Latin taking pride of place because it was considered highly prestigious to have a knowledge of that language.

The fact that exactly the same methodology was used to teach French, a living language with a large speech community regionally and worldwide, as that used to teach Latin during the greater part of the first half of the twentieth century, created a generation of teachers who did not speak the language. In fact, French was taught early in the century by a "spelling method", which meant that the language was not heard in a continuous flow by the students, and words were not even pronounced but spelled out. Vocabulary was acquired in this way with the L1 equivalents of words and phrases always supplied, and the teaching of structure was paramount. Consequently, students were able to read and write French but not speak it because, in effect, the methodology in operation here was the grammar-translation method as inherited from the Renaissance, when scholars were taught to decipher valuable Latin and Greek texts in European libraries through knowledge of structure and vocabulary only.

## The Teaching of French in the English-Official Caribbean from the Early Twentieth Century to the Present

Such a situation in the English-speaking Caribbean bred a group of teachers who, as a consequence, could not teach their students to speak French, but who could, and did, very successfully, teach them to translate and to write grammatically correct French. Further, standard English, which is the variety officially claimed to be taught in Caribbean schools, but which is not the L1 of the vast majority of Caribbean children, was also taught in this way and helped to reinforce the knowledge and understanding of structural concepts in French.

The language-teaching situation as it existed in schools, outlined above, continued until about the sixties and early seventies, with English grammar being carefully taught. At this point, Latin was taught only in some Caribbean grammar schools that were patterned off British grammar schools because, in addition to the intellectual and social prestige it carried, the prevailing opinion was that it provided a good structural and lexical base for both English and foreign languages such as French and Spanish. However, Latin began to lose ground as it fell out of use even in the Roman Catholic Church, and it was gradually phased out altogether, except in very few schools in the English-speaking Caribbean. From the time of the Second World War, when oral competence in several languages became literally a life-and-death matter and crucial to national security, there was a shift away from the emphasis on the teaching of structure in the developed countries which have the greatest influence on the English-speaking Caribbean, namely, Britain and the United States. The new language-teaching methodology which emerged began to lessen the emphasis on structure, and methods which emphasized oral competence began to evolve as societal needs changed drastically.

In the 1940s through the 1960s, a number of new methods arose in Britain and the United States. The most important among them to help us understand our situation regarding the change in teaching methodologies of standard English were the oral approach and situational language teaching in Britain and audio-lingualism in the United States, which sought to help students develop oral competence. Although structure was considered important for correct expression, it was not the primary focus as it had been before.

The teaching of English grammar was gradually phased out in our primary and secondary schools in the English-speaking Caribbean, and language arts developed in its place in the late 1960s and early 1970s. This gave rise to a generation of students and teachers who were not familiar with the concept of language structure, as this was not addressed at the basic level in the primary-school language arts curriculum. This fact impacted negatively on the learning and teaching of foreign languages in general, and, as it is the purpose of this chapter to illustrate, on the learning and teaching of French.

## The Current Status of French in Schools in the English-Official Caribbean

Furthermore, the teaching of French, while it continued to flourish in many schools in Barbados and the other territories of the English-speaking Caribbean itself, in which English is the official language, began to be phased out in favour of Spanish, which is really the majority language of the Caribbean, in demographic terms, followed by French Creole.

French began to be considered as too "difficult" in regard to both pronunciation and structure for children in the "newer" secondary or comprehensive-type schools of Barbados, as well as in comprehensive-type secondary schools in territories such as Jamaica and Guyana. Spanish, on the other hand, in addition to being recognized as the majority foreign language of the Caribbean, was also perceived as being easy to pronounce and easier to learn than French (the latter assumption is clearly a myth). As a result, while most schools in Barbados teach Spanish, not all of them teach French, and the same is true in Guyana and Jamaica. In Guyana, foreign languages in general have suffered greatly, for a number of reasons which are more political than educational, a statement which would be better addressed in a separate article. On the other hand, territories like Trinidad, St Lucia and Dominica still have a fairly strong French-teaching tradition because of their settlement history; the French occupation, which was quite prolonged, influenced their culture and, therefore, their language.

This, then, is the situation, in outline, in which French as a foreign language finds itself today in the English-official Caribbean in general.

## Problems Encountered in the Teaching of French

A number of problems emerge in the teaching of French in our schools today, caused by the following factors:

1. the phonological and morphological peculiarities of the French language;
2. the lack of knowledge of the concept of structure in general and certainly of the structure of the standard variety of English;
3. the structural peculiarities of the non-standard vernacular which is the L1 of the majority of Barbadian and other English-speaking Caribbean students; and
4. teachers' inability to deal with the three abovementioned problems because of their own deficiencies in the French language. These stem from various factors, including lack of preparation in, and practice of, the spoken language; lack of knowledge of language structure; and insufficient knowledge of the principles of second language acquisition.

Some common examples of the first problem – namely, the phonological and morphological peculiarities of the French language – are found in the following errors, collected from a sample of five schools here in Barbados, both "older" or grammar-type schools and "newer" secondary schools.

### Phonological Peculiarities

1. The vowel sound /ə/, as found in *me, te, le, de*, pronounced by students like /e/ in Caribbean and other varieties of English
2. The vowel sound /ɔ/, as found in *alors, robe, note, force, homme*, and pronounced like /o/ as in *go* in Caribbean and other varieties of English

3. The vowel sound /y/, as found in the words *tu, du, rue, plume, utile,* which are pronounced like /u/ in English
4. The vowel sound /û/, the allophone of /u/, which is slightly more closed than the above sound, as in the word *sûr.*

## Pronunciation of Combined Vowels or Diphthongs

1. /ɛ/, as in *mais* and *lait,* which is more closed than <è>, but is pronounced [e] as in English *day* by most students
2. /o/, which is equivalent to the /o/ sound in English *go* and which is often pronounced /ɔ/ by students in words like *pauvre, sauf* and *cause*
3. /ø/, as in *deux, feu* and *peu,* which has no equivalent in English and which tends to be pronounced by students like English /o/
4. /œ/, as in words like *soeur, boeuf* and *coeur,* which also has no equivalent in English and which is often pronounced like English /u/.

Students often experience great difficulty in the pronunciation of nasalized vowels, such as those in the following examples:

1. /ã/, as in words like *an, sans, France, en, envie, accent, camp* and *temps,* which tend to be pronounced like the open [a] or the open [ɛ] in English
2. /ɛ̃/, as in words like *fin, faim* and *simple*
3. /ə/, as in words like *le, me* and *ne*
4. /œ̃/, as in words like *brun, chacun* and *lundi.*

Students also tend to have difficulty in recognizing that when /n/ and /m/ come between vowels they are pronounced differently, and there is overgeneralization on the part of students, who apply the same pronunciation to words like *fin* and *impossible,* which leads them to pronounce *inutile,* for example, as /ɛ̃nytil/ instead of /inytil/.

## Pronunciation of Consonants

Consonants – such as French /g/ before the vowels /e/ and /i/ as opposed to before /o/, /a/ and /u/ – also create many problems for students. Similarly, and this applies to Barbados in particular, many people cannot reproduce the sound [ʒ] but render it as [ʤ], so that the French *je* becomes /ʤe/. Perhaps /ʁ/ is the most difficult French consonant to pronounce for Caribbean students from territories where the variety of English is *r*-full, as in Barbados, Jamaica and Guyana, rather than *r*-less, as in Trinidad, St Lucia, Dominica, St Kitts and Grenada, where French influence was comparatively strong. Consequently, there are renderings of the French words *rouge* as /ɹuʒ/ instead of /ʁuʒ/, and so on.

Some final consonants in French provide a strong challenge for the comparatively few Barbadian and other anglophone Caribbean students who speak mostly Caribbean standard English. The fact that most English final consonants are pronounced, such as /t/ and /d/, carries over to the French pronunciation of words like *ils sont*, *dans*, *alors*, *petit* and *gris*.

In some cases, the teachers themselves are not competent enough in spoken French to correct all the phonological errors made by students because they do not use the language enough – they do not seek to interact with native speakers both inside and outside of Barbados or other anglophone Caribbean territories, and so lack practice – or because they have not been sufficiently well prepared in the language.

## Morphological Peculiarities

The variety of French nouns and their different endings tends to produce a great deal of confusion in the minds of secondary-school students who are not properly introduced to them via the principles of word formation. For example, there is a class of nouns which end in the suffix -*et* and which are usually masculine, such as in the examples below.

**-et** /e/
*le parquet*
*le ballet*
*le sachet*

Conversely, there is a class of nouns which are usually feminine and which end in the suffix -*ette*:

***-ette*** /ɛt/
*la toilette*

*la baguette*
*la serviette*

Another class contains nouns which are usually masculine and which end in the suffix -*eau:*

-**eau** /o/
*le manteau*
*le chapeau*
*le bureau*

There are also adjective paradigms which have different forms in the masculine and feminine which involve complete orthographical changes, such as:

| | | |
|---|---|---|
| *beau* | *bel* | *belle* |
| *vieux* | *vieil* | *vieille* |
| *nouveau* | *nouvel* | *nouvelle* |

The student has to understand when and why the special form of the masculine adjective in the middle column is used before a masculine noun beginning with a silent *h* or a stressed vowel.

There are other adjectives which double their consonants before adding *e* to form the feminine, such as:

| | |
|---|---|
| *bon* | *bonne* |
| *gros* | *grosse* |
| *bas* | *basse* |
| *gentil* | *gentille* |

In addition, there is the phonological fact that the final consonant in the feminine form of these adjectives is pronounced because of the addition of a final vowel /e/, which poses difficulties for students.

There are adjectives which simply add *e* to the masculine to make it feminine, such as:

| | |
|---|---|
| *mauvais* | *mauvaise* |
| *gris* | *grise* |
| *grand* | *grande* |
| *intelligent* | *intelligente* |

As in the previous example, the final consonant in the feminine form of these adjectives is voiced because of the addition of the final vowel /e/.

There are adjectives which end in -*x* in the masculine and undergo a spelling change to end in -*se* in the feminine. The same principle applies in this sample of adjectives as in the previous two samples cited above.

| | |
|---|---|
| *dangereux* | *dangereuse* |
| *heureux* | *heureuse* |
| *merveilleux* | *merveilleuse* |
| *paresseux* | *paresseuse* |

The fact that such types of adjectives exist and that there is grammatical gender in French adds to the students' confusion and leads to errors of noun–adjective agreement, especially as there is no grammatical gender in English and no need for morphological changes in adjectives to mark that gender. The adjective remains the same regardless of the noun it describes, and regardless of the particular characteristics of that noun, such as whether it is singular or plural. The descriptive adjective *beautiful*, for example, undergoes no morphological change to differentiate between *a beautiful house* and *beautiful houses,* or *a beautiful house* and *a beautiful person.*

Similarly, morphological changes in French verbs to denote differences in tense constitute another feature of the language which is baffling and often frustrating to secondary-school learners of French. Take, for example, the spelling change which occurs in a commonly used verb like *s'appeler*, a seemingly straightforward regular -*er* verb in the present tense, where the verb is written *je m'appelle, tu t'appelles, il/elle s'appelle* in the singular and *ils/elles s'appellent* in the third-person plural of the present indicative and the present subjunctive. The first- and second-person plural follow the normal morphological pattern of an -*er* verb: *nous appelons, vous appelez.* Additionally, there are changes of accentuation in high-frequency regular verbs such as *acheter*, where a grave accent has to be written on the first *e* of the first-, second- and third-person singular and the third-person plural of the verb, resulting in the spellings *j'achète, tu achètes, il/elle achète* and *ils/elles achètent.* There are also spelling changes in other high-frequency regular -*er* verbs such as *employer, nettoyer* and *envoyer,* to name one group, and in other verbs such as *manger* in which the word-medial <g> changes to <ge> before the vowels <a> or <o>.

In addition, the numerous irregular verbs, most of which are high frequency, are bewildering in their morphological peculiarities. Examples are the verb *aller,* with its irregular present indicative, subjunctive, future and conditional tenses, as well as the fact that, being a verb of motion, its *passé composé* is conjugated with the verb *être* and not the verb *avoir*; the verb *acquérir*, with its irregular present indicative, subjunctive, imperfect, future and conditional tenses and its irregular past participle; the verb *s'asseoir*, which is irregular in almost all its tenses, both indicative and subjunctive, and which has an irregular past participle; and the verbs *avoir, être, dire, devoir, pouvoir, vouloir, boire, connaître, savoir, mourir, partir* and *sortir*.

Additionally, a structural concept such as the subjunctive, which is not marked in English except in fast-disappearing phrases such as "if I were" and "lest he fall", poses a problem for teachers and students of French. Since teachers themselves have difficulties with these concepts, due to the way in which they themselves were taught, we cannot therefore be surprised that their own deficiencies in these areas are transferred to their students.

Furthermore, if we now reflect on the fact that the majority of Barbadian and Caribbean children do not speak standard English but a non-standard variety of English, and that some Caribbean children speak French Creole, the problems are compounded. Indeed, as Roberts (1983) points out, what some people in the Caribbean (and this includes teachers of English) identify as standard or non-standard English does not necessarily fit those respective categories, so that the identification by teachers of successful learning is not as general nor as certain as is sometimes supposed.

In the case of Barbados, the non-standardized dialect better known as Bajan, which evolved out of an early creole,[1] is so close to the standard dialect that this poses problems for the teaching of English, which are then carried over to the teaching of French. Burrowes, in collaboration with Allsopp (1983), points out a number of structural creole-type features at the linguistic levels of phonology and morphology in Bajan, the former being also manifested in Caribbean speakers generally, such as the reduction of final consonant clusters and the palatalization of /k/ and /g/ to /kj/ and /gj/, respectively. With regard to morphosyntax, some of the features most likely to be reflected in French and found not only in Bajan but in other English-speaking Caribbean territories where creole speech is still fairly common, such as Guyana and Jamaica, are the lack of pluralization of nouns, Ø case marking on pronouns, Ø copula with predicative adjectives, the lack of inflection for tense differentiation, the lack of inflection for possessives, the use of habitual *does* /doz/, the use of other auxiliaries /don/ and /did/ and the special treatment of passivity.

Fields (1992) and Rickford (1992) cite some additional features, such as pluralizing *dem*, no person–number agreement, locative copula and copula *been* with adjectives. It is clear that, in the case of Barbados, as in other territories, a creole did exist in the early years of plantation slavery which decreolized earlier than elsewhere in the Caribbean and of which residues are found even in contemporary Bajan, as they are found in the non-standard dialects of other English-official territories.

## Implications of the Caribbean Language Situation for the Teaching of French

What then are the implications of this situation for the teaching of French in the English-speaking Caribbean? Even before coming to the linguistic realities of teaching French, one of the major strategies that has to be adopted is to convince students of the need to learn French in a region where the French speakers in French departments alone outnumber the number of English speakers in the Caribbean, for example.[2] Another is to point out the demographic power of French as a world language by teaching students about the countries included within the sphere of "francophonie" – a term used to indicate the fact that the French language and culture is the language and culture of these countries. A third is to indicate to students the advantages that they would have in terms of being more marketable in the context of their own economies, which are tourist-centred, and also in terms of the global economy, which is drawing countries of diverse languages and cultures ever closer. Add to this the fact that, from a personal point of view, students would be better equipped to travel to a number of different countries where French is spoken and where young people like themselves live in the French language and do exactly the same things that they do in English – eat, drink, learn similar subjects, participate in sports, engage in a variety of leisure activities, shop for food, clothes and other items, become ill and so on – but they do these things in a different linguistic code.

This type of conditioning is not only necessary before actually introducing the language but has to be continually reinforced in various ways in the French classroom by actually creating the conditions for making the French language live. Of course, one of the primary requirements for so doing is that teachers use French in their classrooms as much as possible and that they ensure that their students hear the best possible French, as the teacher is the primary role model and possibly the only one, barring any native speaker who may be invited from time to time to address students. Teachers therefore have to keep themselves at the cutting edge as regards the use of the target language.

Another linguistic requirement that is just as vital is that, since it is both desirable and practical that there be an integrated approach to foreign language teaching between the L1 and the target language, all language teachers should be aware of the fact that there is such a thing as Caribbean English; that this encompasses two varieties, a standard variety and a non-standard variety; and that the non-standard variety, with regional variations, is the mother tongue of most English-speaking Caribbean students, whether they are in Barbados, Jamaica, St Vincent or St Lucia. Such knowledge is needed for all language teachers to be able to teach in an informed way and to deal with the way in which English language structure and usage have evolved in the Caribbean. Moreover, as English is the L1 of our students, whether they use the standard or non-standard variety, its influence on the learning of a second or foreign language cannot be ignored. Perhaps most importantly, teachers should know how to use the two varieties creatively to exploit the positive influences of both in their teaching of the foreign language, in this case French.

With regard to understanding the principles of second language acquisition, the acculturation model[3] of second language acquisition based on the linguistic theories of pidginization and creolization is most applicable to the Caribbean language situation in terms of why the students' L1 is either a creole or a non-standard dialect of English, given the historical facts. Continuing from there, the concept of psychological distance contained in this theory, which has to do with the affective factors concerning the learner as an individual, such as language shock and motivation, is highly applicable to the learning of foreign languages such as French. In other words, unless students clearly see the need to acquire French, they will not be motivated to do so and their affective filter[4] will remain high and their French pidginized, unable to progress from being an interlanguage. Students must therefore be encouraged to both learn and acquire French as naturally as possible despite the lack of a speech community to support the natural process of acquisition, as opposed to learning which is formal and rule-bound.

Craig (1999) points to the fact that the locality and the speech community in which learners operate strongly influence the phonological and morphosyntactic characteristics of their speech, so that the non-standard features of the L1 majority of our French students are likely to impact heavily on the foreign language that they learn, namely French. These observations serve to demonstrate more clearly why Barbadian and Caribbean learners of French generally have difficulties with pronunciation, intonation and morphosyntax.

Similarly, in relation to structure, French teachers need to be well acquainted with that of both standard English and non-standardized vernaculars, whether they be creoles, as exist in Jamaica or Guyana, for example, or whether they be dialects of English with residual creole features, as in the case of Barbados. Unfortunately, however, this is in many instances not the case. The primary syllabus in Caribbean primary schools adopts a skills-based approach to the teaching of English, termed "language arts", seeking to develop linguistic skill in each pupil based on the level of his or her potential in the four language skills (listening, speaking, reading and writing) – an aim that is in total harmony with foreign language teaching. Nevertheless, there is no provision for the relation of spelling to structure, for example, nor any provision for equipping the student with the knowledge of grammatical function or of any type of structural analysis, two basic and compulsory requirements when learning a foreign language such as French.

## Some Suggestions for Remediation of the Problems Encountered

### The Role of Methodology in the Teaching of French

Based on the preceding observations, it is clear that in order to teach French as a foreign language successfully in Caribbean schools, some structured methodological approach is needed. "Methodological approach" here means an understanding of what the long-term goal of the teaching is, how the teaching is done and what texts are used to achieve the stated goal. There is no doubt that for a long time, French (as well as Spanish) was taught using one traditional method, the grammar-translation method, whereby the teaching of the target language was done through the explanation of rules and through testing to ensure that the rules were known via translation from and into the target language. Indeed, this method still prevails today in too many of our schools, but now it is tempered by aspects of the audio-lingual method (with the use of the tape recorder), by pattern and substitution drills, and by an inductive approach to the teaching of structure. The language laboratory is not widely used in Caribbean schools in general, but some schools do have such a resource, and in those schools that do not, some teachers in foreign language departments simulate the conditions of the language laboratory.

At this point in time, there are three widely used methodologies identifiable in foreign language teaching in most anglophone Caribbean schools. These are

1. the grammar-translation method, modified by the inclusion of elements of the audio-lingual and other methods, as noted above;
2. the cognitive-code approach, a form of the grammar-translation method, in which syllabuses are grammar based, but in which communicative-type activities are used; and
3. communicative language teaching. This approach, with its structural/functional methodology, is currently being promoted both by the CXC syllabus which presently dominates foreign language teaching in many Caribbean schools and by the new foreign languages curriculum which is being used in a number of Barbadian secondary schools at present.

Some teachers are also making an effort to include computer-assisted language learning (CALL) in foreign language teaching and in other subject areas. However, regardless of the teaching methodology used (an eclectic approach combining different methods is recommended), it must take into account the Caribbean language situation as described earlier in this chapter and must also involve an understanding of second language acquisition, which is an area of weakness in our foreign language teachers. Unless teachers are trained to understand the factors which impact on the teaching and learning of French and other foreign languages, much progress will not be made in solving the problems outlined above.

Similarly, the texts or methodological kits used in foreign language programmes should demonstrate an understanding of the Caribbean language situation as outlined above, but those used in our secondary schools hardly do that, since they are largely produced by European teachers. Caribbean French teachers should begin to develop French texts or methodological kits for their students.

Within the framework of the overall methodology used, what teachers need to do at the phonological level is to get the students to imitate as far as possible the way in which French is pronounced by first getting them to listen to individual sounds, then sounds in combination and, finally, words. Students should be assisted to discriminate between sounds that may seem fairly similar to them but which are not. One useful tool is the minimal-pair sound-discrimination exercise, in which lists of words with similar vowel or consonantal sounds are contrasted and students must choose the word that they hear. In a methodology project which this researcher did with a team of foreign language teachers in about eight secondary schools in Barbados, a set of methodology modules was produced and the first module,[5] which deals with showing students how to acquire listening and speaking skills, involves such an exercise: teachers give the students lists of words and sentences which sound alike, and they listen and choose the sound that they actually hear.

*six* /sis/, /si/ (before a consonant) *seize* /sɛz/
*poison* /pwazɔ̃ /          *poisson* /pwasɔ̃/
*Il a **faim**.* /fɛ̃/          *Il a une **femme**.* /fam/

Oral reading is also strongly recommended, especially in simple verses which emphasize sounds that students need to practise, and so are short prose passages with words containing sounds that are similar to each other. Students can repeat and memorize these words, using the pronunciation of other words with similar sounds that they have learned as a guide. By providing listening and reading material on subjects in which the students are likely to be interested, teachers can increase their motivation to master the sounds of the French language.

In addition to oral reading, teachers must orally demonstrate the use of language appropriate to various situations, and students need to be encouraged to put this into practice in the classroom. This practice must be ongoing and not simply artificially learned in the fifth year of secondary school shortly before the CXC oral examinations. Dramatization or role play should accompany such practice as often as possible, for we know that drama usually appeals to students of all ages. Songs are also most useful in getting students to practise good French pronunciation, and the level of language in the songs chosen should be made to coincide appropriately with the students' level of proficiency.

As far as structure is concerned, an integrated approach to the teaching of French structure with that of the L1 is certainly to be recommended. Roulet (1995) points out the soundness of such an approach, denouncing the artificial separation between the teaching of different languages:

> Si l'on admet que l'enseignement du nouveau gagne à s'appuyer sur le déjà connu, comme l'écrivait déjà Lancelot dans sa *Grammaire latine* en 1644, et si l'on veut bien admettre aussi que les langues, au-delà de différences de formes et de structures de surface évidents, reposent sur des structures et des principes largement communs, comme l'ont démontré les recherches récentes dans les domains de la syntaxe et du discours, on ne peut manquer de s'étonner de ce cloisonnement, qui ne peut être que préjudiciable à l'élève.

[If one admits that the new method of teaching benefits from the support of what is already known, as Lancelot had already observed in his *Grammaire latine* (*Latin Grammar*) in 1644, and if the admission is also made that languages, beyond obvious surface structural and formal differences, are largely based on structures and principles that are quite common, as has been illustrated in recent research into the domains of syntax and discourse, one cannot fail to be surprised at this compartmentalization, which can only be prejudicial to the student.]

One of the ways in which structure can be taught is through the teaching of spelling without burdening the student with heavy grammatical definitions of various word classes, but rather, one should, as several French linguistic researchers[6] recommend, "remplacer une conception traditionelle, prescriptive, limité par une conception plus pragmatique qui prend en compte les règles de fonctionnement social de la langue" ["replace a traditional, prescriptive notion, underpinned by a more pragmatic one which takes into account the rules of the social functioning of the language"]. In other words, teachers should try to get students to reflect on their L1 and the target language, with a view to establishing connections in relation to usage rather than learning fixed grammatical rules.

For example, structural analysis can be approached by word-formation devices such as affixation, whereby students are taught that the meaning and function of words can be altered by prefixes, suffixes and roots, collectively known as affixes. Teaching affixes helps greatly in vocabulary building, as the student can make associations with meaning and actually see how words are formed. For example, the teacher can point out that the suffix *-erie* in French gives the meaning of what we would call a type of shop in English: *la pâtisserie, la boulangerie, la confiserie, la papeterie, la boucherie* and so on. Similarly, the agential suffixes *-ier* and *-ière* refer to someone who does something – *le fermier* from *la ferme, le bijoutier* from *le bijou, l'infirmière* from *l'infirmerie* – and these are paralleled in the L1 by the suffix *-er*. The suffix *-ier* added to the names of fruits can be used for trees, such as *le bananier, le cocotier, le manguier, le tamarinier*. The prefix *-re* usually means 'again' and is often found before verbs such as *recommencer, revenir* and *remettre*, referring to performing some action over.

Verb paradigms can be approached in the same way in the case of regular verbs. Compound nouns formed from verb–noun combinations can also be taught in this way, such as *le passe-temps, le porte-parole, le gratte-ciel* and so on. The concepts of tense and mood, so difficult for both standard and nonstandard speakers of English, can be explained as time referring to past, present and future, and as definite and indefinite actions. Adjectives of nationality can be taught in the same way through affixation, as can various classes of nouns and their genders.

## The Contribution of French Caribbean Lexicography to the Teaching of French

Caribbean teachers must be equipped not only with the linguistic understanding of the factors that influence their French students, but also with the proper tools to assist them to keep their students motivated. Reference works in Caribbean French are of great importance in this area. Here reference is made to the *Caribbean Multilingual Dictionary of Flora, Fauna and Foods* (Allsopp 2003), compiled by this researcher with a team of research assistants in Barbados and throughout the Francophone, Franco-Créolophone and Hispanophone Caribbean.[7] Since French Caribbean lexicography is concerned with chronicling thematically the Caribbean French equivalents of various Caribbean English words and phrases, it contributes to helping the students build a vocabulary in context which will enable them to express their Caribbean reality in a way that metropolitan standard French cannot, because the reality that it embodies is totally different.

The *Multilingual Dictionary* will also help students with the concept of gender of nouns, since each item is gender identified and will serve to reinforce the notion of grammatical gender in French.

The word formation process of compounding, which assumes peculiar characteristics in Caribbean French, also evident in the *Multilingual Dictionary*, will assist students to see how words are formed. While on the one hand, there are items such as the names of trees which preserve the morphological norms of standard French by adding the suffix *-ier* to the name of the fruit, as in *sapotillier, pomme-cannelier, corossolier* and so on, there are others which involve calquing, such as *mahot-bord-de-mer, griffe-chat* and many others which combine standard items with creolized items.

Students will also notice an overlap of words in Caribbean English and Caribbean French and the application of a single name to several items because of shared physical characteristics, which will help them to better understand the labelling processes that took place in this region and how historical factors affected them.

Finally, this text will help to make students aware of the difference between Caribbean standard French and French Creole; the latter occupies a place in the dictionary, as a French Creole equivalent is supplied wherever possible. The fact that students can go to a dictionary and find Caribbean French equivalents will hopefully serve to enhance their feeling of pride in their region and in themselves; in turn, this will motivate them to seek to master the French language, in order to communicate with their peers in Caribbean Francophone territories and beyond.

## Conclusion

It is clear that the teaching of French as a foreign language in the English-speaking Caribbean is fraught with problems. It is equally clear that there are quite creative solutions to such problems. The answer lies in fully equipping teachers of French to recognize the problems, to understand why they occur and to be able to move towards solving them creatively via appropriate teacher-training programmes which stress the following areas: competence in the French language; linguistic understanding of the Caribbean language situation; methodologies which are suited to the Caribbean student; appropriate supportive teaching materials that reflect the Caribbean environment and culture; use of technology via suitable computer programmes for students; and a Caribbean reference work supplying equivalents in Caribbean French, which will both reinforce vocabulary-building and provide a better understanding of the morphosyntax of the French language.

## Notes

1. A number of researchers, among them Roberts, Fields, Rickford and Handler, have shown, with examples, that a Bajan creole did exist during the eighteenth century and up to the early nineteenth century.
2. Demographically speaking, according to the Information Services of the Caribbean Development Bank (1999), the number of French and French Creole speakers outnumbers the entire number of English speakers in the English-speaking Caribbean as a whole, with over 12 million French and French Creole speakers compared with the 6.2 million English speakers.
3. Klein (1986) has pointed out that in the learning or acquiring of foreign languages, it is the social and psychological conditions in which the second or foreign language is processed that are important.
4. Krashen and Terrell (1983) have defined the affective filter as the degree of motivation shown by a foreign or second language learner. If motivation is high, the affective

filter is said to be low, because the learner is open to acquiring the target language; if motivation is low, the affective filter is said to be high, because the learner is resistant to acquiring the target language.

5. The present researcher, together with a group of foreign-language teachers, produced a set of methodological modules for the teaching of foreign languages, the first of which dealt with strategies for teaching the phonology of both French and Spanish and which gave a number of ways in which to deal with phonological problems faced by students of those languages.

6. Roulet, Dahlet and other French researchers have made the point that teachers should encourage their students to see the cultural and usage links between the L1 and the target language, so that the target language becomes more meaningful to them.

7. This multilingual dictionary is geared to the entire education system of the whole region, spanning three of the official languages of the Caribbean, including the French-lexicon creole of Haiti.

## References

Allsopp, Jeannette. 1995. Foreign Language Methodology in the Caribbean: A Historical Survey. *Dialog on Language Instruction* 11 (1–2): 13–32.

———. 2003. *The Caribbean Multilingual Dictionary of Flora, Fauna And Foods, in English, French, French Creole and Spanish*. Kingston: Arawak.

Allsopp, Richard, and Jeannette Allsopp. [1983]. Some Problems of Learning to Speak French and Spanish for Speakers of Barbadian English. Paper for the Barbados Ministry of Education seminar on the teaching of foreign languages, Bridgetown, Barbados.

Craig, Dennis R. 1999. *Teaching Language and Literacy: Policies and Procedures for Vernacular Situations*. Georgetown, Guyana: Education and Development Services.

Klein, Wolfgang. 1986. *Second language acquisition*. Cambridge: Cambridge University Press.

Krashen, Stephen D., and Tracy D. Terrell. 1983. *The Natural Approach: Language Acquisition in the Classroom*. Oxford: Pergamon.

Roulet, Eddy. 1995. *Langue maternelle et langues secondes: Vers une pédagogie intégrée*. Paris: Hatier.

# 14 | Educating the Creole-Speaking Child in the North American Classroom

Ian Robertson

*University of the West Indies, St Augustine*

The guiding axiom of this chapter is the assumption that the primary responsibility of every education system is the preparation of its charges for maximizing their contribution to the wider society. Under normal circumstances, students are educated within a sociocultural context which is native to them or, at the very least, one with which they are familiar. In this typical situation, a number of assumptions may be made based on the assumed knowledge and understandings of the society and the type of student it could be expected to provide for the educational system.

The immigrant, however, is by definition different, and if these differences are not properly investigated and subsequently factored into the education system, considerable wastage of human and financial resources might occur. At the very least, the failure to take into consideration the background of the immigrant is likely to become a major source of frustration to immigrant students and their attempts to become integrated into the new matrix culture. This chapter addresses some of the issues which relate to the creole-speaking immigrant from the Caribbean into North America.

Two of these issues are of central concern to this chapter. The first is the considerable difference in school culture, and the second is the exceedingly complex set of background linguistic factors and their impact on attempts to prepare the creole speaker for the new realities of his or her existence.

The primary subject of this chapter is the immigrant from what has been referred to euphemistically as the anglophone Caribbean. Instructive parallels may be drawn with the Francophone and Netherlandic Caribbean territories as well.

## Education Systems

Education systems in the territories under focus may be characterized by the following:

1. a highly centralized administration system with responsibility for such areas as policy, training, evaluation and examination;
2. low levels of teacher participation in issues of policy formation and curriculum planning and development;
3. a high degree of teacher-centred programme delivery;
4. resultant of (3), a passive student role, with little student initiative and independence;
5. an academic/examination-oriented curriculum;
6. the placing of a high premium on examination success and a corresponding lack of opportunity to recover from failure;
7. a high degree of focus on product-oriented writing skills with a correspondingly low emphasis on oracy; and
8. an exceedingly complex and dynamic set of linguistic behaviours, attitudes, beliefs and practices.

One overriding strength of the system is the fact that the teachers are drawn from the very Caribbean societies and, as a consequence, bring their intuitive knowledge and understandings of these societies to bear on the delivery of the curriculum.

Students who migrate to North America must therefore adjust to a number of systemic differences and assumptions. Along with the many social and economic factors which now impact upon their education, immigrants from the Caribbean must come to terms with the following:

1. a change in status from linguistic majority to linguistic minority or even marginal group;
2. a less centralized system of education administration;

3. a less examination-oriented focus, with greater opportunity to recover from failure;
4. lower levels of teacher-centredness;
5. a greater emphasis on student initiative and independence; and
6. a rearranged set of linguistic dynamics, in which the matrix culture imposes a target language that is different from the particular standard English dialect to which Caribbean students had been exposed in their original education system. This new cultural complex also presents considerable barriers to communication in the new classroom environment.

## Linguistic Issues

The second set of issues to which the Caribbean immigrant must adjust is in the realm of linguistics. There is a misleading and inaccurate tendency to link Caribbean territories linguistically to their last colonizing European power through the use of terms such as *English-speaking, French-speaking* and *Dutch-speaking.*

While it is true that in each of the territories under consideration here the language of official documents, education, the legal system and all other formal communication is a Caribbean standard English, the language of widest communication is one or another version of Creole. The sets of social, linguistic and discourse relationships between the Creole and the official language are dynamic and exceedingly complex. They present considerable challenge to the education systems in the Caribbean and, therefore, even greater challenges when transferred to the new and considerably more complex matrix system.

In the Caribbean contexts, the creole languages may be considered as relatively new language systems constructed to service the need for inter-ethnic communication within a plantation culture. The sociohistorical contexts of colonialism and slavery created societies in which relatively homogenous linguistic groups of Europeans (British in the relevant cases, but also Portuguese, Dutch and French in parallel cases) had to interact with a culturally homogenous but linguistically heterogenous set of West Africans. Given the power structure of the plantations, the degree of social stratification and the more overt linguistic similarities to the European languages, the creole languages have attracted considerable negative stereotyping. The earliest descriptors of these languages saw them as "bastardized versions" of European languages, "un baragoin", "langage voluntairement corrompu pour faciliter sa compréhension", based on the assumption that the slaves lacked the human capacity to acquire a European language.

Creole languages continue to be associated with the lower socio-economic classes and, as a consequence, with poverty, dependency and a lack of progress. These languages have only been used formally in an experimental way in the relevant education systems. They do not have a sustained literary tradition sufficient to create the critical mass for further validating their linguistic status, though oral verbal artistry of considerable skill does exist in all these communities. The fact that the majority of their lexical items are drawn from European source languages helps to sustain the caution and doubt which many people, even the speakers of the creoles themselves, cast on the linguistic status of creole.

This particular stigma underlies the negative linguistic self-concept of the creole speaker. It manifests itself in linguistic self-denial and even rejection. There is the persistent misconception on the part of the creole speaker that his language is just "broken French" or "English spoken badly". These perceptions are at the root of the frustration which Caribbean administrators and classroom teachers face in addressing virtually all areas of education. Such misconceptions continue to misinform educators and education systems, and they underline the need for careful, sensitive approaches to the linguistics of educating the native creole speaker from the Caribbean.

There is virtual consensus among Caribbean linguists on the linguistic status of the Caribbean student. Alleyne (1985, 1) notes that "the languages of the Caribbean are often categorized and characterized by means of labels referring to the four European powers that dominated the region during the colonial period – *English-speaking, French-speaking, Spanish-speaking* and *Dutch-speaking.* These terms provide only approximate references. If they are taken literally, they may be misleading, inadequate or inaccurate, in some cases, and they certainly mask a great deal of linguistic complexity."

For the education system to be maximally effective, it must ensure that policy and practice are informed by the considerable range of available information. Persons responsible for the education of the immigrant from the Caribbean also need to be made fully aware of the precise nature of that student's linguistic and associated cultural background.

A considerable amount of data and human resources now exists to provide a reasonable guide to the systems of education in the Caribbean. The distinct nature of the differences between the European languages and their lexically related creole counterparts has been documented by a number of linguists (Allsopp 1962, 1979, 1995; Carrington 1969, 1976; Craig 1976). These differences are discoverable at all the levels of the systems and subsystems of these languages. The examples given here are mainly from the English-lexicon creoles, but parallels with the French-lexicon creoles do exist. What is of considerable importance is the fact that the semantic and grammatical systems of the respective creoles show remarkable similarity despite their obvious lexical differences.

At the level of sound, the English-lexicon creoles follow, in the main, the sound patterns of English. There are, however, some important differences. As a general rule, the consonants remain the same, with the exception of the interdental fricatives written in English as *th*, the alveolar nasal in final position written as *ng*. In some cases, the sound written as *h*, is often deleted in initial position and inserted before vowels in the same initial position. The following list provides examples.

| Creole | English |
|--------|---------|
| *tin* | thin |
| *den* | then |
| *tree* | three |
| *turnin* | turning |
| *buildin* | building |
| *elp* | help |
| *happle* | apple |

Some of these very low-level differences have the obvious potential to present barriers to intelligibility on the part of speakers of the lexical donor languages, since items may not be readily recognized as cognates in the stream of speech and hearing.

In addition to these, there is a tendency to simplify initial and final clusters of consonants, such as those in the following examples.

| Creole | English |
|--------|---------|
| *trang* | strong |
| *ben* | bend |
| *tess* | test |

This latter set of differences does have considerable influence on issues such as subject–verb concord in English.

A number of phonemic distinctions also disappear in the creole, leaving homophones where none existed in the lexical source language; for example, the English *tree* and *three* would become *tree*. Some new words are created, such as *ben*. As a consequence of such differences, new areas of potential misunderstanding arise, as is exemplified by the following incident. In a North American classroom, a teacher sealed the classroom and had the entire class searched because a student had reported that "Di chirren keepin naiz in di class". Literally, that would be "The children keeping [making] noise in the class" – "noise", not "knives", as the non-Caribbean teacher interpreted. The search revealed that there were no knives in the class. The potential for misunderstanding could not be more clearly demonstrated, as both the creole idiom "keeping naiz", which is good creole for "being noisy", and the standard interpretation of "keeping knives" are determined by the grammatical and semantic possibilities of one or the other of the languages.

Apart from these sound-level differences, there are also semantic differences, even where the items used are of obvious English origin or may be readily derived from a number of English sources. The following list exemplifies some of these.

| Creole | English |
|---|---|
| *favour* | resemble |
| *miserable* | troublesome |
| *hand* | arm |
| *foot* | leg |
| *bittle* | food (victuals) |
| *breakfast* | lunch |
| *tea* | breakfast / any warm (milk) drink |

In a similar way, creoleword-formation devices differ from those of the principal lexical donor language, English, in a number of ways, sufficient to warrant their being considered different languages.

| Creole | English |
|---|---|
| *bossman* | boss (male) |
| *bosslady* | boss (female) |
| *murderation* | widespread murder and mayhem |
| *stupidness* | nonsense |

Some of these word-formation devices are well known in English, though they are used quite differently in the creole system.

The combination of semantic, morphological and phonetic differences noted here would render mutual intelligibility difficult, as can be seen from the following examples.

They say I *favour* my mother. (English)
They say I *resemble* my mother. (Creole)
They say that I *show a preference* for my mother. (English)
I decided to *take out* my father. (English)
I decided to *take a photograph of* my father. (Creole)
I decided to *defeat* my father. (Am. English)

Detailed analyses exist of a wide range of Caribbean creole languages of different lexical bases (e.g., Allsopp 1962; Bailey 1966; Bickerton 1975; Carrington 1967; Robertson 1996).

Any study of the syntax of these creole languages indicates that the systems under consideration are different from those of the lexical donor languages. A look at the noun system would suffice for the purposes of this chapter. As in the European lexifier languages, the nouns in creole may be sub-classified into count and non-count. However, membership in the various classes is not the same in the two systems. *Bread, pants, police* and *money* are all count nouns in the English-lexicon creoles, but non-count in English. *Teeth, buns* and *mice* indicate that the base form in creole need not be the singular form in the donor language but could be the plural. Nouns in creoles do not inflect for plurality or for case. The former is signalled in creole by the use of a separate pluralizer similar in phonetic shape to the third-person plural form of the personal pronoun. Thus, *di pikni dem* means 'the children'. Possession is signalled by word order, with the possessor preceding the possessed in English-lexicon creoles. *Di gyrl moda* means 'the girl's mother'. At the most remote creole levels, gender differences are not signalled on the third-person pronouns, as is the case in the lexical donor languages. Consequently, there is no possibility of gender concord between the pronoun and its antecedent, as is done in English.

This necessarily brief and illustrative sampling of the differences between Creole and English gives some idea of the deep-seated differences which exist between the two systems. Linguists continue to argue that though creole languages can be, and frequently are, misclassified, it is necessary to recognize that the speaker of Creole is put at a severe disadvantage in any education system which misclassifies him as a speaker of English. A system of education which is premised on this assumption is likely to be incapable of fulfilling its axiomatic role of maximizing the potential of the creole speaker. The real danger is in those areas of superficial similarity. For example, "From a boy I learnt that" would be understood as "I learnt that from a boy" by an English speaker and "I learnt that since I was a boy" by a Jamaican Creole speaker.

The extent to which a student could negotiate and experience concepts and abstractions in symbolic form is the major determinant of educational success. Teaching may be regarded as guiding and facilitating, setting the appropriate conditions, enabling the student to learn. The important dimensions of this process are creating an environment that facilitates learning; finding the appropriate media for presentation; and assessing the effectiveness of the lessons. In each case, language is the most important element.

Language and language issues must therefore be a *sine qua non* of the education system. If one accepts this, then the North American education system faces some special problems when it comes to educating the creole-speaking student from the anglophone Caribbean. The major issues that arise may be summarized in the following questions:

1. What languages are available for the education of the creole speaker in North American schools?
2. What are the social factors governing their use?
3. Which language(s) is (are) appropriate for education?
4. What effects would languages not chosen have on the education processes?
5. What perceptions do immigrants themselves have about their language?
6. What perceptions do immigrants have of themselves as language users?
7. What are the appropriate classroom policies and practices for dealing with the immigrant from the creole-speaking anglophone Caribbean?

The analysis presented here narrows the possible choices of language to the relevant version of both standard English and creole. Since the ultimate goal is to facilitate integration into North American society, the long-term goal should be to develop a facility with English that is sufficient for social interaction in those communities. At the same time, it must be borne in mind that creole speakers possess a sense of linguistic inferiority which may be linked directly to the complex linguistic and social background out of which they have come. This situation is exacerbated by the fact that they are now in a minority situation in a new matrix culture. It is therefore important that they develop a more positive linguistic self-concept if their potential is to be maximized.

The absence of a positive or informed linguistic self-concept will be most clearly reflected in the oral interaction patterns in the classroom, since the student who is unsure of the bona fides of his speech is likely to stand apart or even to be ridiculed by his peers for his lack of conformity. In these contexts, participation in oral activity is likely to be restricted. This restricted participation is not to be mistaken for lack of cognitive ability but rather should be seen as an indication that the student does not possess the necessary linguistic skills in English, though these may well be present in creole. The creole speaker who refers to his upper arm as his "hand" is not unaware of his body parts; he simply has another way of signalling them.

The classroom must therefore be made to reflect a high level of informed open-mindedness to these differences. This requires a great deal of teacher and student awareness on issues of language. The development of these must be part of a careful and systematic plan for developing this kind of awareness on the part of both teacher and student.

In the contexts under consideration here, there are only two possible choices for a language for education: English and creole. Within these two choices, Craig (1980) lists a number of policy options: bilingualism, monoliterate (in one language or the other) bilingualism, transitional bilingualism (from creole to English), monolingualism (creole or English). Given the common reasons for migration, the ultimate choice for a language of education is likely to be English. Whatever the choice, the major issue then shifts to the role which the language not chosen is allowed to play in the process of education. Creole-speaking students, whatever their linguistic self-concept may be, perform effectively in creole a number of tasks that are identical or similar to those required in the standard English classroom. As an example, ritual abuse, a form of public verbal contestation and abuse, or "tracing" as it is called in Jamaica, requires the participants to listen carefully to the adversary's comment or retort, select the most useful point on which to base their own retort, and frame that retort in such a manner that the response is seen as appropriate. Since the contest is usually intended for public exposure and consumption and even determining a winner, it clearly requires relatively sophisticated comprehension and selection skills, in line with the kinds of choices necessary in classroom contexts. It also requires considerable skill at character sketching. Yet these cognitive and linguistic skills are never used to facilitate the acquisition of the same or similar skills in the classroom language, English.

A study of popular belief systems carried out in Trinidadian schools (George 1995) indicates that the teaching of scientific concepts may be influenced positively as well as negatively by the belief systems associated with creole languages and their speakers. These belief systems and their corresponding linguistic media cannot simply be wished away. They must be approached in a very structured way if they are to allow for the leap of faith required by the transfer from one sociolinguistic and cultural context into the other.

The creole speaker must be convinced, beyond mere lip service, that the different language paradigms each have a validity of their own. Anything short of this is likely to provide minimal returns to the education system.

## Some Directions

Perhaps the single most important factor in the education of the creole speaker in North American education systems is motivation. No person would willingly participate in a system in which there is a sense of alienation. This may best be addressed through a heightening of the levels of language awareness on the part of both the teacher and the student. In the case of the former, there are three key goals that should be a part of training: to expose teachers to the nature of creole languages and how they work, to sensitize them to aspects of the cultural background and experiences of the creole speaker, and to seek to provide some clear guidelines for the implementation of these in the classroom situation.

In the case of the students, there is an urgent need for the development of an informed linguistic self-awareness that is sufficient to ensure that they develop a balanced understanding of creole languages and of their efficacy as media of communication and cultural identification.

Finally, there is a need to produce new materials which would facilitate the types of activities advocated here. This would require that conscious attention be paid to those issues raised earlier as well as to the needs of both teachers and students.

## References

Alleyne, Mervyn. 1985. *A Linguistic Perspective on the Caribbean*. Washington, DC: Latin American Program, Woodrow Wilson International Center for Scholars.
Allsopp, Richard. 1962. Expressions of State and Action in the Dialect of English Used in the Georgetown Area of British Guiana. PhD thesis, London University.
———. 1979. Caribbean English and our schools. *Caribbean Journal of Education* 6 (2): 99–109.

———. 1995. *Dictionary of Caribbean English Usage*. Cambridge: Cambridge University Press.

Bailey, Beryl Loftman. 1966. *Jamaican Creole Syntax: A Transformational Approach*. Cambridge: Cambridge University Press.

Bickerton, Derek. 1975. *Dynamics of a Creole System*. London: Cambridge University Press.

Carrington, Lawrence D. 1967. *St Lucian Creole: A Study of Its Phonology and Morphosyntax*. PhD diss., University of the West Indies.

———. 1969. Deviations from Standard English in the Speech of Primary School Children in St Lucia and Dominica. *International Review of Applied Linguistics in Language Teaching* 7 (3): 165–84.

———. 1976. Determining Language Education Policy in Caribbean Sociolinguistic Complexes. *International Journal of the Sociology of Language* 8: 127–43.

Craig, Dennis R. 1976. Bidialectal Education: Creole and Standard in the West Indies. *Linguistics* 175: 93–134.

———. 1980. Models for Educational Policy in Creole-Speaking Communities. In *Theoretical Orientations in Creole Studies*, edited by A. Valdman and A. Highfield, 245–65. New York: Academic Press.

George, June. 1995. An Analysis of Traditional Practices and Beliefs in a Trinidadian Village to Assess the Implications for Science Education. Phd thesis, University of the West Indies, St Augustine.

Robertson, Ian E. 1996. Towards a Rational Language Education Policy for Caribbean States. In *Caribbean Language Issues, Old and New*, edited by P. Christie, 112–19. Kingston: University of the West Indies Press.

# 15 | Teaching English to Vernacular Speakers in US and Caribbean Schools

JOHN R. RICKFORD AND ANGELA E. RICKFORD

*Stanford University and San Jose State University (respectively)*

Although it has not become generally known as yet – and thankfully, it has not generated the media frenzy that the Oakland Ebonics resolutions did in 1996 – California has taken radical strides to incorporate the perspectives of linguists into its elementary language arts textbooks, requiring among other things that all publishers (including SRA/McGraw-Hill, Houghton Mifflin and others) provide contrastive analysis and other strategies to help students who speak African American Vernacular English (AAVE) master standard English and improve their performance in reading and writing (see section 1 below). The challenges of teaching literacy and the language arts to creole-speaking students in the anglophone Caribbean – the focus of much of Dennis Craig's lifetime research, culminating in his 1999 book *Teaching Language and Literacy* – of course differ in some respects from the challenges of teaching speakers of AAVE in the United States. Nevertheless, there are similarities between the situations, suggested first of all by the subtitle of Craig's 1999 book (*Policies and Procedures for Vernacular Situations*), and by the fact that he discusses the situations together in his opening chapters. Craig's (1999, 1) appreciation for these similarities derives in part from his conviction that "the Caribbean and the AAVE [varieties] can be regarded as derived from a single North and South American and Creole language system that has been linked historically with the African diaspora". But beyond this historical issue, there is also the fact that

> the commonalities between the AAVE and the Caribbean language situations were recognized ever since the nineteen-sixties (e.g. Stewart 1962); and . . . language education studies in the two geographically removed situations have a common relevance. It is obvious that what we are here concerned with is a problem which, in its generalized form, can be conveniently designated: "Teaching English to Speakers of a Related Vernacular" (TESORV), since, in all instances, it will be the relatedness of the vernaculars to English that will create the special characteristics of the language education situation. (Craig 1999, 3)

The similarities between the anglophone Caribbean situations and AAVE include the negative attitudes that teachers and the general public have about the Creole or vernacular varieties – perhaps not as extreme now as reported in the 1960s through the 1980s (see Le Page 1968; Carrington and Borely 1977; Rickford and Traugott 1985), but still a far way from linguists' recognition of them as "systematic, rule-governed communication systems, equal in efficiency to standard languages" (Craig 1999, 13).[1] The similarities also include the fact that many teachers and educational authorities in both the Caribbean and the United States continue to believe that no special methods are required to help vernacular speakers acquire literacy and master standard English, or what Craig (1999, 3) refers to as "Internationally Accepted English".

We share with Craig a concern for the poor academic performance of precisely those students in both regions who are most likely to speak the vernacular (compare his statistics on academic performance in the Caribbean with ours for the United States). And we share with him the conviction that special methods that take the vernacular into account are required; that whole-language or communicative-language teaching methods – while valuable in some respects – are not sufficient (Craig 1999, 76); and that approaches that explicitly focus on the sounds and structures of the varieties involved are most likely to be successful. Craig's "augmented language experience approach" builds on but goes beyond the contrastive analysis approach discussed in this chapter.[2] Craig had expressed the hope (1999, 19) that "the Caribbean, with a less complex and less contentious set of sociolinguistic issues than that of the AAVE scenario, [might be] a good workshop for designing classroom procedures that could be efficacious with creole-influenced vernacular speakers everywhere." We agree with him, and hope that researchers working on literacy and language-education issues involving AAVE and other vernaculars will turn to his work for inspiration and ideas. In the spirit of his comparative approach, we also hope, more humbly, that what we have written here for US educators trying to move forward with the education of vernacular speakers might also be of interest and use to educators working with vernacular and creole speakers in the anglophone Caribbean. (See now Rickford et al. 2013.)

## 1. Why Should English and Language Arts Teachers Care about AAVE?

The new *Imagine It!* readers meet the California Department of Education's requirement for a "deeper focus on the instructional needs" of several categories of students, including "students who use African American Vernacular English" (California Department of Education 2006, 451). But why did the State of California include this requirement, and why should teachers working with African American students care about AAVE?

The answer is that African American students, on average, consistently underperform white students in reading, writing and the language arts, both in California and in the United States as a whole. One reason for this disparity appears to be the vernacular that many African American students speak, and the way in which teachers respond – or fail to respond – to this vernacular in teaching them standard/academic English and in helping them to become more accomplished readers, writers and speakers more generally.

Let us begin with the idea of the "black–white achievement gap". Figure 15.1 shows results from the English–Language Arts component of the 2008 Standardized Testing and Reporting (STAR) programme in California. Since the STAR website notes that "the target is for all California students to score at proficient or above",[3] in this and subsequent charts we show the percentage of students who meet this target. In figure 1, 31 per cent fewer African Americans than whites meet this target, at every grade level. But while 43 per cent of African Americans score at the proficient or advanced level in grade 4, that number drops by half, to 22 per cent (about one in five), by grade 11.

Note that while these are statewide averages, in some districts, the disparities are even wider. For instance, in Oakland, the gap between the percentage of African Americans and whites who scored at the proficient level or above at

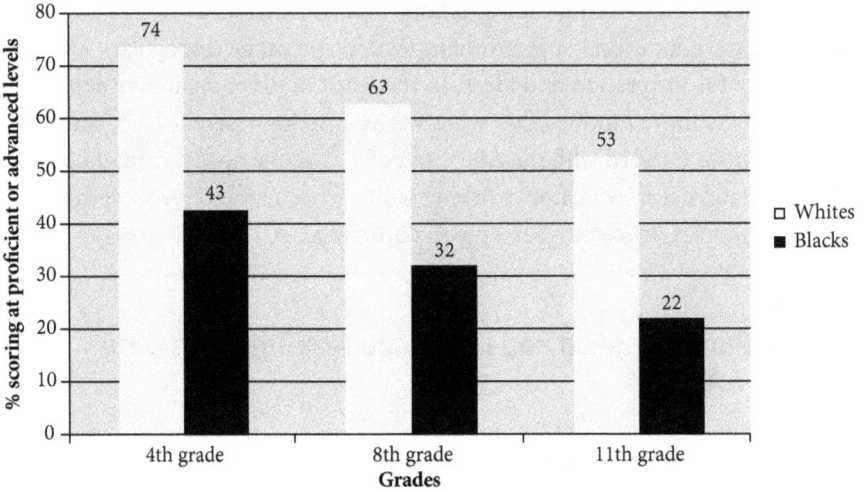

**Figure 15.1:** 2008 STAR English language arts results, California, proficient and advanced levels

the grade 8 and 11 levels was not 31 per cent, but 61 per cent. The percentage of whites who scored as proficient or above in grade 8 was 79 per cent, and at grade 11, 72 per cent; for African Americans, the percentage in the same categories in grade 8 was 18 per cent, and in grade 11, only 11 per cent.

Results from the 2007 National Assessment of Educational Progress (NAEP) assessments in California for reading and writing – shown in table 15.1 – paint a similar picture, with 25 to 27 per cent fewer black students scoring at the proficient or advanced levels in each case. (Writing results for grade 4 in 2007 are not available.)

That this achievement gap exists nationally and not just in California is clear from the NAEP nationwide reading scores for 2007: the average score for whites in grade 4 was 231, and for African Americans it was 203 (28 points less); in

**Table 15.1:** 2007 NAEP Results for California, Reading and Writing: Percentage Scoring at Proficient or Advanced Levels

|  | Reading, Grade 4 | Reading, Grade 8 | Writing, Grade 8 |
|---|---|---|---|
| **Whites** | 40% | 37% | 40% |
| **Blacks** | 15% | 10% | 13% |

grade 8, the average score for whites was 272, and for African Americans it was 245 (27 points less). Moreover, this is not a new phenomenon, but an old and persistent one. For instance, Michael Casserly, executive director of the Council of the Great City Schools (which includes fifty of the nation's largest urban public school districts), reported to a US Senate subcommittee[4] in 1997 that in 1994, nine-year-old African American students in the Great City Schools were, on average, 29 points behind their white counterparts in reading proficiency (on a 500-point scale). By the age of thirteen, that gap had increased to 31 points. And by the age of seventeen, the gap was greater still, with African American students a full 37 points behind their white counterparts.

The reasons for this persistent nationwide disparity include several factors that have little if anything to do with language. Among these are the fact that the schools attended by African Americans and other students of colour usually have more limited facilities and teachers who are more poorly trained and lower paid than those attended primarily by whites; that the students tend to come from lower socio-economic backgrounds and be subject to stereotype vulnerability (Steele 1992); and that their teachers tend to have lower expectations for them, which are often linked to lower achievement (Tauber 1997; Brophy 1998).[5] Understanding and overcoming these and other factors is essential to trying to close the black–white achievement gap (Darling-Hammond et al. 2008; DeShano da Silva et al. 2007; Downey et al. 2009; Ferguson 2007). However, we believe, along with the California Department of Education, that if these other factors are held constant, a language arts programme that takes the linguistic background of AAVE speakers into account is more likely to succeed than one that does not. It should come as no surprise that with subjects like reading and writing in which language is central, the *kind* of English that students bring to the classroom and how teachers respond to it might be relevant. But there is now more than thirty years of evidence on the relevance of AAVE and other non-standard varieties to the teaching of standard or academic varieties and school success. Let us consider some of it now.

## 2. The Relevance of AAVE and other Vernaculars to School Success

Ann Piestrup's (1973) study of 208 African American first-grade children in Oakland, California, was one of the first to show that *how* teachers responded to their students' AAVE pronunciations and grammar influenced the students' success in reading. She identified six different teaching styles, but the most important were the "Interrupting" and "Black Artful" styles. Teachers using the Interrupting style "asked children to repeat words pronounced in dialect many times and interpreted dialect pronunciations as reading errors" (p. iv). Such teachers had a stultifying effect on their students' reading development, reflected not only in the fact that children taught by this method had the lowest reading scores, but also in the fact that some children "withdrew from participation in reading, speaking softly and as seldom as possible". By contrast, teachers in the Black Artful group "used rhythmic play in instruction and encouraged children to participate by listening to their responses. They attended to vocabulary differences of the children and seemed to prevent structural conflict by teaching children to listen for standard English sound distinctions." Children taught by this approach participated enthusiastically in reading, and also showed the highest reading scores.

Other research (e.g., Williams 1976; Politzer and Hoover 1976; Granger et al. 1977) has shown that teachers evaluated students who spoke or read with non-standard or vernacular pronunciations much less positively than those who did not. This may be because people believe, mistakenly (see section 3 below), that AAVE and other non-standard varieties are irregular or unsystematic, and that their speakers are ignorant, careless or lazy. But sometimes it is just because the speech identifies the speaker as black or Hispanic, and elicits deeper prejudices towards those ethnic groups. Shepherd (2009) shows, for instance, that teachers evaluate the same response more negatively when they think it is from a minority student than when they think it is from a white student. And when Justice Joiner found the Ann Arbor (Michigan) School District at fault for failing to take the "black English" of their pupils into account, his opinion was that the district had failed not so much because of features of the variety itself, but because of the negative attitudes and expectations teachers and administrators had towards this variety and its speakers (see Smitherman 1981).

Other research has suggested that it is not enough for teachers to correct their misconceptions and prejudices about AAVE and other vernaculars. They could do more by *using the vernacular* to teach students to read, write and even speak in the standard or mainstream variety that schools (and employers) require. One strategy for doing so that was championed in the 1960s and 1970s but that is rarely advocated nowadays was the use of "dialect readers" – like the *Bridge* readers created by Simpkins, Holt and Simpkins (1977), which would begin with passages written in AAVE, transition through a mixed variety and then end up with standard English. Even though experiments showed that this method boosted reading scores among African American students more than conventional methods that made no reference to students' vernacular (Simpkins and Simpkins 1981), making such extensive use of AAVE was considered too radical and was viewed too negatively by teachers, parents, district officials and community leaders.

The more benign and widely advocated method of using the vernacular to teach the standard is through contrastive analysis. This involves explicit comparison between the features of each variety, to help students understand the differences more clearly and to improve their ability to switch between them (Wheeler and Swords 2006).

The first rationale for contrastive analysis as a means of teaching standard English is that speakers of vernacular varieties of English – and their teachers – are typically *not* aware of the systematic differences between them. As Le Page (1968, 487) noted forty years ago in relation to the creole Englishes of the Caribbean, "The teachers *are* in most cases aware of the fact that the vernacular of the lower-middle-class and working-class homes is different from the language they are supposed to use in the classroom, but they are not able to formulate in any methodical way where the differences lie or what they are due to." Feigenbaum (1970, 91), referring to AAVE and other vernaculars in the United States, similarly observed, "By comparing the standard English structure to be taught and the equivalent or close nonstandard structure, the student can see how they differ. Many students have a partial knowledge of standard English, that is, they can recognize and produce it but without accurate control."

The second rationale for contrastive analysis is that this method allows for increased efficiency in the classroom, as teachers can concentrate on the systematic areas of contrast with standard English which cause difficulties for vernacular speakers rather than taking on the more daunting task of teaching *all* of English grammar. The standard English features of contrast and potential difficulty (for instance, possessive -*s* for speakers of AAVE, who may write "the mother name" instead of "the mother's name") can then be brought under conscious control through identification, translation and other drills. Feigenbaum (1970) provided several examples of such drills, and there are hundreds of examples in the substantial handbook of the Standard English Proficiency Program for Speakers of Black Language that has been in use in California since the 1980s. Students, however, can find the overuse of drills boring, and the more recent trend has been to draw the contrasts between varieties and develop students' linguistic versatility through extensive use of literature and song (see Rickford and Rickford 2007).

The third and perhaps most important rationale for using contrastive analysis to improve the teaching of standard English is that where it has been systematically compared with other methods, it has shown itself superior. Taylor (1989) reports, for instance, that African American students at Aurora University who were taught standard English through an eleven-week programme of contrastive analysis showed a 59 per cent *decline* in the intrusion of ten AAVE features in their standard English writing, while a control group taught by conventional methods over the same period showed an 8.5 per cent *increase* in the use of AAVE features in their standard English writing.

Similarly, as table 15.2 shows, fifth- and sixth-graders in Kelli Harris-Wright's bidialectal programme in DeKalb County, Georgia (outside Atlanta), who learned to switch between "home language" and "school language" through contrastive analysis, showed improved scores on the reading composite of the Iowa Test of Basic Skills each year. By contrast, students in control groups, who were taught by other methods, showed less improvement (1995–96) or actually did worse (1994–95 and 1996–97) between their pre- and post-tests. In an article in the *Atlanta Constitution* (9 January 1997), Doug Cummings noted that DeKalb's contrastive analysis programme won a "Center of Excellence" designation from the National Council for Teachers of English, and that students in the programme improved at every school.

Other evidence in support of the contrastive analysis program comes from recent studies of writing in elementary classrooms that have used contrastive analysis techniques, although they sometimes label it by different names. In studies by Maddahian and Sandamela (2000) of Noma LeMoine's Academic English Mastery Program in the Los Angeles Unified School District, by Fogel and Ehri (2000) of a three-way experiment in two northeastern schools, and by Sweetland (2006) of a three-way experiment in two schools in Cincinnati, Ohio, the contrastive analysis method proved superior to all others in terms of

**Table 15.2:** Pre- vs. Post-Test Changes in Reading Scores on the Iowa Test of Basic Skills for Bidialectal Contrastive Analysis (CA) and Control Students in DeKalb County, Georgia

| Group | 1994–95 | 1995–96 | 1996–97 |
|-------|---------|---------|---------|
| **Bidialectal (CA) Students** | +2.68 | +2.68 | +3.89 |
| **Control (non-CA) students** | –0.37 | +2.0 | –0.05 |

improvements in students' writing scores and evaluations, and their ability to translate between AAVE and standard English.

Contrastive analysis is incorporated in several places in the *Imagine It!* readers, including in some of the "Teacher Tips" that occur in each book, contrasting specific AAVE and academic-English features that are illustrated in specific stories or that may come up in students' speech and writing, and in the contrastive analysis charts for pronunciation and grammar that appear in some of the *Imagine It!* materials.

Finally, even where reference is not specifically made to the vernacular of AAVE-speaking children, studying the specific reading errors they make and tailoring lesson plans to address them has proven very effective in reducing or eliminating the black–white achievement gap. Labov (2001) showed that dramatic reductions in reading decoding errors could be achieved through the individualized reading diagnostic and training strategies that he and Bettina Baker developed at the University of Pennsylvania. And more recently, Labov (2006) has shown that the differential between black and white reading scores (as measured by the Woodcock-Johnson III Letter-Word Identification test and other measures) can be removed by using a modern variant of the individualized reading method.

In all the cases discussed in this section, reference has been made to specific features of students' vernacular language use or reading performance, either to report that these trigger prejudiced reactions, diminished expectations and counterproductive pedagogical practices in teachers; to show how they have been utilized in contrastive analysis to improve students' reading, writing and mastery of standard English; or to demonstrate that they significantly reduce decoding errors and help to eliminate the black–white differential in reading performance. It is for reasons like these that the *Imagine It!* series, in keeping with the 2009 adoption criteria of the California Department of Education, includes a "deeper focus on the instructional needs" of "students who use African American Vernacular English".

Before we go on to discuss specific features of AAVE and suggest how teachers might best approach the teaching of AAVE speakers, it should be emphasized that the *Imagine It!* series also incorporates the best available knowledge about the teaching of reading through phonemic awareness, systematic phonics, vocabulary development and other means. Children who speak AAVE are not being offered a reading programme that consists only of the insights that linguists and educators have gleaned from over forty years of studying AAVE and its reception and use in schools. These insights are being harnessed, in this series, to what researchers consider the *very best means of teaching reading* to children everywhere, to increase the chances that African American children will overcome the persistent and insidious black–white achievement gap and perform closer to the peak of their potential.

## 3. AAVE: Vocabulary, Pronunciation and Grammatical Features?

"AAVE" refers to the vernacular or non-standard variety used by many African Americans in informal conversation. It is referred to by other names as well (Ebonics, African American language), usually reflecting the ideologies of its users, but AAVE is the name most linguists use, and is the one used by the California Department of Education in its adoption guidelines. For various reasons – its distinctive features, controversies about its history, its interest for students of sociolinguistic variation, its relation to educational issues – AAVE has been the subject of numerous linguistic studies over the past forty years, with "more than five times as many sociolinguistic publications devoted to it than any other ethnic or regional dialect" (Schneider 1996, 3).

It is not possible in this chapter to list, much less discuss, all of the features of AAVE.[6] What we will try to do instead is describe *some* of the distinctive features of AAVE's vocabulary, pronunciation and grammar, beginning with a brief example from the work of two-time Pulitzer Prize winner August Wilson, whose plays are replete with examples of AAVE. Although he didn't draw on the vernacular when he first began writing plays about African American life, Wilson changed once he realized that "art is within the language of the people" (Rickford and Rickford 2000, 29), and his vibrant use of AAVE is an important element in the authenticity of his dialogue and his characters.

Here, for instance, is an extract from the first play that won Wilson a Pulitzer prize, *The Piano Lesson* (1989, 9):

| | |
|---|---|
| Boy Willie: Oh Doaker look at her, she **done** got big. **Ain't** she got big? | 1 |
| Doaker: Yeah, she Ø gett*in'* up *d*ere. | 2 |
| Boy Willie: How Ø you do*in'*, sugar? | 3 |
| Maretha: Fine. | 4 |
| Boy Willie: This Ø your uncle Boy Willie, from down South! Hey, that | 5 |
| there Ø Lymon. He Ø my friend. | 6 |
| Maretha: Hi. | 7 |

Lymon: How Ø you do*in*'? You look *jus'* like your mama. I remember    8

[when] you **was** wear*in*' diapers.    9

Using the 1995 Hallmark television performance of this play (released as a VHS video in 1999) as our guide, we have represented distinctive features of AAVE pronunciation in this extract in italics, and distinctive grammatical features in boldface.

## 3.1 Vocabulary

The first thing to note is that there are no distinctive vocabulary features to talk about, apart from words like *done* and *ain't*, which have grammatical functions. This extract is indeed very representative of AAVE more generally, with most of the vocabulary shared with other varieties of American English. Many teenagers and young adults do use distinctive slang words (like *bling-bling* for 'expensive jewellery'), but these can vary a lot from one region of the United States to the other, and almost by definition, slang changes quickly. More enduring, less varied by age and region, and ultimately of more interest to linguists is a small set of words that African Americans use, but without realizing that most whites don't use or recognize them, at least not with the same meanings. The set includes *ashy* for "the whitish or grayish appearance of [black] skin due to exposure to wind and cold", *kitchen* for "the hair at the nape of the neck, inclined to be the most curly (kinky)" and *cut-eye* for "a visual gesture which communicates hostility, displeasure, disapproval, or a general rejection of the person at whom it is directed".[7]

## 3.2 Pronunciation

Of greater interest to linguists than AAVE vocabulary, and of more relevance to teachers, are the distinctive features of AAVE pronunciation. The *Piano Lesson* extract includes the following features:

a. simplification of word-final consonant clusters, as in "jus'" (line 8)
b. realization of -*ing* in present-progressive verb suffixes as -*in*' ("doin'", line 3)
c. realization of voiced *th* as *d* at the beginnings of words, as in "dere" (line 2).

There are several other AAVE pronunciations not found in this extract, such as:

    d.  the deletion or vocalization of *l* after a vowel, as in "he'p" for 'help'

    e.  the deletion of vocalization of *r* after a vowel, as in "sistuh" for 'sister'

    f.  the realization of voiceless *th* as *f* or *t* at the ends of syllables: "teef" for 'teeth'

    g.  the realization of voiced *th* as *v* or *d* at the ends of syllables: "bave" for 'bathe'

    h.  the merger of short *i* and *e* before nasals, as in "pin" for 'pin' or 'pen'

    i.  the pronunciation of the /ay/ diphthong as a long monophthong: "Ah" for 'I'

    j.  stress on the first rather than second syllable in some words: "PO-lice", "HO-tel".

About these pronunciations, several things need to be said. The first is that, contrary to widespread misconceptions, they are *systematic and rule-governed*. For instance, feature (a), the simplification of word-final consonant clusters, only applies to clusters in which *both* consonants are either voiced (like *friend*) or voiceless (like *just*), but not to clusters like *pant* or *jump* in which the first consonant in the cluster is voiced (*n*, *m*) and the second voiceless (*t*, *p*). That is, you will never hear an African American speaker pronounce *jump* as "jum'", or *pant* as "pan'".

Second, the "rules" that speakers follow to simplify or reduce some clusters and to keep others intact are not consciously taught or learned. No one sits an African American child down at the age of four or five and explains that in voiced sounds the vocal cords in one's larynx are held together and vibrate noisily (say "zzzzz" with your fingers in your ears and you will hear it clearly), while in voiceless sounds, they are held apart, and the air from the lungs passes through them without the same deep vibration (say "sssss" with your fingers in your ears and you will notice the difference immediately). Nor that this voicing distinction is something they will need to know about for other features too, such as (c), (f) and (g) above (voiced *th* becomes voiced *d* or *v*; voiceless *th* becomes voiceless *t* or *f*).

Third, several of these pronunciation rules have grammatical effects. For instance, the deletion or vocalization (vowel-like pronunciation) of *l*, as seen in feature (d) above, can remove the contracted remnant of future *will*, converting "He'll be here tomorrow" to "He Ø be here tomorrow." And consonant cluster simplification can remove the -ed suffix, making *moved* sound like "move" and *baked* sound like "bake", even though AAVE normally marks its past tenses quite faithfully, as you can see in the ubiquitious strong pasts like *came* or *saw* that are not affected by consonant cluster reduction.

Fourth, many of these features are shared with other American English dialects, especially Southern dialects, and white vernacular or colloquial varieties more generally. But they tend to occur more often in AAVE. Most of them do not occur 100 per cent of the time, however. This is evident even in the short *Piano Lesson* extract, for "there" in line 6 doesn't become "dere" (by rule [c]), and "friend" in line 6 doesn't become "frien'" (by rule [a]). In general, the lower the socio-economic class from which speakers come, and the more informally or agitatedly they are speaking, the more frequently you can expect these and other AAVE features to occur. But you should not expect students in the classroom, or writers, preachers, comedians in the larger world, to use them 100 per cent of the time.

## 3.3 AAVE Grammar

Let us turn now to distinctive *grammatical* features of AAVE in the *Piano Lesson* extract above:

- k. the absence of the copula *is* and *are*, as in "He Ø my friend" (line 6)
- l. the use of preverbal *done* to mark completion: "she done got big" (line 1)
- m. the use of *ain't* as a generalized negative marker: "Ain't she got big?" (line 1)
- n. absence of subject–verb agreement, as in "you was wearin' diapers" (line 9).

There are several other grammatical features of AAVE not seen in this extract, including

- o. the use of invariant habitual *be* for recurrent events: "He be walkin' every day."
- p. the use of stressed *BIN* for events that happened a long time ago ("I BIN paid him his money") or for states long ago initiated ("I BIN had that car")

q. the use of *be done* for future perfect: "Before you know it, she be done gone."
r. use of *finna* ('fixing to') for immediate future: "She finna leave."
s. absence of third-person singular present tense -*s*, as in "He walkØ home."
t. marking possession by juxtaposition, without 's, as in "JohnØ house."
u. absence of plural -*s* (more in writing than speech): "three boyØ"
v. multiple negation, marking the negative on the verb *and* on the negative indefinite or quantifier, as in "He don't know nothing."
w. inversion of a negative auxiliary and an indefinite subject to make a positive, often emphatic statement, as in "Didn't nobody leave." ('Nobody left.')
x. use of *it* rather than *there* for existentials: "It's a bee in the house."

Again, this list is not exhaustive, but many of the points made in discussing the pronunciation features apply here as well. For instance, the systematic, rule-governed nature of AAVE is evident in the fact that the absence of the copula affects only *is* and *are*, not first-person *am* (which is often contracted, but not deleted), and not past-tense *was* or *were*, nor forms of *is* or *are* that are stressed or come at the end of a clause, as in "That's what he is" (that is, you cannot say "That's what he Ø"). Moreover, although you can only see this if you begin to count how often these features occur, it is evident from any longer sample of AAVE speech, virtually anywhere in the United States, that *are* is deleted more often than *is*, and that both forms are deleted more often when they come before a progressive or future verb (as in "She Ø getting up there" or "He Ø gon' leave") than before a noun (as in "He Ø my friend"). These and other complex regularities about AAVE are not consciously taught, and they cannot be articulated by native speakers, but they are followed and exemplified day in and day out, across the country.

Although it is true that some of these grammatical features, like their pronunciation counterparts, are also found in white vernaculars, especially in the South, some of them, like invariant habitual *be* (o) and copula absence involving *is* (k), are so much more frequent in AAVE, and so rare in most white varieties, that they seem to be unique to AAVE. Certainly, their use by African American writers and comedians is often sufficient to make the character in a story or skit seem "authentically" black.

These grammatical features also stratify the African American community more dramatically than some of the pronunciation features do, with middle-class speakers more likely to avoid (and even condemn) them as grammatical shibboleths. At the same time, they come to the fore most frequently in informal conversation among familiar peers.

## 4. Making the Best Use of Information about AAVE in the *Imagine It!* Materials

The *Imagine It!* readers include two resources for teachers seeking to improve the teaching of English or language arts to students who speak AAVE. One is the comprehensive contrastive analysis chart included in the materials, which provides information about the corresponding AAVE equivalents of academic English pronunciations and grammatical features, including special notes about where and when they occur, and how teachers might take them into account in the classroom. For instance, regarding the realization of voiceless *th* as *f*, as in "bafroom" for *bathroom*, and of voiced *th* as *v* or *d*, as in "breave" for *breathe* or "dis" for *this* (see features [e] and [f] above), the contrastive analysis chart notes that this is "more of a problem in spelling and speaking rather than in learning to read", and suggests that if teachers want to tackle it, they "use contrastive analysis to have students differentiate between /th/ and /f/ [or /v/, /d/, etc.]. Write several words in Informal English and contrast those with the spellings in Academic English. Have students identify the sound that /th/ makes in Academic English, and have them practice with additional words."

The other resource for teachers are the "Teacher Tips" and "Universal Access" notes that occur throughout the teachers' editions of the readers at each level, either in relation to a narrative in which AAVE is used (for example, "The Pretty Pennies Picket" in the grade 6 reader, or "From Miss Ida's Porch" in the grade 5 reader), or in relation to exercises in which AAVE pronunciations or grammatical features might emerge. For instance, in the grade 1, unit 1 reader, the following "Universal Access" note is provided in lesson 8 (p. T255) for teachers who have AAVE speakers in their classes:

> **IF** . . . students are using informal subject-verb agreement as they read and write their sentences, **THEN** . . . use one of their sentences as an example to do a contrastive analysis. For example, if their sentence states *I have fun with my friend Alisha when we plays at school*, write their sentence on the board. Then rewrite the sentence using " . . . *Alisha when we play* . . ." Have students contrast your sentence with the student example. Ask them how the two sentences differ (*play* has an *s* added in Sentence 2), then have them choose which sentence is written in Academic English.

For another example, this time involving pronunciation, here is a teacher tip from the grade 5 reader (p. 96 of the teachers' edition):

> Speakers of AAVE and dialects may pronounce the unstressed verbal participles in Line 1 [which includes the words *bordering, growing, hanging* and *selling*] with *-in* instead of *-ing*. This is a widespread characteristic of colloquial English around the world (such as in Australia, England, the United States), but it's more frequent in AAVE than other US dialects. If your focus is on the grammatical *structure* of the words (base verb + inflectional ending), as it is in this routine, you should not simultaneously discuss pronunciation, which may divert attention from word structure. But if you later want to develop students' ability to produce *-ing* pronunciations consistently, use as models non-participle words like *thing*, or *sing*, which are always produced in AAVE with *-ing*.

In keeping with the evidence and explanations provided in this chapter up to this point, it should be clear that the intent behind these notes and tips is to help teachers develop the linguistic versatility of AAVE-speaking students, especially with respect to reading and writing (and, to a lesser extent, speaking) in standard or academic English. But a few cautions are in order. The first is that not every African American child speaks AAVE, and teachers should check for the presence of AAVE features (such as those discussed in section 3.2 and 3.3) in their students' speech or reading or writing before launching into contrastive analysis and similar techniques. If an African American child is already fluent in standard or academic English, these techniques are not needed.

Second, teachers have to be careful not to *overdo* the practice of identifying AAVE features in students' speech and writing and pointing out their academic English equivalents, especially if it is not relevant to the primary lesson focus (for example, word structure rather than pronunciation, as in the grade 5 teacher tip above). This would lead to constant interruption of the flow of students' classroom offerings and, as Piestrup's 1973 research showed (see section 2 above), to resentment, disinterest and poor performance.

Moreover, the goal of contrastive analysis is not the elimination of AAVE (which is not likely to succeed anyway, given that AAVE may be widely used by students' friends and family members and others in the community, and is often an important part of their identity), but the addition of standard or academic English to their repertoire. It is not necessary to eliminate AAVE to learn academic English, just as it is not necessary to eradicate English to learn French or any other foreign language. Developing bidialectalism (parallel to bilingualism) and linguistic versatility (Rickford and Rickford 2007) should be our goal. And, especially for older students, the suggestion that AAVE is a "problem" to be corrected and eradicated may lead to reduced interest and even hostility.

Some of the AAVE-related tips (for example, in relation to vernacular features in narratives) are provided so that teachers and students might fully understand and appreciate the meaning of the narratives, and so that teachers might understand that AAVE is regular and systematic and not underestimate the intelligence of students who speak it (the evidence is clear that low expectations lead to low performance). Teachers should encourage students to discuss their reactions and responses to the use of AAVE features in the narratives in which they occur. Some questions they might pose to students are: "Do you enjoy reading stories with dialect or vernacular features in them? Why or why not?" "Does the language used in this story remind you of anyone you know or have heard who sounds like that?" "How do you feel when you hear it?"

In leading discussions about language, teachers should take care to keep an open mind about the subject, not to sanction or articulate prejudicial perspectives, and to encourage positive perceptions of difference in dialects and languages. Teachers and students alike should develop a positive respect for the rule-governed and expressive nature of their students' vernacular speech, and for the AAVE used in stories in the *Imagine It!* readers and in the literature of African American literary giants like Maya Angelou, James Baldwin, Lucille Clifton, Paul Laurence Dunbar, Langston Hughes, Sonia Sanchez, John Edgar Wideman, Alice Walker and August Wilson, among others. Teachers should encourage interested students to conduct further research into these authors, and to read some of their works. All of these writers display the exemplary ability to switch back and forth between AAVE and standard English that we should help AAVE-speaking students to develop. And some of them are loud in their praise of the vernacular. James Baldwin, writing in 1979, referred to AAVE as "this passion, this skill . . . this incredible music". Toni Morrison, two years later, claimed that "the worst of all possible things that could happen would be to lose that language" (see Rickford 1997).

To summarize and clarify: The goal of this *Imagine It!* series is to combine the best available knowledge about how to teach reading, writing and the language arts to *all* speakers with the best available knowledge about how to do so with AAVE speakers, especially insofar as this involves developing linguistic versatility, adding academic English to their repertoire and becoming the best readers, writers, speakers and listeners they can be. In the age of Obama, this is not an impossible dream.

## Acknowledgements

This chapter is a modified version of a white paper that we were asked to prepare for SRA/McGraw-Hill and users of their *Imagine It!* elementary-level readers, especially the California edition released in 2009. We are grateful to publisher and editor Ruth Cochrane of SRA/McGraw-Hill for permission to use this paper in this festschrift for Dennis Craig.

## Notes

1. This is actually Craig's version of an LSA resolution that was developed by William Labov and "accepted and reaffirmed by the Linguistics Society of America" in 1974 (Craig 1999, 33n4). Interestingly enough, in 1997, the LSA approved a resolution on the Ebonics issue introduced by John R. Rickford that was very similar (although independently created), insofar as it emphasized that AAVE/Ebonics was "systematic and rule-governed like all natural speech varieties".
2. Although Craig's index does not include "contrastive analysis", his (1999, 233–36) Syllabus Resource One (SR1) identifies "Basic Morphological and Syntactic Contrasts Between Internationally Accepted English (IAE) and English-Based, Creole-Influenced Vernaculars" and his Syllabus Resource Two (1999, 236–41) does the same for "Sounds, the Alphabet, and the Vernacular".
3. See http://star.cde.ca.gov/star2008/help_scoreexplanations.asp. "Proficient" corresponds to a mean scale score of 350 out of 600. Mean scale scores for whites at grades 4, 8 and 11 are 382.7, 364.7 and 350.4 respectively; corresponding scores for blacks at grades 4, 8 and 11 are 340.9, 321.4 and 302.5 respectively. Asians as a group score higher than whites at each grade level (391.3, 376.1, 360.4); Latinos/Hispanics score about the same as blacks at each grade level (339.7, 322.9, 305.8).
4. Casserly testified before the US Senate Appropriations Subcommittee on Labor, Health and Human Services, and Education on 23 January 1997.
5. See Rickford's (1999, 5–9) study for further discussion of these and other factors.
6. For more details, see studies by Green (2002), Rickford (1999), Rickford and Rickford (2000), and the references to earlier studies therein.
7. Definitions of *ashy* and *kitchen* are from Smitherman 2000; the definition of *cut-eye* is from Rickford and Rickford's (1976) work.

# References

Brophy, Jere, ed. 1998. *Expectations in the Classroom*. Greenwich, CT: JAI Press.

California Department of Education. 2006. Criteria for Evaluating Instructional Materials: Reading/Language Arts/English Language Development, Kindergarten through Grade Eight. http://www.cde.ca.gov/ci/cr/cf/documents/rlafw.pdf.

Carrington, Lawrence D., and Clive B. Borely. 1977. *The Language Arts Syllabus 1975: Comment and Counter Comment*. St Augustine, Trinidad and Tobago: School of Education, University of the West Indies.

Craig, Dennis R. 1999. *Teaching language and literacy: Policies and procedures for Vernacular Situations*. Georgetown, Guyana: Education and Development Services.

Darling-Hammond, Linda, Brigid Barron, P. David Pearson, Alan H. Schoenfeld, Elizabeth K. Stage, Timothy D. Zimmerman, Gina N. Cervetti and Jennifer L. Tilson. 2008. *Powerful Learning: What We Know about Teaching for Understanding*. San Francisco, CA: Jossey-Bass.

DeShano da Silva, Carol, James Philip Huguley, Zenub Kakli and Radhika Rao. 2007. *The Opportunity Gap: Achievement and Inequality in Education*. Cambridge, MA: Harvard Educational Review.

Downey, Carolyn J., Betty E. Steffy, William K. Poston, Jr. and Fenwick W. English. 2009. *Fifty Ways to Close the Achievement Gap*. 3rd ed. Thousand Oaks, CA: Corwin.

Feigenbaum, Irwin. 1970. The Use of Nonstandard in Teaching Standard. In *Teaching Standard English in the Inner City*, edited by R. Fasold and R. Shuy, 87–104. Washington, DC: Center for Applied Linguistics.

Ferguson, Ronald F. 2007. *Toward Excellence with Equity: An Emerging Vision for Closing the Achievement Gap*. Cambridge, MA: Harvard Education Press.

Fogel, Howard, and Linnea C. Ehri. 2000. Teaching Elementary Students Who Speak Black English Vernacular to Write in Standard English: Effects of Dialect Transformation Practice. *Contemporary Educational Psychology* 25: 212–35.

Granger, Robert C., Marilyn Mathews, Lorene C. Quay and Rochelle Verner. 1977. Teacher Judgements of the Communication Effectiveness of Children Using Different Speech Patterns. *Journal of Educational Psychology* 69 (6): 793–96.

Green, Lisa. 2002. *African American English*. Cambridge: Cambridge University Press.

Labov, William. 2001. Applying Our Knowledge of African American English to the Problem of Raising Reading Levels in Inner City Schools. In *Sociocultural and Historical Contexts of African American English*, edited by S. Lanehart, 299–317. Amsterdam: John Benjamins.

———. 2006. Spotlight on Reading. Presentation to various groups, including the West Philadelphia Tutoring Project and America Reads, and to the Voices of African American Students group of educators in Los Angeles. http://www.ling.upenn.edu/~wlabov/Spotlight.html.

Le Page, Robert B. 1968. Problems to Be Faced in the Use of English as a Medium of Education in Four West Indian Territories. In *Language Problems of Developing Nations*, edited by J. Fishman, C.A. Ferguson and J. Das Gupta, 431–43. New York: John Wiley.

Maddahian, Ebrahim, and Ambition Padi Sandamela. 2000. Academic English Mastery Program: 1998 Evaluation Report. Publication No. 781, Program Evaluation and Research Branch, Research and Evaluation Unit, Los Angeles Unified School District.

Piestrup, A.M. 1973. Black Dialect Interference and Accommodation of Reading Instruction in First Grade. Monographs of the Language Behavior Research Laboratory, #4. Berkeley: University of California Press.

Politzer, Robert, and Mary Rhodes Hoover. 1976. Teachers' and Pupils' Attitudes toward Black English Speech Varieties and Black Pupils' Achievement. Research and Development memorandum no. 145. Stanford, CA: Stanford Center for Research and Development in Teaching.

Rickford, Angela E., and John R. Rickford. 2007. Variation, Versatility, and Contrastive Analysis in the Classroom. In *Sociolinguistic Variation*, edited by R. Bayley and C. Lucas, 276–96. Cambridge: Cambridge University Press.

Rickford, John R. 1997. Suite for Ebony and Phonics. *Discover* 18 (12): 82–87.

———. 1999. *African American Vernacular English*. Oxford: Blackwell.

Rickford, John R., and Angela E. Rickford. 1976. Cut-Eye and Suck Teeth: African Words and Gestures in New World Guise. *Journal of American Folklore* 89 (353): 194–309.

Rickford, John R., and Russell J. Rickford. 2000. *Spoken Soul: The Story of Black English*. New York: John Wiley.

Rickford, John R., Julie Sweetland, Angela E. Rickford, and Thomas Grano. 2013. *African American, Creole, and Other Vernacular Englishes in Education: A Bibliographic Resource*. New York and Urbana, IL: Routledge and National Council of Teachers of English.

Rickford, John R., and Elizabeth Closs Traugott. 1985. Symbol of Powerlessness and Degeneracy, or Symbol of Solidarity and Truth? Paradoxical Attitudes toward Pidgins and Creoles. In *The English Language Today*, edited by S. Greenbaum, 252–61. Oxford: Pergamon.

Schneider, Edgar W., ed. 1996. *Focus on the USA: Varieties of English around the World*. Amsterdam: John Benjamins.

Shepherd, Michael. 2009. The Effect of Perceived Ethnicity on Teachers' Evaluations of Students' Spoken Responses. Paper presented at the annual meeting of the American Dialect Society, San Francisco, January.

Simpkins, Gary A., Grace Holt and Charlesetta Simpkins. 1977. *Bridge: A Cross-Cultural Reading Program*. Boston: Houghton Mifflin.

Simpkins, Gary A., and Charlesetta Simpkins. 1981. Cross-Cultural Approach to Curriculum Development. In *Black English and the Education of Black Children and Youth*, edited by G. Smitherman, 221–40. Detroit: Center for Black Studies, Wayne State University.

Smitherman, Geneva, ed. 1981. *Black English and the Education of Black Children and Youth*. Detroit: Center for Black Studies, Wayne State University.

Steele, Claude M. 1992. Race and the Schooling of Black Americans. *Atlantic Monthly* 269 (4): 68–78.

Tauber, Robert T. 1997. *Self-Fulfilling Prophecy: A Practical Guide to Its Use in Education*. Westport, CT: Praeger.

Taylor, Hanni U. 1989. *Standard English, Black English, and Bidialectalism*. New York: Peter Lang.

Wheeler, Rebecca S., and Rachel Swords. 2006. *Code-Switching: Teaching Standard English in Urban Classrooms*. Urbana, IL: National Council of Teachers of English.

Williams, Frederick. 1976. *Explorations of the Linguistic Attitudes of Teachers*. Rowley, MA: Newbury House.

www.ingramcontent.com/pod-product-compliance
Lightning Source LLC
Chambersburg PA
CBHW021810270326
41932CB00007B/126